Beyond the Icefall

Beyond the Icefall

Sorrel Wilby

CLOUDCAP
SEATTLE

Above: Most of the team and support crew at Base Camp.
Front cover: Paul Bayne, an agile and confident member of 'Pat's Rats', scales a block of ice in the Icefall.
Endpapers: Sunrise over the Dudh Kosi Valley, below Namche Bazaar.
Half-title: The black summit pyramid of Chomolungma (Everest).
Title: Everest in-situ, rising behind Nupste.
Contents: The last rays of sunlight strike the summit of Tamserku.
Back cover: Sorrel Wilby, with Chomolungma in the background.

Dedicated to the memory of Tim Hughes

First published in North America in 1989 by
Cloudcap
Box 27344, Seattle, Washington 98125
Simultaneously published in Australia by
Child & Associates Publishing Pty Ltd
Edited, designed and typeset in Australia by
Child & Associates Publishing Pty Ltd
© Sorrel Wilby 1989
Printed in Singapore by Toppan Printing Co. (S) Pte Ltd
Typesetting processed by Deblaere Typesetting Pty Ltd

Cataloguing-in-Publication data

Wilby, Sorrel.
    Beyond the icefall.

    Includes index.
    ISBN 938567-16-0

    1. Australian Bicentennial Everest Expedition (1988). 2. Mountaineering—Everest, Mount (China and Nepal). 3. Everest, Mount (China and Nepal)—Description and travel. I. Title.

915.49'6

All photographs taken by Sorrel Wilby unless otherwise indicated in photo caption.

Foreword

In the first chapter of her story of the Australian Bicentennial Everest Expedition, Sorrel Wilby poses the question: 'A lot of people might wonder what sane person with a will to live would put themselves at the mercy of this mountain, this known killer of climbers?'

It's a good question, but her answer is just as good: 'Climbers do not have some bizarre death wish; rather, a life wish; a need to experience all that is offered within the framework of their own limitations.'

And that's just the short answer. In fact it takes the whole length of this enthralling book to provide the full explanation of what truly motivated the members of the Australian Bicentennial Everest Expedition. This is the story of the determination, the courage, the excitement, the disappointment and finally the triumph of a group of dedicated Australians seeking to climb the world's highest mountain.

Chomolungma—the Tibetan name for Mt Everest, meaning Goddess Mother of the Universe—has exerted an irresistible attraction on adventurers for a hundred years before it was finally conquered by Edmund Hillary and Tenzing Norgay in 1953.

In 1984 Tim Macartney-Snape and Greg Mortimer became the first Australians to reach the summit. The members of the Bicentennial Expedition were determined to be the second group of Australians to make this historic ascent, and I readily agreed to be one of the patrons of this climb.

Expedition members, through their courage and success, have given all Australians something of which to be proud, and have set new goals for others to follow. This expedition was the first to climb Chomolungma without the support of high altitude Sherpa porters.

Sorrel Wilby's account takes the reader through all the stages of physical and psychological endurance and exaltation experienced by the expedition members.

It gives her personal account of the trials and difficulties of such an endeavour as well as an insight into the detailed arrangements involved in planning and undertaking such a large and difficult expedition.

I am proud that the Government was able significantly to support the expedition through the Australian Bicentennial Authority grant and the assistance of our Defence Forces.

I extend my personal congratulations to Sorrel Wilby for

putting together an exciting book accompanied by her brilliant photographs. This enthralling story will instil the exhilarating experience of climbing Chomolungma into the hearts of all those who read it.

R. J. L. Hawke, AC, MP
Prime Minister of the Commonwealth of Australia

Contents

Chomolungma, the Goddess Mother of the Universe, is crowned by sunset hues of gold.

1
Because It's There

Chapter One

Because It's There

There was the challenge, and we would lay aside all else to take it up.

John Hunt,
writing of the 1953 British Expedition

Terry McCullagh and Zac Zaharias at Camp One.

I just *knew* it was going to be one of those days! I rolled over, wrestled with the zipper on the tent fly and peered outside. Another still-born morning, longing for the kiss of light! The sun was rising behind Chomolungma, the Goddess Mother of the Universe, but it would be hours before its rays revived her ice-cold Cwm. I wriggled back into my sleeping bag, caught the end of my plait in the hood drawstring and knocked over a half full saucepan of soup. Thank God it was frozen!

Jim Van Gelder was snoring, oblivious to the day's ominous beginning and the proximity of my right ear to his face. Damn tents never seem to be comfortable, least of all spacious. It was a choice between 'kgnoooor shoooo ahhh' at full force or the dreaded damp spot. I opted for the former, and turned up the volume on my thoughts to block out the din.

Whoever named this place 'Everest' lacked more than an imagination. Fancy this sacred, timeless peak, this celebration of nature at her wildest, most breathtaking limit, condemned forever to bear the name of some otherwise unmemorable surveyor-general of the Great Trigonometrical Survey of India, Sir George Everest. I mean *really!* we are talking about *the* Goddess of the Universe—Chomolungma or, as the Nepalese call her, Sagarmatha, meaning 'Brow of the Oceans'. Surely the English-speaking world could have come up with something more venerable. I guess we're lucky Sir George's surname wasn't Smith. At least 'Everest' has a certain ring to it.

I tried to visualise the deliciously ethereal origins of the mountain—to picture it rising from a vast sea of rainwater suspended in space; or to picture the goddess riding on her red tiger. I was high on a cloud, about to drift off into legend-land, when Jim suddenly snorted so loudly, he woke even himself.

Back on Planet Earth, I heard the rest of Camp One stirring. In another Gore-Tex dome-home about 10 metres away, Austin Brookes and Brian 'BJ' Agnew were rummaging around in a ration pack for food. The head of a match grated against the flint-side of its box and ignited with a short hiss. I could hear the gas cooker being primed and lit as if it were inside my eardrum; the crackling of cellophane as it was ripped away from a row of dry biscuits very nearly broke the sound barrier. Normally imperceptible sounds were being magnified in the still, rarified air. Things were getting noisy up here in the great 'Valley of Silence'.

'Hey, do you want a cup of tea, Grandma?' Austin called affectionately. 'Grandma' ran a respectable second in the nickname stakes. 'Moo' (as in the cow) was by far his favourite, and I don't remember ever hearing him call me Sorrel. 'Yeh, do you wanna bring it over to me?' I drawled hopefully, knowing full well he wouldn't. I emerged out of my sleeping cocoon, pulled on my boots, dived over Jim and somersaulted out the door.

I first met Austin in 1985 in Lhasa, the enchanting capital city of Tibet. He was about to lead a team of New Zealand climbers up the North Face of Chomolungma and I was preparing for a 3000 kilometre solo trek across the western and central regions of the country. To familiarise myself with the lay of the land and the harsh conditions I would encounter, I joined Austin and his merry band of mountain men on their week-long journey to the Rongbuk Valley Base Camp. I didn't see or hear from him again until New Year's Eve 1987 when he phoned to ask me to take part in the Australian Bicentennial Everest Expedition (ABEE).

As I sipped my brew, I looked at Austin—a softly focused cameo framed in the steam rising from my cup. He hadn't aged since 1985—just weathered a little. The landscape of his remarkable face oddly resembled a Himalayan map. Each line held a river of experience, each ridge a shining success or defeat. Thirty years' worth of expeditions and hair-raising misadventure reflected in his crystal clear eyes. To be climbing with such a mountain of a man was an honour.

BJ dished out three portions of hot stewed apple without spilling or knocking over anything. I was impressed. I was born clumsy and found it impossible to do anything vaguely dextrous

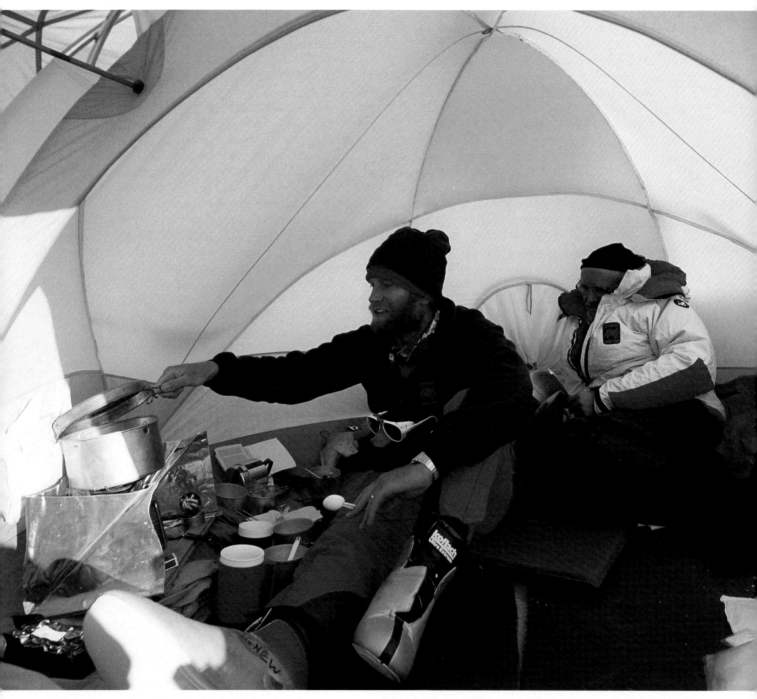

Brian 'BJ' Agnew and expedition leader Austin Brookes, prepare breakfast in the cramped confines of their Camp One tent.

in an empty tent—let alone a crowded one. After trying various alternatives, BJ had finally resorted to poking his long legs out the door. Austin's knees were wedged into the small of my back, and I didn't have any room to so much as scratch my nose. I tried to eat my breakfast.

'Hmmm, this is good!' BJ murmured. I told him he was obviously suffering from cerebral oedema. Enjoying dehydrated food is the first sign of severe high altitude sickness and victims should be forced to descend before their brains and tastebuds are irreparably scrambled. But BJ wouldn't have a bar of it, and scoffed down what was left of my meal as well.

When he finished his cuppa, Austin let out a satisfied sigh and prodded me in the ribs. 'Well Moo, you better get your crampons on,' he quipped. I was a newchum in this climbing game; and naturally Austin's star pupil. His next comment revealed all. 'And this time put them on the right feet, OK?' The day before, I climbed through the Khumbu Icefall with my spiked steel crampons strapped to my boots incorrectly. Not realising, I had to walk like a bow-legged cowboy to stop the buckles from locking together. I had no intention of spending another day tripping my way to social ridicule or, worse still, an early icy grave.

The long, winding route through the Western Cwm to Camp Two had a reputation for hidden dangers—bottomless chasms and ice avalanches posed a very real threat, and I was forced to take myself seriously for a change. A week before, BJ had disappeared down a hidden crevasse somewhere up there. He lived to tell the tale by being well-prepared and adequately equipped. I remembered the adage Terry McCullagh, another of the boys in our eighteen-man climbing team, had often chanted: 'There are old mountaineers and bold mountaineers,' but there aren't too many old bold mountaineers,' and I checked my harness and screw gate as well as my crampons.

Terry and two of his team mates, Bruce Farmer and Zac Zaharias, were in the tent next door to Austin's getting ready to ferry loads up to Camp Two. They were, no doubt, envious of my pack-free position on the team. I was a photographer not a masochist, and carting oxygen cylinders and equipment up to the higher reaches of the mountain was definitely not on my contract. If I stand forever in my team mates' hearts as the expedition's biggest wimp, so be it. At least I will be able to stand *straight*.

Jim wandered over to join the three hunchbacks and I went back to our tent to grab my camera and spare film. The sun still hadn't stripped the frigid shadows from our route up through the

Dwarfing climbers, Nupste flanks the right-hand side of the Western Cwm.

Cwm, so I put on an extra pair of padded gloves and a woollen beanie. The range of temperatures one could encounter on a single day in this vast 'Valley of Silence' defied belief. It was well below zero now, but if the sky remained cloudless and the wind abated, by mid-afternoon the Cwm could reach a sweltering 40°C.

Austin was chafing at the bit—conscious of my sluggish pace and anxious to complete the 'Camp One to Camp Two and back' circuit before nightfall. I wasn't the fittest member of the expedition, but I prided myself on being the slowest. Carrying 15–20-kilogram loads, the boys were making their forays through the Icefall and Western Cwm in a little under half my record time. I had to stop and take pictures, and change film, and walk backwards and forwards to get the right compositions, and … well, to be honest, I had to stop a hell of a lot to catch my breath. I buckled up my harness, attached myself to the fixed rope and plodded on up the hill behind my mentor.

Austin was a good 20 metres ahead of me, racing through an area the boys called the 'Gunbarrel Highway'. You were meant to speed like a bullet between and over the crevasses below the steeply sloped, and therefore avalanche-prone, West Shoulder. But I was sticking to my tried and tested pace. It was exhilarating

As Paul Bayne emerges over the top of the Icefall, the peaks of Khumbutse and Lingtren form a spectacular backdrop.

to stop and leisurely take in the magnificent panorama. It was hard to believe this beautiful place had so much potential for disaster.

I looked back over the cracked lip of the Icefall, towards the sunlit peaks of Pumo Ri and Lingtren. It was so silent, I could hear my own heart beat. God, it was good to be alive; to feel so small and insignificant.

Suddenly a loud cracking sound interrupted my inner dialogue. I quickly focused on a ramshackle row of ice terrace houses clinging to the massive broad West Shoulder above me, anticipating a frigid brick or two would come hurtling down. My hand went limp around the lens … my mouth fell open and the camera fell away from my eye. The whole building was falling down—the entire icy street; crumbling in slow motion, as if it had been charged by dynamite. I couldn't believe it. I couldn't move. Austin was running for his life, and I couldn't unhook myself from the fixed rope. Tears were streaming down my face. I just couldn't move. I had nowhere to go anyway; I was on a long frozen island between two gaping chasms. Great blocks of ice weighing thousands of tonnes were plummeting towards me, crashing close … too close. This scene was taking forever to end. I hadn't read the script; I had no idea if I would live or die in it. I threw myself down on the ground and made a feeble attempt to shield my face. Clouds of powder snow, stirred by the ice

avalanche, were swirling from the demolition debris. I sensed at last I was out of range from the falling ice, but the spindrift could be just as fatal if I breathed it into my lungs. I waited until the world fell silent again and stood up, shaking like a leaf and crying—more with relief now than fear.

Austin was brushing himself free of snow. He looked down at me and screamed, 'Don't just stand there—*move!*' Trouble was he meant onwards and upwards—not a retreat to Camp One. It didn't take a genius to figure I wanted to tuck my tail between my legs and get the hell out of there. This climbing game was *dangerous!* I'd seen that for myself now, and I wanted *out*.

Why on earth was I there in the first place? Why were any of us there for that matter? Chomolungma had been climbed before by every conceivable route. It had been climbed solo, without oxygen, and nigh on 200 people had stood on her lofty summit. Over 100 climbers and their Sherpa companions had perished on the mountain and God knows how many had lost toes and fingers up there. At 7986 metres the South Col was reputed to be the world's highest garbage dump; the legacy of some 120 separate expeditions. I can't even begin to tell you what Base Camp looks like when the snow melts … Most climbers will tell you the mountain, by its most popular routes, isn't a particularly difficult technical exercise anyway … but they'll keep coming back, again and again, till they've made it to the top. Chomolungma or Sagarmatha—or Everest if you insist on calling her that—is, and always has been, something of an obsession.

For centuries man's relationship with this mountain was

13

purely spiritual; to the Tibetan, and later Sherpa, people who knew of her, she was the Goddess Mother of the Universe. Many mountains in the Himalayas were considered by these devout Buddhists to be mighty deities: Makalu was the Goddess of Destruction; Gauri Shankar, the home of Shiva and his consort, Parvati; Annapurna, the Goddess of Plenty; and Khumbila was so revered, one only had to speak his name to be comforted. Ironically, Sherpas believe that to scale great mountains is to intrude among angels. When Tenzing Norgay reached the summit of Chomolungma with Sir Edmund Hillary in 1953, he made a little hole in the snow and placed a small offering in it—a bar of chocolate, a packet of biscuits, a handful of lollies and a blue pencil from his daughter—to appease the gods.

Western society's affair with the peak began in 1852, when an official of the Great Trigonometrical Survey of India, apparently charged into Sir Andrew Waugh's Dehra Dun office declaring, 'Sir! I have discovered the highest mountain in the world!' Waugh had succeeded George Everest as surveyor-general and under his direction the numerous observations and calculations taken of the peak in 1849 (under Everest's supervision) had finally been analysed and computed.

The tiny kingdom of Nepal, wedged strategically between the two great nations of India and Tibet, was not accessible to Westerners in those days, so the lofty peak had to be surveyed from the Plains of India. The Nepalese rulers were distrustful of all foreigners and had closed their borders following upset over the 1816 British 'Treaty of Friendship'. They were furious with the eastern and western Nepalese border revisions, not at all happy about Sikkim being made a British protectorate, and resentful of the British resident consequently established in Kathmandu. The idea of a resident irked the Nepalese so much that they settled him on land they believed to be lethally malarious and infested by spirits. The resident and his successors were the only aliens within Nepal's frontiers for well over a century.

Chomolungma's inaccessibility led to continual controversy over the mountain's height and name. The figure given for the peak was 29 002 feet (8840 metres), 695 feet (212 metres) taller than Kanchenjunga, the mountain previously believed to be the world's tallest. Not surprisingly, the measurement was inaccurate, but remained the official height until 1955 when results from a survey taken at closer range computed it to be 29 028 feet (8848 metres).

The naming of what the British initially referred to as 'Peak XV', caused quite a stir. Waugh wanted to name the mountain for his predecessor, but even Everest himself had reservations: his name could not be written in Persian or Hindi, and the natives of India could not pronounce it. The official policy of the day, supported by the leading geographical societies around the world, was that mountains should be given the name by which they were known locally. Waugh communicated his contrary intention to the Royal Geographical Society, and justified it by claiming he would not be able to track down a regional name as long as he and his officers were denied entry to the kingdom.

Tenzing Norgay on Everest, 29 May 1953. He and Sir Edmund Hillary were the first to reach the summit of the highest mountain in the world. (Royal Geographic Society)

A spectacular aerial shot of the Everest region, part of the vast Himalaya mountain system which extends 2400 kilometres across southern Asia. Chomolungma is on the left. (William Thompson)

Suggestions that the Sherpas called the mountain Devadhunga, or later, Gauri Shankar, were, in time, dismissed. They were in fact names of other peaks in the jumble of Himalayan giants. The Society adopted the name Everest in 1865, but many of its members were far from satisfied. Douglas Freshfield, one of the group's leading figures wrote in 1882:

> I trust that all geographers, or at any rate all mountaineers, will revert to the ancient and natural name for the mountain. With every respect for the worth of the 'Indian Survey' it is impossible to acquiesce in the attempt permanently to attach to the highest mountain of the world a personal and inappropriate name in place of its own.

Interestingly, proof that the mountain's name was Chomolungma was completely ignored by Waugh and his 'pro-Everest' cronies. As early as 1733, based on the work of a group of monks who had lived in and travelled through Tibet, a company in Paris had published a map which marked the correct position of the mountain and labelled it 'Tschoumou-Lancma'. The Survey of India eventually modified their idea, and agreed 'Chomolungma' should be used when referring to the whole mountain massif … but Everest remained the name of its peak, or summit.

All that fussing over altitude and appellations saw Chomolungma into the early 1920s; and that's when climbers cut in on the geographers' long measured waltz with the world's tallest mountain. The height and name game would continue, but the Goddess Mother of the Universe had a new set of suitors.

The first Reconnaissance Expedition to Everest took place in 1921. The sport of climbing was considered an admirable pursuit by then. In the mid-1800s, British and European scientists had justified their jaunts in the Alps, touting research and exploration as their aim, but by the turn of the century, good old-fashioned international contention had asserted its validity. Mountains were being climbed purely for the achievement, and Britain powered into the Himalayas to take the ultimate prize.

Nepal was still closed to outsiders, so the summit of Everest was pursued from the north. For political reason the British were not in a position to negotiate an expedition into Tibet until after World War II. The British had had a consul in Tibet since 1904 and that, coupled with their control of India, virtually guaranteed them an exclusive right to 'take' Everest. No other nations had a chance to even try, until Nepal reopened its borders in 1951.

In 1921 Tibet was not as well set up as it is today to receive

Base Camp on the Tibetan side commands an uninterrupted view of Chomolungma's Northern Face. (Peter Allen)

expeditions. For a start, there was no such thing as an international airport, nor a motorable road leading from Lhasa all the way to the glacier at the foot of the mountain. The first Everest Reconnaissance Expedition members had to travel across Europe by train to the Middle East, cross the Indian Ocean by ship, train it again from Bombay to Calcutta then drive to the British Hill Station at Darjeeling, near the Indian-Sikkim border. From there it was a foot-slog, all the way through the steamy, leach-infested jungles of Sikkim, then across the dry, wild wastes of Southern Tibet to the ancient Rongbuk Monastery. Sitting at 5030 metres, commanding an uninterrupted view of the loftiest mountain in the world, the monastery had been earmarked as the starting point for the reconnaissance and Base Camp was established close by. One of the team members, George Leigh Mallory, a thirty-five-year-old schoolmaster who did much of the exploratory work of the expedition, wrote of his first view of Everest:

> We asked no questions and made no comment, but simply looked … There is no complication for the eye. The highest of the world's great mountains, it seems, has to make but a single gesture of magnificence to be lord of all, vast in unchallenged and isolated supremacy.

There were no summit aspirations; the purpose of the 1921 expedition was to find the approach route and assess the climbing conditions, in preparation for the following year, when a second expedition, with the sole intention of climbing the peak, would return.

That first all-out 'assault' on Everest in 1922 mixed triumph with tragedy; a sobering cocktail served on so many of the expeditions that would follow. Two of the climbers in the expedition, Geoffrey Bruce (who'd never been mountaineering

before) and Australian scientist, George Finch, reached a height of 8320 metres—a new altitude record. However, seven of their Sherpa porters were killed by an avalanche below the North Col.

The only veteran from the first expedition to join the second was George Leigh Mallory. His name became inexorably linked to Everest. Britain needed a hero to match the might of the mountain, and they chose Mallory: striking good looks, athletic build, young; not the greatest mountaineer around, but that wasn't the point …

Mallory's greatness was indeed thrust upon him. He was selected for the third expedition and a few days after his team leader, Lieutenant Colonel Norton, had reached a height of 8580 metres without oxygen, Mallory and mate, Andrew Irvine, set out from their Top Camp for the summit. They were never seen again.

Somewhere above 8450 metres they paid the ultimate price for a crack at the ultimate mountain. Britain, however, wanted to believe the dynamic duo had reached the summit and perished somewhere on the way down. This 'maybe' secured Mallory a place in the Everest epoch, as did his famous few words: 'Because it is there.'

The fourth, fifth, sixth and seventh British expeditions followed, keeping mountaineers busy between 1924 and 1938. World War II wiped out or maimed many of Britain's better climbers and the English bid for Everest was not resumed until 1951. During that earlier time, two other bizarre solo expeditions took place. In 1934 Maurice Wilson, an ex-captain of the British Army, set out to prove that nothing was impossible. Bent on flying himself into Tibet, he studied and received his pilot's licence in England and then flew to India. Authorities grounded him, so the wacky yet enterprising Wilson went to Darjeeling, hired himself a handful of Sherpas and trekked, in disguise, into Tibet. His body was found on the mountain the following year, en route to the North Col at 6400 metres.

The second loner was Earl Denman, a Canadian who, in 1947, disguised as a Tibetan, made an illicit journey across Tibet to Everest and climbed to just below the North Col; a height of 7150 metres. Unlike Wilson, he lived to tell the tale. It was comforting to know Mother England didn't have a monopoly on eccentricity … or, for that matter, the mountain.

1950–51 heralded a new era in the pursuit of Everest. Tibet had been taken over by the Chinese and once again sealed off from the outside world. Thousands of Tibetan refugees fled to Nepal, and it seemed that the challenge between man and the mountain had reached an anti-climactic stalemate. But a remarkable twist of fate quickly brought the players back to the game. For the first time in 101 years, the King of Nepal moved aside a few of his nation's political pawns and effectively reopened the other side of the board.

King Tribhuvan established diplomatic relations with many countries, and consequently paved the way for other Everest-obsessed nations to seriously compete in the race for the summit. A small Anglo-American party were allowed access to the Solu

A historic photograph of the 1922 British expedition, showing George Mallory and Lieutenant Colonel Norton climbing at 8225 metres. (Royal Geographical Society)

Khumbu region in 1950 and reconnoitred the route to the Khumbu Glacier and beyond to the foot of the Icefall. The Alpine Club and Royal Geographical Society sent a second Reconnaissance Expedition in their footsteps the following

year. They explored the Nepal approaches to Everest and, after negotiating most of the imposing Icefall barring entry into the Western Cwm and thus the peak of Everest, they returned to England, convinced they would be able to reach the summit by this route.

While they toiled over their quixotic plans for yet another all-out British bid to conquer the mountain, two expeditions

Edmund Hillary and Tenzing Norgay as they start from Advance Base for the second assault. (Royal Geographical Society)

18

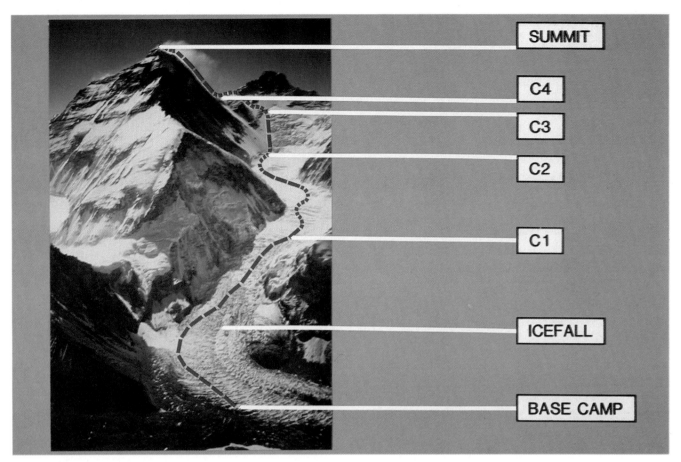

The route taken by members of the Australian Bicentennial Everest Expedition (ABEE) on their successful ascent, which was achieved without the help of Sherpa porters. (Army Audiovisual Unit)

sponsored by the Swiss Foundation for Alpine Research received permission to test their skill on the 'hill'. They flew directly to Kathmandu, met their Sherpas and sirdar, Tenzing Norgay, and reached the mountain in twenty-three days. Confidence was running high. The Brits had their noses put out of joint, but the 1952 attempts, although reaching a record height of 8595 metres, were unsuccessful. The Swiss went home and England breathed a long sigh of relief.

The pressure was on. It was obvious the mountain would be climbed, and soon. If the British were going to pull it off, it was now or never: the French had been allocated a permit for 1954 and the Swiss held another for 1955. Potential climbers for the 1953 British assault were picked and packed off to practise on another Himalayan giant, the 8153-metre Cho Oyu. Among them, of course, was Edmund Hillary, the strong, lanky bee-keeper from Auckland, New Zealand. He was a veteran of the 1951 British Reconnaissance, and considered from the outset to be a summit hopeful. The appointed 1953 expedition leader, John Hunt, wrote in retrospect:

> His testing in the Himalaya had shown that he would be a very strong contender, not only for Everest, but for an eventual summit party … Quite exceptionally strong and abounding in a restless energy, possessed of a thrusting mind which swept aside all unproved obstacles, Ed Hillary's

personality had made its imprint on my mind, through his Cho Oyu and Reconnaissance friends and through his letters to me, long before we met.

Hillary became a living legend. On 29 May 1953, he and Tenzing Norgay stood on top of the world. They (as Hillary so crudely put it) had 'knocked the bastard off'. It was ironic that neither of the two summiteers were British nationals, but that failed to quell the wave of pride which swept across England. The news had been received in London on the eve of Queen Elizabeth's Coronation.

The success did not put an end to the Everest obsession; on the contrary, it broadened it. Climbers from all over the globe, inspired by Hillary and Norgay, sought glory for their country and selves. More difficult routes than the 1953 South Col ascent were found and forged in pursuit of recognition within the sport of mountaineering, now being played at an internationally competitive level. There were the first Indian climbers to stand on the summit, the first Americans, Japanese, Argentinians and so on. Then there were the first ascent of the West Ridge, first traverse, first post-monsoon success, first ascent by a woman (Junko Tabei) and finally the first ascent without supplementary oxygen by Reinhold Messner and Peter Haebler, members of the 1978 Austrian Expedition. In 1980, Messner pushed his mental and physical abilities to the absolute limit and set the ultimate mountaineering precedent: he climbed Everest again without oxygen, and this time alone.

That same year, China reopened the now Autonomous Region of Tibet, so mountaineers knocked up another impressive list of firsts. Australia, flat barren land that it is, even got two to the top;

Tim Macartney-Snape and Greg Mortimer climbed a new route without oxygen in a light-weight ascent.

Improvements in climbing equipment and clothing led to this new, lightweight mountaineering style. Gone were the tweed trousers, felt hats and heavily insulated leather boots; the bulky canvas tents and hurricane lamps. Instead there were new fabrics, Gore-Tex and down, dehydrated foods and aerodynamically designed tents. Characterised by a small, close-knit and often self-supporting team, alpine and lightweight-style climbing was radically different to the tried and tested philosophy of past large-scale expeditions, and quickly became popular in the elite mountaineering arena. That's not to say huge expeditions had had their day; using all the mod cons, ours was a twenty-five member team, and the Tri-Nation Expedition sharing our Base Camp had a total of 252 people involved; the largest expedition in Himalayan history. They were attempting to climb the mountain from both sides, rendezvous on top, and send out the first television telecast from the summit. At a cost of $17 million, it would probably be the most expensive expedition on record as well. If they succeeded millions of people around the world would see the Japan-China-Nepal Expedition triumph *live!*

The thirty-five-year marriage of Westerners to the mountain, for better or worse, has not only changed the lives of the people who have stood on her summit, not to mention the thousands who have risked or forsaken their lives trying, it has changed, irreversibly, the face of a nation. The economy and lifestyle—and in places, the landscape—of so much of Nepal and the Nepalese/Sherpa way of life has altered since foreign climbers first took to their hills.

The highest mountain in the world has gained a new name as well, 'Sagarmatha', meaning 'Brow of the Oceans'; yet the purists, like me, cling doggedly to the local Tibetan and Sherpa title 'Chomolungma'. Only in history do I call the Mother Goddess of the Universe 'Everest', as in Sir George. The name is totally inappropriate; always has been, always will be. I am a disciple of Douglas Freshfield, the long-gone man of ethics in the Royal Geographical Society, and I sense I have less chance of converting the public to his view than he did in 1882. But bear with me, for this is a personal obsession of mine ...

Another person with a recent passion to change popular belief was American astrophysicist, Professor George Wallerstein. In 1986 he shocked the world by announcing a new more accurate survey technique had revealed that K2—previously the second highest peak on the globe—was 8860 metres high, 12 metres taller than the Goddess herself! The ensuing debate led to an eight-man Italian team mounting an expedition to both mountains, and using computerised radio receivers and a system of timed signals from a network of overhead satellites they calculated the exact latitude, longitude and altitude of each receiver. K2 measured in at 8618 metres—7 metres higher than its long-standing measurement—and Chomolungma remained queen at

For thirty-five years Sherpas have risked their lives carrying equipment, consolidating routes and establishing camps for foreign expeditions. While the Tri-Nation Expedition sharing our Base Camp continued this tradition, our own climbers chose not to.

8874 metres, 26 metres loftier than her history records.

Over the decades Chomolungma has seen the works ... short of helicopters or chairlifts ferrying tourists to the summit, it seems as if we've exhausted all possible ways of challenging the world's tallest mountain. What now could impress a saturated public into supporting yet another expedition to Chomolungma? Why on earth would anyone want to go there now anyway? 'To go where no man has gone before' used to satisfy the inquisitive pragmatists ... to get there first had obvious, if nationalistic, validity ... but now, what sane reason is there to risk lives and money on an exercise of very little, if any, social merit? What is it that these climbers of today, and tomorrow, seek?

I guess I've talked to a lot of people about this; and read thousands of books and magazine articles. Public recognition rarely comes into it. Lincoln Hall, a member of the first Australian expedition to Chomolungma wrote:

> It is not the thirst for fame nor the fires of competition which drive me to climb. In the dangerous world of mountaineering such petty desires are tempered by the need to survive.

Sobering words, indeed! A lot of people might wonder what sane person with a will to live would put themselves at the mercy of this mountain, this known killer of climbers? To those people I offer that climbers do not have some bizarre death-wish; rather, a *life*-wish; a need to experience all that is offered within the framework of their own limitations.

When a peak is climbed, when man stands on the summit of any mountain, there is a great sense of achievement, triumph and exaltation. The physical conquest provides part, but by no means all, of the joy in fulfilling that urge which is within all of us: that which impels us to rise above our environment. Mountaineering, the sport that American climbers dubbed 'nine-tenths hell and one-tenth beauty' is part of the eternal quest for adventure; the passion for exploring hazardous and unknown terrain.

Climbing the highest mountain in the world may not be an *adventure* in the eyes of the public anymore, but for every new climber, every new addict to the sport, it is; Chomolungma is a known entity but the height of an individual's limits are, until tested, riddled with uncertainty. It's not so much a matter of climbing the mountain 'because it is there' that counts; more importantly, it becomes 'because *I* am there'. Shallow criticisms such as, 'It's been done before!' aren't going to taint the enthusiasm of someone lusting after their own *personal* 'experience of a lifetime'. To push one's self to the limit of one's mental and physical abilities has nothing to do with the public; nothing to do with history or nationalism; it is purely a *personal challenge*, and in every generation, in societies where the struggle for the right to live is not an everyday battle, there are those who will rise to meet it.

> *Those Himalayas of the mind*
> *Are not so easily possessed:*
> *There's more than precipice and storm*
> *Between you and your Everest.*
>
> C. Day Lewis.

*Buddhist prayer flags fly from the 500-year-old Great Stupa of
Bodhnath, one of the biggest stupas in the world.*

2
Kathmandu Revisited

Chapter Two

Kathmandu Revisited

Still the world is wondrous large—
seven seas from marge to marge—
And it holds a vast of various kinds of man
And the wildest dreams of Kew
are the facts of Khathmandhu …

Rudyard Kipling,
in *In the Neolithic Age*

The all-seeing eyes of Buddha, adorning the great Stupa of Sway-anbhunath, gaze compassionately over the city of Kathmandu.

For the 1534th time, I scrawled my signature across an official expedition postcard. I looked up from the never-shrinking pile of 'sponsored' correspondence balanced on the tray table wedged between me and the seat in front, and looked out the porthole-sized window. Nepal at last! We were finally flying over the world's only Hindu kingdom; a small but spectacular rectangle just 800 kilometres long and 90–220 kilometres wide. 'There's Kanch! Kanchenjunga!' Jim Van Gelder called above the constant roar of the 747's engines. His voice rang like a bell dismissing class. The autographing session stopped abruptly and all the team members raced to the right-hand side of the plane to gaze at the 8598-metre peak. Craning our necks, more of the northern Himalayas came into view, rising behind a sea of blue foothills like the foaming crest of a daunting tidal wave.

'Which one is Chomolungma?' I asked innocently. Jim looked at me like I was some sort of moron, pointed at a huge black peak disappearing into the clouds and went on staring longingly at Kanchenjunga. He had climbed, but not summited the mountain in 1986 with James Strohfeldt and three others, then had a second go at it in late 1987 with Terry Tremble. The majestic, isolated peak, although the third highest in the world, is infrequently climbed. There is a huge amount of mystique surrounding the mighty mountain, and Jim claimed that its spiritual significance had prevented anyone from ever standing on the highest of its five summits. Climbers always stopped a few metres short of the sacred top. 'Everest is a social phenomenon—it's no different from a City to Surf marathon; you climb it for other people, not for personal reasons,' Jim said, still mesmerised by his beloved Kanch. 'It doesn't matter that I haven't been successful on Kanch yet—that's great! It means I get to go back again.' He dreamily recalled the beauty of the walk-in and the herd of deer feeding peacefully around the lush green Base Camp. The reason behind his being on the Everest Expedition had more to do with not wanting to miss out, than it did with Chomolungma-mania.

Jon Muir, the hottest of the hot climbers, was chainsmoking

and laughing. 'That's it. That big black one there,' he giggled, almost as high as Everest itself. 'I ought to know—I only left the place three months ago!' He laughed so hard he fell into the lap of an incredulous yuppie-looking American tourist—and that simply added to his hysteria. When a 'take-off and landing phobia' (even one diluted with enough beer to knock a horse unconscious) is coupled with a glimpse of the world's highest mountain, extreme emotions surface; especially when the paranoiac is on his way to climb the giant for the third time. Acutely aware of how ridiculous his obsession seemed, the red-headed freckle-faced ace from Natimuk, Victoria, had finally cracked up. He was ready for a straightjacket—not a climbing harness.

The seatbelt sign went on and the plane began its descent. I strapped Jon in and sat next to him, holding his hand. Below us the Kathmandu Valley shone like an emerald. Every facet was highlighted by the red-tiled roofs of Nepalese farmhouses, increasing in number as we inched towards the city. Neo-classical palaces, built during the kingdom's despotic century-long Rana oligarchy, were stark, obvious landmarks in the ochre urban sprawl of Kathmandu/Patan. The tarmac suddenly rushed to meet us and Jon squeezed hard on my fingers. He regained most (which wasn't much) of his former composure as the plane taxied slowly towards the terminal.

The Tribhuvan Airport 'Arrivals' room was as spartan and dilapidated as I remembered from my last visit. The stench from the squat toilets brought back a million memories; as did the long wait for our luggage. With the plush furnishings and efficiency of Bangkok Airport and adjoining hotel still fresh in their minds from a stopover there, the newchums to the Asian continent were clearly stunned, if not overcome.

When the first barrels and kitbags appeared on the carousel I spied Australia's attractive ambassador to Nepal, Di Johnstone,

*Snow-covered peaks, rising to meet the clouds, dominate the horizon
behind Kathmandu's emerald green valley.*

in the corner furthest from the offensive toilets, welcoming a '60 Minutes' television crew to the kingdom. She presented the crew, producer and anchorman—who had come to film the dynamic blonde from 'Down Under'—in action on the 'Roof of the World'—with flower garlands, and then helped them get their cameras and film stock through customs. She left Brian Pullen, the embassy's right-hand man, to similarly aid the expedition, and disappeared out of the concrete hovel with a gay, 'See you all at the cocktail party.' The reason for having to bring a 'dressy pair of trousers and a shirt (tie optional)' was at last made clear. 'Lady' Di was throwing a party in our honour.

Austin had a carton of cigarettes and a bottle of whisky on hand just in case Pullen couldn't charm the custom's officials as easily as Ms Johnstone. With the exception of seventy-five disposable lighters distributed in our personal gear, we didn't have anything to hide; we were just trying to avoid paying duty and the time-consuming inconvenience of opening over eighty packs and barrels for inspection. After asking Jon and I to unlock our camera cases and politely requesting Rheinberger for the key to one bulging duffle bag, the officer in charge signed and stamped a lot of papers. Pullen smiled (as only a public servant

Six tonnes of expedition equipment and supplies preceded our own arrival at Kathmandu's Tribhuvan Airport. (Zac Zaharias)

can) and we were free to drag our swags and selves out onto the street. Children with beaming smiles and ragged dusty clothes mobbed us for 1 rupee notes (about 4 cents), and begged to help us with our luggage. They were all shorter that the average kitbag, but hung around laughing and looking at the huge pile of gear until our Mountain Travel 'Courtesy Bus' arrived in a choking cloud of dust.

Once loaded, the bus revved and laboured its way along the road to the Shangrila Hotel. I don't believe there are road rules in Nepal; merely suggestions. One: don't look where you are going too often; two: don't drive on the correct side of the road for more than thirty seconds at a time; and most importantly, three: never ever hit a cow. Since the beast we mercilessly reduce to hamburger mince is sacred in Nepal, knocking one off—even by accident—is an offence punishable by law. Bovines have right of way over buses, and if one decides to slump down in the middle of the road and create a traffic hazard, so be it.

With my back-seat-driving nerves about to short-circuit, I tried to relax and enjoy the passing glimpses of semi-rural landscape on the edge of the city. Orange-red brick houses were surrounded by pitiful rice paddies, struggling to grow in the heavily polluted air. Women squatted by streams, washing and beating their families' clothes and bed linen, then drying the sheets and saris by laying them flat in an abstract pattern on the

Colour floods the streets of Kathmandu as traders display their wares outdoors.

Cauliflowers and radishes cover the steps of a small shrine in the busy market area of Thamel.

canvas of the land. In the suburbs, exhaust fumes blended with the smell of cooking oil bubbling sluggishly in huge vats on the roadside stalls and in the doorways of poky, unlit cafes. Electricity, punctuated by frequent power cuts, has been available on a twenty-four-hours-a-day basis in Kathmandu since 1982, but shops and eateries off the regular tourist beat rarely turn anything on until the evening.

Life floated past, like frozen frames in a movie. A group of women … a tiny face peered out from the folds of a pink sari embroidered with silver thread … a huge pair of eyes, as big as Buddha's and ringed with kohl stared upward … a grubby hand clutched the string of a burst balloon and a little pink lip quivered, close to tears … a pair of tired chubby legs dangle from another hip and lolled to the rhythm of a mother's graceful movement … a nose ring glittered here, a toothless smile flashed there. Each silent image I savoured in slow motion.

By Nepalese standards the Shangrila Hotel in the Lazimpat district rated at least four stars. I'd never stayed in a real hotel in Kathmandu before; the one-dollar-a-night-bed-bugs-included doss houses and 'trekkers' lodges' had always served me and my budget well. After recovering from the initial shock of uniformed (and white-gloved!) bellboys and perfectly groomed receptionists, Jill, the expedition cook, and I relished the luxury of having someone carry our bags up to our room. They'd put us together on the top floor because we both looked like we could use the exercise of the stairs. I was glad to have Jill for a room-mate, and we were mutually happy to have each other on the expedition.

We had already shared an enormous bed in Bangkok, so I knew she didn't snore. We pulled open the curtains in our room, made sure the hot tap in the shower wasn't an illusion, and walked off for an afternoon in Thamel, the trekker's mecca.

Jill had been to Nepal less recently than I, so she was even more dumbfounded by the changes in the country's capital city. A mediaeval township suddenly launched into the twentieth century, it could not fail to show the startling effects of 'progress'. It was impossible to imagine what the place must have looked like before the mass-immigration of mountaineers and hippies in the '60s, for so much of the Kathmandu we had known so well had already changed beyond recognition in the short space of a few years.

For some reason the streets had been swept almost clean; a rare, possibly hallucinated, dust-free image which made me pinch my arm in disbelief. Really! The streets were swept! Last time I was in Kathmandu it was the monsoon season and the streets were ankle-deep, and in places calf-deep, in muddy water. Flower petals, plastic bags, torn wrappers from chocolate bars and glucose biscuits, tufts of hair and horns from dismembered goats, banana peels and bidi (cigarette) butts; you name it, it floated on the surface of the city's seasonal canal system. It looked so different I had trouble remembering the well-trodden route to Thamel.

A huge new concrete and brick shopping complex—more in keeping with the drab style of modern Indian or Chinese architecture than the space-age, no-expense-spared designs of the West—now dominated the left-hand side of the main artery leading into Thamel's taxi- and rickshaw-cluttered heart. It also had a squeaky-clean façade and the pseudo-European pastries for sale in the first of an anticipated twenty retail outlets and offices not only looked but tasted like plastic. Adding insult to injury, the building dwarfed the ancient pagodas still standing right alongside it.

The inner chambers of Thamel, thank God, had withstood the test of time. Since tourism became a big industry in the kingdom, Kathmandu has overdosed on Westernisation and society has largely become service orientated. Without losing an ounce of charm, Thamel gradually established itself as an area of town functioning totally for the benefit of the on-a-shoestring travellers of the '80s; here is the Freak Street of the hippie era, conservatively tailored to suit our very different modern wants and needs. That's not to say you can't still buy tee-shirts emblazoned with 'The Grateful Dead' and 'Woodstock Lives On', nor shoulder bags, crushed velvet waistcoats, secondhand leather sandals and cheap paper prints of Yin and Yang symbols or spiritually enlightened erotica. That stuff will always be there, tucked somewhere behind the rows of handmade, designer-look jumpers dyed in the current fashion shades and the latest and greatest mountaineering and backpacking equipment.

Anywhere else in the world, I'd probably shy away from such a place; always preferring to romantically immerse myself in the authentic, traditional—as opposed to recently manufactured—culture. But not here. Not in Kathmandu. I fell in love with Thamel and its unique personality, evolved from the blending of East and West, and all the Nepalese people who contribute their character, not to mention their goods and chattels, to the mayhem and madness of the place.

After negotiating the traffic-jam of tooting taxis and brightly painted honking rickshaws in the tiny square in the middle of the Thamel district, we stood for a minute on the doorstep of a trekking shop (there are no footpaths). We looked up at the communication-congestion of signs and telegraph wires similarly competing for space above the level of the crowded street, then looked across at the *thangka* shop, still displaying several hundred hand-painted religious scrolls, both outside and within its 2 metres by 3 metres space. We watched a constant parade of blonde, red and curly brunette heads pass; listened to a dozen different languages and accents, then smiling at each other we sighed simultaneously, 'Now *this* is more like it!' Absorbed in the colour and chaos, I stepped down from the shop's threshold and straight into the path of a speeding black-framed bicycle. The rider swerved, knocked another tourist into a fruit seller who wobbled and dropped a few already bruised apples from his bamboo basket onto the road. A mangy, thin dog immediately darted forward to chase it and ran in front of a taxi which veered out of the way and ran over my foot. Yep, that *really* was more like it! Jill and I laughed and like human dominoes, we joined the throng and toppled into the restaurant-studded single-lane street leading to Le Bistro.

Every step was countered by 'You buy carpet?', and 'Change money?—I give you good rate!' If I had a dollar for every time those words were whispered at me, I wouldn't *need* a good rate. If it's not 'Change money,' it's 'Hashish—you want hashish?' or 'Massage? I give good massage!' If it wasn't so annoyingly constant, and the touts were older than the average age of eleven, it might actually be funny. I saw one tourist attempting to prevent

Souvenir shops stock everything—thankas, carpets, hand-made sweaters, shoulder bags and Lindt chocolate! You name it, you can buy it!

the pint-sized blackmarketeers from continually bombarding him with their parroted sales-pitches; he had a tee-shirt printed with a list: 'No hashish, No shoeshine, No carpet, No change money, No massage, NO PROBLEM!!!' I saw a hashish-kid I recognised from 1985. He was still working the same beat, still hanging out with the legless beggar on the skateboard and still pushing drugs. He'd grown cheekier as well as taller, and now offered more than just a 'rub down' on the massage deal. At fifteen, I guess he thought he had substantial credibility!

Jill and I lingered outside Helena's Restaurant for a moment, drooling over the tempting lemon meringue pie and thickly iced chocolate cake exhibited in the window. A curio peddler tried to sell us a rather dubious string of coral and turquoise beads, claiming they were genuine antique Tibetan jewels. All things Tibetan were currently in vogue and fake-gem-encrusted jewellery and artifacts littered every second street stall. Anything authentic cost an arm and a leg, from the silver-lined human skull bowls to the appliqué felt wedding boots, outrageous prices were not only being sought, but *paid!* Tibetan traders are the best in the world; you can wrangle with them till you're blue in the face, and you'll never beat them down. Not surprisingly, the majority of trekking and mountaineering stores in Thamel are owned by shrewd Tibetans living in Kathmandu since they or their families fled their homeland after Tibet's unsuccessful revolt against tightening Chinese control in 1959. Despite the normal six- or seven-day trading week, many of the outfitting businesses we passed were closed. Hand-written notices stuck on the bolted wooden doors reminded me that it was Tibetan New Year. Obviously the proprietors were down at Bodhnath Stupa, or off

Buyers beware! Fake turquoise and coral stud the 'genuine antique' Tibetan jewellery on this stall in Thamel.

visiting relatives and friends, welcoming in the Year of the Fire Dragon with plenty of chang, dancing and feasting. Jill and I quickened our pace; we had a bit of visiting to do as well, not to mention drinking and eating.

I glimpsed my old friend, Ganesh Pandey, through the dusty window of his restaurant, Le Bistro. He was smiling from ear to ear, framed by his blackboard menu: the image was a carbon copy of the one I had carried around in my head for a few years. Absolutely nothing had changed; not even the worn faded tablecloths and matching burnt-orange seat cushions. I pulled the wire screen door open and ran in to greet my old buddy and introduce him to Jill. When I was held up in Kathmandu for three weeks in July 1985, trying to convince the Chinese Embassy to allow me into Tibet via Kodari on the Nepal-Tibet border, Pandey used to console me with huge slices of yak cheesecake and thick papaya *lassi* shakes. It was comforting to see he still had them on the bill of fare. I thought I may have consumed his lifetime supply when, on returning from my long trek across Tibet, I spent an additional two weeks in Kathmandu joyfully pigging out, using Christmas and a 13-kilogram weight loss for my new excuse. It's a great feeling to walk into a restaurant at the other end of the world, after years of next to no contact, and say, 'I'll have the usual, please.'

Jill got on as famously as everyone did with Pandey. We gave him two huge jars of Vegemite to appease his favourite brand of clientele, and spent the rest of the afternoon telling tales from more recent adventures and reliving some special shared memories. The night Pandy's diminutive, but volatile, wife chased me out of the restaurant, wielding a housebrick seemed like only yesterday. Tears of laughter trickled down my cheeks as I recalled how she had assumed I was her husband's mistress!

Jill was splitting her sides over the story, the sun was pouring down into the courtyard and I didn't have a single care in the world. Ahhh, Kathmandu … Thamel. It was so damn *good* to be back!

Many other team members were similarly occupied that afternoon. Jon Muir and Mike Rheinberger had gone to see Elizabeth Hawley, the executive officer of Sir Edmund Hillary's Himalayan Trust. Jon had left a few items of climbing gear with her after his last expedition. Her office had become a meeting place for mountaineers and her files bulged with reports and documentation on every major Himalayan expedition ever undertaken. Jon said his hellos, retrieved his kit and returned to the hotel uncharacteristically despondent. It seemed Ms Hawley, a resident of Kathmandu for over twenty years, a journalist and 'one-woman Himalayan mountaineering institute' was in danger of being kicked out of the kingdom. She was writing for *Time* magazine and Reuters news service and had recently scribed some criticism which so offended the powers that be that her residency status was cancelled and replaced with a two-week tourist visa.

In other parts of Thamel a few of the guys were discovering the varied delights of the exotic Asian capital for the first time, testing their cast-iron constitutions by dining anywhere and everywhere from lunchtime right through to dinner.

Before sunrise the next morning, Jill and I coaxed Zac Zaharias and Paul Bayne out to watch the day dawn from Swayanbhunath, the famous 'monkey temple', which commands a magnificent view from the top of a hill just west of Kathmandu. Legend has it that the valley of Kathmandu was once a calm turquoise lake. A beautiful lotus, with a venerable blue light shining out from its heart, floated on its surface. The flower was said to be the manifestation of the primaeval Buddha, Swayanbhu. People came from all over Asia to contemplate and adore the fiery flower. The patriarch Manjushri wanted to worship it more closely, so he took his flaming sword of wisdom and sliced the valley wall damming the lake. All the water drained out and the lotus settled on the valley floor. Manjushri built a shrine there, which grew into the Great Stupa of Swayanbhunath.

Zac and Paul got out of the taxi at the top of the hill and entered the stupa's sacred grounds the easy way. Jill and I wandered down the road winding to its base for the more meritorious approach: straight up the wide ramp of 300 muscle-flexing flagstoned steps. The steep aisle soared upward through the monkey-riddled forest blanketing the hillside and was flanked on both sides by pairs of huge stone animals. The notoriously mischievous monkeys of Swayanbhunath were hitching a ride on the backs of these fearsome 'vehicles of the gods', trying to antagonise passing groups of their two-legged descendants, slowly lumbering towards enlightenment. Reminiscent of the Australian Kooris' stories of creation, the pesky primates were supposed to be the result of Manjushri once cutting his hair at Swayanbhunath: each falling hair became a tree, and every little head louse became a monkey.

Crawling up the last few steps, Jill and I collapsed beneath the

A colourful archway frames the first of 300 flagstoned steps leading up to the hilltop stupa of Swayanbhunath.

The first rays of sunrise set the stupa's spire of thirteen gilded rings ablaze. Swayanbhunath is one of eight sites in Nepal included in UNESCO's World Heritage list.

all-seeing unblinking eyes of Buddha. Zac came over and joined us. The first rays of sunrise set the stupa's spire of thirteen gilded rings ablaze. We squinted to block out the glare, but Buddha didn't bat so much as one of his eight eyelids. Painted on all four sides of the block crowning the whitewashed hemispherical mound of the stupa, the eyes gazed compassionately over the Kathmandu Valley in all four directions. Between each curved set of eyebrows a yellow circle represented the mystical third eye, a symbol of true wisdom. The Nepalese character for number one, a symbol of unity, featured as Buddha's nose, and the glistening gold rings denoted the thirteen degrees of knowledge and the ladder to nirvana—manifested here as an ornate gold umbrella.

Right of the giant staircase, in a large low ceilinged shelter recessed into a wall, devotees were waking their gods with music. The haunting, strained notes of a *saringhis*—a four-stringed viola carved from a single piece of wood—lilted to the bend of a musician's bow. A second pair of leathery hands thrummed upon a worn hand-drum hide, and the timbre of a singer's nasal voice was miraculously transformed as it echoed

32

in the acoustic recess. It was a joy to watch Paul, with such uninhibited, almost child-like wonderment, absorb the sound, light and entire visual spectacle of pilgrims, monks and mangy dogs making their way around the stupa. It was even more satisfying to realise experience had not contracted my own goggle-eyed sense of awe.

We joined the parade of prayer-wheel-spinning worshippers moving clockwise around the stupa. An old woman appeased the gods by sprinkling a ritual offering of rice grains, red powder and tiny yellow flower petals on each sunlit bronze deity she passed and a pre-schooler tempted fate by reaching for a wayward monkey's tail. Pigeons cooed and fluttered around the gold nirvana then winged their way towards the valley, carrying the message of daybreak to the streets of sleepy Kathmandu. We took a few photographs then stood together at the top of the stairs and watched the rising sun pull back the misty pink covers blanketing the city. We stood for some time, watching the early morning serenity completely dissolve beneath a haze of exhaust fumes and dust. The last ritual melody wafted from the temple chamber and lost itself in the orchestration of horns and purring motors below. Zac and Paul went straight back to the hotel for the 8.30 a.m. strategy meeting, and Jill and I detoured to Narayan's Restaurant in Thamel for some cinnamon rolls. Narayan's was

The view over Kathmandu from Swayanbhunath at sunrise.

a kind of halfway house or purgatorial transit lounge between the lofty Swayanbhunath and the down-to-earth business of expedition administration.

Naturally, our indulgence and subsequent tardiness added fuel to the hellish fires of our antagonists. There were those among the rank with public bar mentalities: they clearly objected to women being included in their macho-man mountaineering manoeuvres. Even Chris Curry, one of the file who regularly voiced his support for Jill's and my own inclusion in the expedition, had admitted his opinion would change as the team advanced to the higher reaches of the mountain. Jill and I were there under sufferance; sticky cinnamon-coated lips and all. I was glad I only had to photograph, not feed, the troop. I wouldn't have swapped jobs with Jill for all the rupees in the kingdom. As cook she was set to cop every scathing criticism imaginable. That Jill could prepare potatoes, eggs and dehydrated or tinned foods 101 different ways wouldn't matter; men under stress have to complain about *something*—that's a fact—and on expeditions, nine and a half times out of ten their frustrations surface at the dinner table. There is never enough food, it's too spicy, too bland, the same menu as the day before, not up to the five-star restaurant standard their stomachs are used to … you name it, they'll complain about it.

Luckily we weren't too late to miss the 'Day One' plan: to get our passports and paperwork down to Mountain Travel's

headquarters, change money and purchase last minute equipment needs from the trekking shops in Thamel. Since I didn't know one end of an ice-axe from the other, Mick Pezet was assigned to accompany me on a 'climbing boots and all' spending spree.

Mick was an instantly likable character—the team's genuine Mr Nice Guy. He worked for his father's Parramatta-based car radiator business and part time as a corporal in the Army Reserve. In the hectic blur of days just prior to the expedition, I remember bumping into Mick in every mountaineering shop in Sydney. In each case he had his girlfriend, Andrea, in one hand and a 2-litre white plastic Jerry-can-shaped pee-bottle swinging from the other. This *pièce de résistance* came courtesy of the medical research unit set to accompany the ABEE. Mick had submitted voluntarily to the blood tests and twenty-four-hour urine sampling, and was far from coy about displaying his latter contribution. When slack shop assistants were annoyingly slow to serve him, he simply lifted his pee-bottle onto their glass display counters and smiled. They couldn't wrap and charge his purchases quickly enough!

On our tour of Kathmandu's second-hand mountaineering gear suppliers, we ran into the team's token Tasmanian—ace-climber and crack comedian Bruce Farmer—and his articulate, charismatic shopping partner, Major Jim Truscott. It seemed Jim was incapable of smiling, and stringing a sentence together without using swear words for conjunctives. I couldn't for the life of me work out why he had such a huge dark cloud floating above his constantly frowning, brow-knotted head. The day we left Sydney he had found out his wife, Collette, was pregnant with their second child, but it was difficult to imagine someone

Mick Pezet and Paul Bayne stop for a snack during a last-minute buying spree in Thamel.

like Jim being so sensitive to a bit of bad timing; besides, Collette still intended walking into Base Camp with the third AAA trekking party in April. No, there was something—some unresolved anger—there, and it didn't take a triple-certificated psychologist to recognise it.

Bruce, on the other hand, couldn't have been happier. He was in haggler's heaven—beating down the price of an ice-axe here, arguing over the blackmarket exchange rate there. His relentless banter had the Nepalese merchants laughing and pleading for mercy. He had the face and temperament of a perpetually happy drunk and as I watched him performing for a carpet seller in the middle of the street, I remembered how much his 'no worries' attitude and bad jokes had contributed to the good feeling at the start of the New Zealand Chomolungma Expedition in 1985. Australian citizenship had not changed him one iota. He was still a solid wall of lunacy, and it was still impossible to picture him being a business-suited general manager of *anything*, let alone an enormous multimillion dollar aluminium company like Comalco.

It took all afternoon to find the cheapest, lightest, best fitting and most suitable models of all the items on our list. The boots were the hardest to come by, and in the end, Mick put a down-payment on a pair he really wanted for himself and agreed to give me his bright-blue expedition issue Koflachs. We went back to the hotel and I spent the evening trying everything on and double checking I had, at last, everything I personally needed to stay warm and safe on the mountain.

Our next morning in Kathmandu started badly. It was Jill's and my turn to take part in the sacrificial blood-letting rite. Carol, the vampire, let herself into our room and prepared the syringes. The first samples had to be taken while we were still lying down and semi-comatose. It was worse than waiting to have a tooth drilled, and while our nervous jokes may have covered up our fear, our telltale pulse rates revealed all.

The whole ordeal proved far more torturous than we could ever have imagined in our wildest of wild nightmares. Jill and I have deepset veins and Carol ain't William Tell ... we suffered, and not in silence. The dart-throwing doctor kept missing her target and my arm was soon bruised and swollen beyond belief. Jill's was worse. Blood had squirted onto the sheets and half a dozen hypodermics, bloodied swabs and all the packaging from the sterile specimen vials and assorted bandages filled the rubbish basket. I half expected the drug squad to burst into our room.

Cinnamon rolls eventually pacified us and Jill ventured off to spend the day buying cooking pots, pans and paraphernalia for her 'walk-in kitchen'. Most of the guys were assigned to 'trial tent-erection duty' and since a degree in engineering was a prerequisite for useful participation, I excused myself and went on a photographic venture to Patan and Bodhnath.

The ancient city of Patan, just south of Kathmandu on a plateau above the Bagmati River, is possibly the oldest Buddhist city in the world. I started re-exploring the temple-riddled streets and plazas just near the city's Durbar Square. From every corner a different cluttered image formed. Doorways and dark passages beckoned and faces in ornate window-frames met my gaze then disappeared into darkness. The roofs of gilded copper temples glistened between the displayed wares spilling from basket shops and *thangka* dealers. Like entrails spewing from the grey gut of a wounded beast, a mass of coloured cords and insulated wiring stretched from telegraph pole to telegraph pole. Every which way I looked there were 'Sincere Supermarket Centres', 'Humane Fit Tailors' and similarly dubious retail outlets and manufacturers. In one back street courtyard I strayed into, a hair-shaving ceremony was in progress. The Nepalese families involved in the initiation-style rite welcomed me, and I sat with them for a joyous half hour, laughing, and crying for, their shaven children. The one-year-old babies dripped huge tears from their khol-smudged eyes and their seven-year-old brothers, draped in thin cotton sheets, sat bald and shivering in a sombre row.

Down at Bodhnath Stupa, the largest in Nepal, a very different tradition was being honoured. The Tibetan New Year celebrations were drawing to a close and a great wave of gay Tibetans, intense-looking Western devotees and stunned tourists, ebbed towards a small temple courtyard near the main bell-shaped stupa. Vats of chang, a fermented barley drink, were opened and large boxes and trays laden with special *lho-sa* pastries were passed or offered around. I felt a little alienated in the crowd and felt a longing to be back in the real Tibet. Even though Kathmandu, with its 12 000 Tibetan residents, is considered a principal centre of Tibetan culture and religious teaching, I sensed something was amiss. There was some protective essence, some completely trusting acceptance that always encompassed me inside the real Tibet, that was missing here at Bodhnath. Perhaps I had been spoilt.

I left the party and wandered back through the maze of monasteries, liquor bars, lodges, chapels, cheese shops and carpet factories surrounding the Great Stupa of Bodhnath. Worshippers were moving around the outside perimeter of the massive whitewashed mound, spinning prayer wheels and reverently touching the 108 images of Buddha set into its base. On the gradually ascending terraces directly beneath the mound,

Tears stream from khol-smudged eyes of a baby during a hair-shaving ceremony in Patan.

Temples and pagodas crowd Durbar Square in the ancient city of Patan, just south of Kathmandu.

brand new prayer flags, streaming like maypole ribbons from the top of the gold nirvana umbrella, were being tied down for the year. I watched the pilgrims prostrating and chanting, then lost myself in fond memories of Lhasa for the rest of the afternoon.

When I finally returned to the present, I hurried back to the Shangrila Hotel. I had completely forgotten about the Embassy 'do' scheduled for the evening. I quickly got my act together, threw on a dress (I didn't have the expected 'shirt, tie optional' garb) and raced down to meet the rest of the gang in the foyer. We all piled into taxis, armed with our embossed invitations and hand-drawn maps directing the way to Di Johnstone's Western-style residence.

Di met the droves of punctual guests at her front door and diplomatically shook every offered hand. The strong tungsten

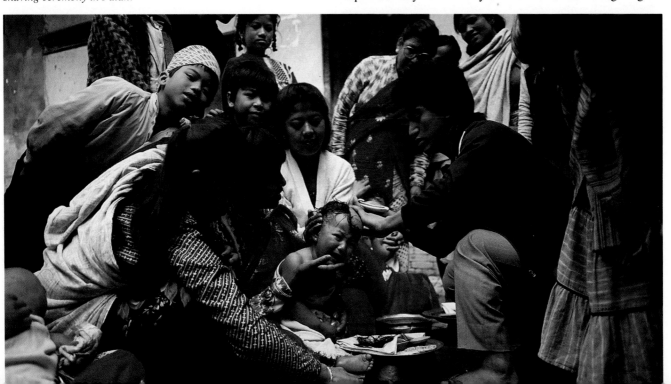

globes of the '60 Minutes' film crew made her forehead gleam with perspiration and her all-covering black sequins danced like stars in the light. Politicians and government representatives never cease to amaze me with the strength of their smiling muscles.

The two Terrys, not wanting to waste any time, grabbed a drink from a passing tray. In the time it takes a normal human being to blink, they had drained three glasses apiece, and were well and truly set to uphold the greatest of all Aussie traditions. The measure of a party's success is how little one can remember of it the following morning. A few formal speeches were made and Austin presented Di with a framed Ansell Adams print of Alaska's Mt McKinley—one of the practice climbs for many of the expedition members. The '60 Minutes' team switched off their spotlights, and within 60 seconds there wasn't a trace of formality and seriousness left in the room.

By breakfast time the following day, the expedition casualty list had predictably grown. Bruce, (Troubled) Truscott and Andrew Smith had missed the ambassador's reception and were still doubled up with stomach cramps, fever and diarrhoea. Jill was hungover and nearly passed out when Chris Curry tried to take blood from her. (The two of us had personally sacked Carol in favour of Chris' better bedside manner.) The two Terrys were bedridden and Paul Bayne had been caught short with the dreaded diarrhoea. Several others were coming down with headcolds, myself included. Mine wasn't bad enough to warrant mollycoddling, so I offered to relieve Jill of her fresh-food

Sorting out supplies and equipment proved a formidable task for expedition members.

shopping duties. Her stomach had decided to spend the rest of the day impersonating a washing machine—alternating between the turning and churning and spinning out cycles.

I met Wanchu the expedition's Nepalese cook, over at the Mountain Travel offices, at 10 a.m. He was mentally calculating what we needed; how many eggs, potatoes, bamboo porter baskets, cauliflowers, kilos of rice and dhal and sacks of carrots and onions. I left him with his sums for a moment and ventured around to the grassy yard behind the neoclassical office building. All available hands were out there, packing equipment and supplies needed on the three week walk-in into 30-kilogram porter-loads. Rheinberger was efficiently distributing clothing and footwear to our Nepalese support crew of cookboys and mail runners and BJ was working out the best way to pack as yet unbroken biscuits. I took several photographs of the busy and colourful scene, then wandered over to console a grumbling Chris Curry, unhappily crouched over a bright orange tarp spread with every drug and diarrhoea suppressant known to mankind. He had been asked to sort through the medical supplies, since the expedition doctor, Tony Delaney, had yet to materialise from the ski slopes of Aspen, Colorado. Chris had wanted no part whatsoever in the doctoral needs of the expedition. As a full-time senior medical officer in the emergency department of Christchurch Hospital, mountaineering trips were his way of escaping the rigours of his profession, not extending his iatric experience. 'I just wanted to be a bum climber,' he moaned, '… check this rubbish out—there are enough anti-diarrhoea agents here to clog up the entire armed forces for a year! What's worse is people will expect me to dish the drugs out.' Chris was a firm believer that pills were a last resort measure, and rarely

administered anything stronger than an aspirin. He was not happy with his new, if temporary, responsibility, nor the stack of medicines at his disposal. I managed to make him smile for a photograph, then rejoined Wanchu, now requisitioning brass stoves from the company's storeroom.

Pasang, the head cookboy, joined us on the shopping venture. Wanchu knew every stall holder on the crowded market streets, and since all negotiations were done in Nepalese, I had no idea what, or how much of it, we were purchasing. Not, that is, until Pasang appeared with three rickshaws and we returned to all the grain stores, vegie shops, butchers, bakers and candlestick-makers to collect our orders. It was amazing how much stuff they crammed into the rear of each rickshaw, after removing the passenger seats. The drivers were initially reluctant to cram their ricketty rollers so full, but eventually agreed when Wanchu offered them a 10-rupee tip. Pasan, Wanchu and I flagged down a fourth richshaw and followed the caravan, labouring along the rough back laneways beneath no less than 11 000 rupees worth of foodstuffs. It was already late afternoon by this stage, so I jumped off at the Thamel intersection to say my goodbyes to Pandey and the gang in Le Bistro.

It rained during the night and 'D-day' dawned clearer and crisper than any I had ever known in Kathmandu. In the hotel foyer, luggage was stacking up faster than Phil Pitham could number and record it. He was getting frustrated and tried to implement some sense of order to the chaos. There was a pile of backpacks and personal gear destined to accompany us on the bus ride to Jiri and thus the walk-in, and there was an even bigger heap of equipment which would fly with Peter Lambert and Charlie Hart to Lukla and be yak-packed to Base Camp well ahead of the main party. Peter Allen and Norm Crookston were already in Lukla, hopefully hiring herdsmen and organising their payments on a per yak basis.

Everyone madly ran around swapping items in and out of different bags and securing their padlocks before they had time to change their minds again. Jon Muir was sitting comfortably on the lounge, putting the finishing touches to his application to climb a new route on Ama Dablan. As if the immediate challenge of Chomolungma wasn't enough! The guy was insatiable. I went over to tell him the bus was leaving, and he just let out one of his manic laughs. 'Third time works the charm!' he said, shaking his head to the beat of an unheard Sony Walkman. He showed me his Ama Dablan application and described the hairy knife-edged route he wanted to climb and film with his wife, Brigette, in 1989.

Jon was by far the most interesting guy on the team; irreverent, crazy, uninhibited, good humoured and so intense his eyes were permanently popping out of their freckled sockets. A thin rat's-tail plait hung down from his closely cropped red hair; if he made it to the summit of Chomolungma, he was going to cut it off and give it to his father. Every time Jon talked about his family, he oozed with love. He wasn't interested in putting up any independent, macho façade—his family meant the world to him, and he wasn't too proud to admit it.

Jon was destined to be a climber: conceived in Scotland, he (and twin sister) were carried to Australia on the P&O *Himalaya*. He was born in Wollongong and his introduction to the climbing game came courtesy of Chris Bonington's television documentary, 'Everest the Hard Way'. Right then and there, in the middle of trying to choose a career for himself, the inspired fifteen-year-old turned to his father and said, 'That's it! That's what I'm going to be! A mountain climber!' And right then and there, that's exactly what he set out to become. First it was library books, then rock-climbing with a mate and his sister's horse rope for safety on Wollongong's Mt Keira, then New Zealand … then a whole heap of other cliffs, mountains, and sea stacks (he climbed one of the Twelve Apostles off the Victorian coastline in 1987), and of course Chomolungma. The tee-shirt he had been wearing since we arrived in Kathmandu was embroidered with the all-revealing words, 'Everest '84, Everest '87, Everest '88—might as well touch the sun.'

We walked out to the bus together with Krondorf—Jon's go-everywhere mascot. I shoved the monster-sized floppy-eared stuffed dog under my flu-heavy head and Jon wired into another of his seventy-odd tapes. All the sickies, clutching rolls of toilet paper, got into the first few rows of hard narrow seats and Austin hopped in last, joining BJ in the bus driver's cabin. The engine revved, and slowly the tyres hissed on the wet bitumen, pulling us away from the comfortable Shangrila. Our journey to Chomolungma, the Mother Goddess of the Universe, was at last under way.

Chris Curry, temporarily in charge of the medical supplies, sorts through a barrel full of bandages and diarrhoea suppressants.

Sunset from Shivalaya on the first day of the walk-in to Base Camp.

3

The Way to Namche

Chapter Three

The Way to Namche

Our land provides the visitor with a continual surprise of change and contrast, of richness and beauty. Its panoramic beauty has, since time immemorial, attracted sages and seers as it does attract modern explorers and tourists.

His Majesty King Birenda,
King of Nepal

Rape (mustard) flowers filled the fields around Bhaktapur.

The rain had washed away the usual thick curtain of pollution draping the valley. Cameras were frantically retrieved from pack tops and passed to the window-seated climbers on the left-hand side of the bus. Fields of brilliant yellow rape (mustard) flower, conducted by the wind, danced before the mediaeval metropolis of Bhaktapur. From the ninth-century city's ochre blur of buildings, the five-tiered Nyatapola Temple stood out on its pedestal like a great maestro commanding an adoring audience. The applause of clicking shutters muted the traffic rhapsody, for beyond Bhaktapur the gentle blue hills rose to a crescendo of snow-capped Himalayan peaks. It was truly a magnificent way to start the day!

I continued gazing at the landscape, trying to imagine what Hunt and Hillary and all the guys on the 1953 expedition would think of today's comparatively short approach march to Chomolungma. A 188-kilometre head-start bus ride to Jiri was out of the question in those days; expeditions started walking from the cobbled streets of Bhaktapur. In the early '70s, when the Chinese road to the Nepal/Tibet border town of Kodari was half completed, Lamosangu became the climbing fraternity's new starting block for the conditioning and acclimatising walk-in to Base Camp, alleviating 78 kilometres of the traditional hard-slog route. The hand-built road to Jiri, sponsored by the Swiss Association for Technical Assistance as part of a regional agricultural development programme, was finally finished in 1984, so jumping-off from the predominantly Jirel village is a relatively recent phenomenon in the 'how to climb Everest' blueprint.

The early morning shadows sculptured the terraced slopes surrounding the vibrant green Kathmandu Valley. As the bus climbed higher, bare sun-bronzed hills, like the chins of impatient adolescents, yearned for the first stubble of spring growth. Higher still, a lather of snow escaped the changing season's razor touch and above and beyond an incredible panorama of the Eastern Himalayas unfolded. Someone called out the names of some of the greater peaks. Someone else disagreed. Whether this

was Langtang and that was Manaslu seemed irrelevant—the whole breathtaking vista loomed larger than life in the crisp clear atmosphere of the morning.

The road switchbacked up, over and down each mountain ridge, crossing the many turbulent rivers between them by means of somewhat precarious suspension bridges. The bus laboured onward, stopping at numerous checkposts for seemingly purposeless and paranoid inspections by pompous self-possessed Nepalese officials, who had little else to do in their paper-pushing, politicking pursuits.

Our dhal and rice lunch stop at the otherwise forgettable three-shack village of Muldi was highlighted by a super-rich chocolate cake Jill had secretly bought from Pandey at Le Bistro. After we finished the last few crumbs, Chris, Mick, Jon and I joined a few of the other climbers on the roof of the bus. The interior of the vehicle was cramped and was starting to fill with nauseating fumes from a leaking fuel container, jammed in with all our trekking gear. The bus roof-rack proved a more spec-tacular mountain-watching platform because of its unrestricted 360-degree views, but it was an unbearably freezing eyrie and after half an hour I welcomed an unscheduled stop and retreated to a seat next to Austin in the front cabin. The worst thing about travelling on that sideways front seat was unavoidably ping-ponging my attention between the dangerous high-speed hairpin corners and the ghastly white pallor of the sick and scared team members being thrown around in the main body of the bus, as it convulsed out of control down each mountainside. No matter how many times I subjected myself to such distinctly Asian bus rides, I would never get blasé about the experience. Fear of a vehicle careering off the road and plummeting down a sheer

The distant snow-capped Himalayas strike a strong contrast to the brilliant green terraces sloping gently down into the Kathmandu Valley.

mountainside is never irrational; the last time I travelled on the Kodari to Kathmandu highway, the truck behind the one I was travelling in slipped off the road and plunged into the icy depths of the Sun Kosi River. Not one of the Tibetan pilgrims on that truck survived. They were making their way out of Tibet to see the Dalai Lama perform a once-every-twelve-years *puja* (a ritual ceremony) at Bodgia in northern India, and no amount of good karma had saved them from the death-by-bad-driving sentence.

We were still alive when our bus rattled down the last forested ridge before Jiri. Heavy cloud accompanied our arrival in the village and Sonam Girme, our expedition sirdar—in charge of organising our Nepalese staff and overseeing their duties—was first off the bus and flustered around to find the team enough space (and hopefully some beds) for the night. Within ten minutes he was back, detailing the various costs of trekkers lodges to Andrew Smith, the on-location ABEE treasurer. Andrew was in no fit state to haggle with his usual zeal, and settled on the large wooden lodge directly beside the parked bus. All he wanted to do was crawl inside, get horizontal and forget how bad his bus-churned, belly-bugged stomach felt. I was worried about him;

the dark circles under his eyes filled me with foreboding. I had this terrible feeling that he wasn't going to make it back from the mountain, and because of that fear, I was stopping myself from getting to know him well. I wasn't famous for my prophetic powers, so I didn't frighten him with my predictions. I told Jill, and we both agreed to keep a kind of motherly eye on him and if the feelings—or the circles—grew any darker, we'd let him know.

The people of Jiri were not at all interested in our party since our arrival coincided with the arrival of a far more fascinating phenomena: electricity. The lights went on and a cheer went up in the kitchen of the trekker's lodge. People were running off the street and into the few privileged hotels and houses connected to the power source for a closer inspection of the glowing globe. The expedition card-players, huddled around the tea table in the lodge's warm dining room, failed to notice the commotion and went on cheating and arguing as they washed down handfulls of stale glucose biscuits with swigs of lukewarm sweet tea. By our

Sorting out porters and porter loads in the main street of Jiri.

standards the light was dim and unless you were standing directly beneath it, there wasn't any real benefit from it being on at all.

Rain hindered our efforts unloading the bus. After the late afternoon tea, all able-bodied team members were sent outside to form a human chain from the bus to the storeroom beneath the lodge, and one by one we relayed all our walk-in kit and kaboodle to safety for the evening. The exercise exhausted me, and since my head was about to blow a gasket, I retired to my bed without dinner. I could hardly breathe through my flu-stuffed nose and I was shivering with cold. I felt sorry for myself so I crawled into two sleeping bags and covered my throbbing head. I listened to the rain falling on the tin roof. The floorboards constantly creaked beneath the booted footsteps of my team mates as they dragged packs of personal gear to their rabbit-warren rooms via the tunnel-like hallway outside my door. Threatening my sanity, a single line of drips from a leaking water pipe plopped with metronome regularity outside my window. Jon's manic laughter, ringing out from the adjoining room, stopped me from going to sleep. I wanted to scream at him, but I couldn't be bothered. It was a hell of a way to be feeling on the eve of a 130-kilometre trek.

Sonam rose early to oversee the hiring of porters and the fair distribution of the loads they would carry as far as Namche Bazaar, some 70 kilometres away. It was Sonam's thirty-seventh Himalayan mountaineering expedition, so he was well qualified to run the show. He reminded me of a skinny Humphrey B Bear, with huge ears and a broad gentle smile. He was always busy, and if he couldn't find something to do, he became very nervous and uncomfortable. He had perfected the art of even-handedness and consequently held the respect of every porter and Sherpa in the Solu Khumbu region as well as every international climbing contingent he had ever worked for. Many young Sherpas looked up to Sonam, for he had served his apprenticeship well and had not forgotten his roots. He could remember his first job as a porter on an expedition in 1962, his days as a high-altitude load carrier, a mail runner, cookboy and finally promotion to head expedition cook. He reached the summit of his profession and the 'local boy from Namche' turned sirdar gradually became something of a living legend. His commitment to mountaineering was so great, even the National Geographic Society had honoured him.

I looked at the enormous pile of gear he was trying to disperse among our seventy-five porters. Phil Pitham stood beside him cataloguing every load as it was issued to the motley crowd of local Jirels, Sherpas and Sherpanis. As they waited for their share of the bulk, the men huddled together in small bow-legged groups, puffing on bidis and rubbing their bristly chins in mock discontent of the wages offered. The Sherpanis sat together silently in the background, hugging their knees and staring towards the slowly diminishing heap of equipment and trek-in food stores. They would carry the same 30-kilogram basketloads as their menfolk and receive equal pay for their labour; the only inequality was their unlucky-last position in the ensuing procession.

As the porters set off over the bridge and up the first of countless steep hillsides, I thought again of the 1953 British Expedition. What an amazing human caravan they would have had! 450 porters were hired at 3 rupees per day to carry some 473 thirty-kilogram loads (some masochistic porters carried double loads for double pay). Funds to pay the porters and cover additional en route costs had to be carried, and since locals outside the Kathmandu Valley preferred coins to paper notes, the money alone amounted to twelve very heavy loads. The bearers were never told exactly what they were lugging for the entire seventeen-day journey from Bhaktapur to the monastic settlement of Thyangboche. Thankfully our modern porters preferred notes; at the inflated rate of 40 rupees per day per porter—plus insurance, union fees and tips—it would have amounted to an enormously heavy load of coins.

The expedition members moved off from Jiri in dribs and drabs, dispersing themselves among the steady throng of panting porters. As Jill and I were about to set off, the bus which had brought us safely to Jiri backfired and slowly bounced its way back through the village. The only wheels we would see turning

From day one of the walk-in we were rewarded with spectacular vistas. This photo was taken between Jiri and Shivalaya.

Seventy porters, each carrying a 30–60-kilogram load, transported the bulk of our expedition supplies from Jiri to Khunde. There, new porters and yaks were hired for the second leg of the long journey to Base Camp.

in the next few months were Buddhist prayer wheels. The only fumes we'd smell would emanate from burning juniper and Jill and Wanchu's cooking pots.

Away from Kathmandu, Nepalese air was so pure, it had an intoxicating effect and the views were almost hallucinogenic. It was impossible to believe that just a week ago, I was wedged inside my tiny office, working up to eighteen hours a day, trying to meet editor's deadlines … It was impossible to believe how furious I'd been when the car conked out and the mechanic hit me with a whopping service and parts bill the same day the telephone, electricity and gas accounts were due … It was impossible to believe I'd been contemplating buying a washing machine and further ensnaring myself in the consumer-culture of the 'Great Tame West' … It was *not* impossible to believe, however, that I had come to my senses, yielded to the 'get back to basics' ideal and willingly left all that crap behind. The only thing I really missed from that world, was my fiancé, Chris.

The human stream flowed steadily over just one 2400-metre pass and bubbled downhill into the Khimti Khola (River) Valley. The track was lined with gnarled rhododendrons and surprisingly, many of the trees were in full bloom. The boughs were bending beneath an uncharacteristically early profusion of brilliant crimson and pink flowers. Already petals had fallen and were

floating in the creek which followed the track down to the river. One by one the Macpacked and porter-basket-laden entourage crossed the long wire and chain suspension bridge leading into the quaint lodge-lined 'street' of Shivalaya. That was as far as we were expected to go for the day; and it wasn't even lunchtime! Distance is not measured by kilometres in this heavily trekked part of Nepal—it is metered by feasibly sized 'porter days'. These are set by the porters' union and everyone—including trekkers and climbers who wish to stay near their beloved goods and chattels—must stick to the routine. The porters dropped their loads and disappeared into the various teahouses, and the climbers made themselves comfortable for the afternoon on the large grassy flats alongside the river.

I sat down to read, but got distracted by a conversation a few of the blokes were having about Telecom, Australia's telecommunications network. They were grilling Mike Rheinberger about the somewhat notorious profit-making monopoly, since he had just retired from thirty years service as one of their leading telecommunications engineers. Mike seemed a lot less relaxed than I remembered from the brief time I'd spent with him in Tibet during the 1985 New Zealand Chomolungma Expedition. Perhaps he was justifiably anxious; this was his third trip to the 'Big E' in four years. He had easily reached the 8047-metre summit of Broad Peak in August 1986, but wasn't about to confuse that success with the greater challenge of Chomolungma. Jon's 'third time works the charm' superstition had no effect on his attitude either; his conservative, methodical thought processes prevented him from jumping to such radical, irrational assumptions. Mike and Jon were great friends and climbing partners, but they were poles apart; the classic 'odd couple' of Australian mountaineering.

Getting to know Mike was like reading through any one of the 200 limericks he knew by heart. First you became aware of his eloquent, conservative infrastructure, then his clever sense of humour surfaced from beneath the somewhat serious exterior. Mike's bottom line, when drunk and off guard, was always terribly smutty. He will kill me for saying that, but it's true. When in his usual serious mode, the bald-headed country boy from Bega, New South Wales, made a point of answering a simple question with a painstakingly articulate answer. Average Joe would say, 'Geez, I don't know,' but Rheinberger would respond, 'I do not feel I am in a position, nor suitably qualified, to comment on that particular point.' He would have made a sensational politician. Mike had spent a lot of years working towards this expedition. I had a lot of respect, and admiration, for him, and I really hoped the Mother Goddess would be kind to him this time around.

Secretly, what he needed was a good woman, not the crown of the elusive mountain goddess … and he would kill me for saying that too, but it's true.

When everyone had had enough inactivity, the mess tent and Gore-Tex sleeping domes were erected for the evening. The picture-book pink sunset pouring through the blue valley was followed by rain, and the great Telecom debate continued on through dinner. I guess it beat listening to horror stories from disaster-struck mountaineering exploits.

The following day, en route to Bhandar, we passed to the left of our first *mani* wall. The walls are elongated piles of stones, textured with the Buddhist Sanskrit inscription, *'Om mani padme hum'*, which literally means 'hail the jewel in the lotus'— a somewhat esoteric mantra or prayer. Each stone had been placed by devotees seeking particular religious or spiritual merit, and anyone passing on the left-hand side of the wall at any time, would also score points. It was a 'rule' I was very familiar with from Tibet, and I adhered to it, more out of respect and superstition than outright belief in Buddhist doctrine. As Chris,

A view of the 7145-metre Gauri Shankar, photographed en route to the Thodung Cheese Factory.

Austin, Jill, Terry McCullagh, Pat and I filed pass the wall, Chris conned us into making a 'small' detour. We climbed away from the main track and up into a rhododendron forest which supposedly led ('just around the next corner') to the Thodung Cheese Factory. Up and up we went, on and on, until we'd run out of suitable Monty Python jokes and energy. Snow still covered the ground in shaded gullies and potholes on either side of the track. The detour took us up over the 3000-metre elevation mark, and eventually ended at the hilltop Nepal Dairy Development Corporation Factory. The view was better than the cheese, and that's saying something! Before hoeing into the hard yak variety, Pat and I stood gawking at the impressive volcanic plug-shaped peak of the 7145-metre Gauri Shankar.

In 1980 Pat led a very ambitious expedition attempting to conquer the mountain via its unclimbed South-East Ridge route. 'When I booked Gauri Shankar, it had never been climbed. We wanted to make the first ascent, but someone beat us to it and climbed up the North Face in 1979,' Pat explained. 'We went for the South-East route, and got as far as Tseringma Peak— 6333 metres. It still hasn't been summited by that route; any mountaineer will tell you—it's one of the most difficult bloody traverses in the Himalaya.' I didn't need any mountaineer, wimpy or bold, to tell me the peak belonged at the bottom of the 'too-hard' basket. Its sheer sides, obvious even from this vast distance, were proof enough.

Pat Cullinan was a lovely man, who personified the adage: 'Don't judge a book by its cover.' If you met the skinny, round-shouldered Army major at a party, you couldn't help but assume he spent his service time chained to a filing cabinet. He had that classic 'boy who gets sand kicked in his face' physique; not the typical or expected build of a crack SAS commando and competent climber. Pat was living proof that success in the sport of mountaineering, or any seemingly insurmountable challenge for that matter, was more dependent on mind than muscle.

There wasn't an egocentric, macho-man bone in his body. He was modest to the point of being flushed with embarrassment whenever anyone complimented him on his recent triumph as leader and summiteer on the 1986 Broad Peak Expedition. I was amazed to learn later—from another climber, of course—that he had won the highly esteemed Star of Courage medal for risking his own life to save that of another climber on Broad Peak. Karl

Faßnacht, a member of a four-man German expedition attempting to scale the mountain at the same time as the Australian expedition, suffered debilitating high-altitude sickness about 100 metres from the summit. At 6 p.m. Pat—weary from his own eleven-and-a-half-hour ascent—met up with Karl, and realising he was desperately ill, forced him to abandon his summit bid. As the pair descended, Karl became exhausted and stopped. It was dark by this stage and far too dangerous for Pat to guide him down the knife-edged summit ridge. Pat found a small, protected hole in the snow and bivouacked with his semi-conscious charge. The next morning they started climbing down again, and at 7900 metres, Pat stopped to boil up some snow and attempted to rehydrate Karl, who was deteriorating rapidly. Karl, who couldn't speak a word of English, wouldn't respond to Pat or take any fluids. At 3 p.m. Pat gave up, put Karl in his bivouac bag and started dragging him down the mountain. A few hours later, the leader of the German expedition and Mike Rheinberger arrived and relieved Pat. It took them another six hours to lower Karl to safety and emergency medical treatment at Camp Four. The two expeditions eventually helped Karl off the mountain five days later; severely frostbitten, he spent the next seven months in hospital having all his toes amputated and relearning how to walk. If it wasn't for Pat's selfless efforts, he would have lost a hell of a lot more than his toes.

Unlike most of the mountaineers on the ABEE, Pat was definitely hanging up his climbing boots after Chomolungma. He had no interest in climbing forever, playing an increasingly risky game of roulette with his life. 'I'm not going to keep climbing until I'm Diemberger's age—I don't believe in climbing mountains 'til an avalanche gets you,' Pat said as we walked towards the cheese shop, glancing over his shoulder for one last look at Gauri Shankar; 'I just want one go at the top [of Chomolungma] and I'll do my absolute best. Then I just want to enjoy life with my wife, Sharon; you know if you've got $10 000,

Pink-backed climbers speckle the route into the Solu Khumbu region.

well, you can have a more enjoyable time spending it than on mountaineering expeditions. A holiday in Europe sounds nice, doesn't it?' he added wistfully. He had plenty of incentive to succeed and I hoped his swansong would not be undertoned by a 'do or die' recklessness. I guessed sheer determination was more in keeping with his methodical character, but then altitude can do funny things to a man's personality and judgement …

The smiling cheesemaker gave us a tour of his small primitive factory. Two huge copper vats, as shiny as old Rheinberger's sunburnt pate, were set into a wood-fuelled fireplace, ready to ferment the dairy's next supply of yak's milk. A pungent maturing-room, lined with rickety slatted shelves, held what remained of last season's 10-kilogram rounds of cheese and a dusty laboratory (by name only) completed the three-roomed operation. It had become very cold in the hilltop factory, so most of us retrieved our packs, paid for our fill of bread, cheese and tea, and began running down a second track to rejoin the main trail supposedly on the ridge separating the Khimti Khola and Likhu Khola Valleys. The predominantly Sherpa village of Bhandar—our scheduled stop for the night—lay in a hanging valley above the Likhu River. We all laughed and talked and joked our way down the slippery muddy track, descending about 1000 metres in under an hour. It was a great feeling, to be part of such a friendly congenial gang!

The first indication I had that we were anything less came two days later, on the trail between Sete and Junbesi. I had stopped to watch Austin help the bare-footed or slippery-soled porters inch their way over the snow-covered, icy 3530-metre Lamjura Pass. The trail tight-roped itself up the hillside to the top of the ridge and the heavily laden porters were having trouble balancing on the suddenly glassy surface. Terry McCullagh caught me up, and we started walking down the other side of the ridge together, behind the ecstatically happy cookboy, Pasang. His 'flying kitchen' load rattled and clanked against his back as he raced downhill and disappeared into the moist mossy forest directly below the pass. As Terry and I weaved our way between the hobbit-like grove of twisted rhododendrons and ancient musty-smelling maple and birch giants, we started talking about ourselves and how we felt about various members of the expedition.

Terry was, of all things, a weapons expert. I couldn't imagine him in any shade of Army green, let alone a uniform with pipped epaulettes! The ferret-faced funnyman totally floored me when he revealed he was not, as I had assumed, a civilian; rather an officer in command of a 'battery', or artillery unit, of 120 people. I could better visualise him in a pub, clowning around harmlessly, bragging and joking about other people's exploits and misadventures. I imagined his 'you should have seen the one that got away!' style stories were melodramatic, Logie-award-worthy epics of hysterical proportion.

Terry struck me as a very easy, down-to-earth guy, so I didn't hesitate to bring up the one thing that had been bugging me for days: Jim Truscott. Initially I thought Jim's perpetual frown and downright anti-social behaviour could be attributed to his untimely departure (considering his wife's pregnancy) from Australia. I had said something to him as he passed me on the track the day before, and asked if Collette's condition had anything to do with his obvious misery, to which he replied flatly, 'Na, I just hate

Junbesi, capital of the Sherpa region known as Solu.

bushwalking.' He didn't stop. He didn't look up at the trees or out at the majestic mountain vistas, he just kept on marching along at a cracking pace and at the end of the day, he buried himself in the pages of a book and only rose from his silent tomb to eat. Talk about a worry!

'It's the blackfella; Zac, the Greek,' Terry said callously, by way of explanation, I was startled by his sudden caustic blatancy. 'Jim hates him. It's hard to explain, Sorrel; it goes back a long way. I don't think much of the b——d either,' he added. I didn't have trouble dealing with a little personal animosity; a build-up of tension on big mountains is something every large-scale expedition has had to contend with in the past. You can't, after all, like all of the people all of the time. But this was not stress-related animosity—this was *hate;* and we were nowhere near the battlefield of Chomolungma! It shocked me to learn that no attempt had been made to resolve the long-standing, petty differences. Apparently part of the problem had something to do with Zac's publicity prowess and Jim not being suitably recognised for his enormous sponsorship-raising efforts. Jim refused to so much as talk to Zac, and I found that very, very difficult to comprehend, particularly in light of the fact that they were heading into a potentially dangerous, possibly life-threatening situation. I certainly wouldn't like to put my life in the hands of someone I didn't like or trust. Clearly, selection of the ABEE team had more to do with AAA (the Australian Army's Alpine Association) politics than commonsense. Criteria for civilian selection had included an analysis of how well each applicant would perform in the large-team situation. If they were not 'personality compatible' they were not included. Perhaps I oversimplified the obvious discrepancy; I never have been able to understand the military mentality.

Terry changed the subject, but I found it difficult not to brood. It was none of my business, of course, but I really liked the broad-smiling, efficient Zaharias—Prince Charles ears and all. He had a very traditional approach to climbing: he was always thoroughly organised, always rationalising something, be it statistics or logistics. He was very reflective and philosophical, but tended to take himself, and life, too seriously. He was a natural leader, and never 'off duty': it would take a long time to know the real, out-of-uniform Zac, but I hoped one day I would. He had the face and physique, the discipline and confidence of the soldier epitomised in media campaigns by the Australian Army's PR department. He attracted the limelight; he didn't seem to thrust himself beneath it.

I was still thinking about him when Terry and I rounded another hillside, which opened out to a magnificent view of Junbesi; the most serene, picturesque village I had ever seen in Nepal. Nestled in a wide vivid green valley beneath the revered 6959-metre Shorong Yul Lha, Junbesi is the capital of the Sherpa region known as Solu. The village is named after Jun, the moon. According to Sherpa legend, a great saint lived in the Solu Valley and loved it so much, he couldn't bear to have it disappear at night; so one evening, he pulled the full moon closer to the earth. His fingermarks remain on it today.

The Solu is part of a 960-square-kilometre region of Nepal called the Solu Khumbu; heartland of the internationally renowned Sherpa people. The area is centred around the upper reaches and tributaries of the Dudh Kosi River. At the headwaters is the high, fan- or lotus-shaped area known as the Khumbu, which channels into the gorges of Pharak and then opens to the fertile slopes and valleys of the Solu. Junbesi marks the northern end of this famous Sherpa region.

The Sherpas are a Mongolian race, who migrated to the Solu Khumbu from Minyak in the eastern Tibetan province of Kham: in local lingo *sher* means 'east', and *pa* means 'people'. The original Sherpa tribes were thought to be nomadic herders, driven south by invading Mongols or the warlike Khampas of east Tibet, nearly 600 years ago. After travelling 1250 kilometres, they crossed into Nepal peacefully and, unopposed, began populating the previously uninhabited high Himalayan valleys. The pass they originally crossed to enter Nepal made a natural trade route, and before long many Sherpas were soon yakking rock salt, wool and skins from Tibet in exchange for grain, cotton and cattle crossbreeds from Nepal and India. In addition to trade, the Sherpas grazed cattle and farmed in crude forest clearings. When they discovered the humble potato, and began cultivating it, they settled permanently in Nepal. The potato was thought to have come from either the colonial gardens of Darjeeling, or courtesy of the 1774 India Company Expedition to Lhasa where the envoy was instructed to plant potatoes at each resting place en route. The Sherpas have a fundamentally ethereal interpretation of their migration and settlement: even the life-sustaining tuber, which is still the staple of the Solu Khumbu, is believed to have come from the precious, all powerful gods.

The Sherpas were Buddhists of the older sects of the Tibetan church, and naturally they brought their religion with them into Nepal. Many of their beliefs and rituals have since been coloured by folklore, but the essence of Tibet's unique brand of Buddhism has been retained. With Junbesi still in view, Terry and I came to a signposted sidetrack detouring to Serlo, a monastery

The newly built temple in Junbesi.

surrounded by apple orchards a short distance above the village of Junbesi. We joined Mick, BJ, Andrew, Zac, Jill and Bruce Farmer in a cosy receiving-room-cum-restaurant, inside the main compound of the monastery. A rosy cheeked, mahogany-robed, enterprising monk was busy in an adjoining unlit kitchen preparing glasses of freshly squashed apple juice and baked apple pies. After gulping down the feast, Mick and Andrew sniffed out a second eatery, with a more extensive menu, and ordered another substantial entrée. It didn't matter what or how much Jill prepared for their meals each day, there was always room for more. The guys were travelling on and for their stomachs, marching from restaurant to restaurant every day, recording little of the spectacular vistas and beautiful villages in their diaries, but much of the culinary delights and frights experienced along the way.

After a quick look around the dark, rancid-yak-butter-odoured inner sanctum of the distinctly Tibetan monastery, I started heading down to Junbesi with Zac. A storm rode in over the hills and by the time we reached the narrow, walled streets of the village, light rain was falling.

Austin had decided we should bunk down in any of Junbesi's comfortable trekkers' lodges, and Sonam sent Jill and her cookboy consortium up in the largest guesthouse kitchen he could find. Together, they transformed a sackfull of boring eggplants into a gastronomic extravaganza.

After dinner, in the large newly timbered dormitory of the Junbesi Teahouse, I lay down to write. One glance around the room restored my faith in the unity of our team. Chris Curry was on the far side of the room, curled inside his sleeping bag giggling to himself as he read Tom Sharpe's *Wilt*. Andrew was in the bed next to him, trying to balance the expedition's expenditure in his cash-flow book. Every time Chris chuckled, Andrew tapped his pencil on the side of his records; it was frustrating stuff labouring over figures when someone else was enjoying their favourite book. Mick Pezet was in one corner of the cosy room writing a letter to Andrea. He stopped to ask me how I first got involved in writing and if I would be scribing a story about the expedition for *National Geographic*. That led on to a brief chat about pre-Chomolungma publicity and somehow keeping a straight face, Mick proudly said, 'Well I'm pretty popular too you know; *People* magazine rang me reverse charges for an interview!' Everyone cracked up, except Bruce—he was fast asleep in the opposite corner, next to Terry McCullagh. The rain falling on the roof shingles eased and the Thai movie and rock stars postered around the room continued smiling insincerely at each other. Pens flew across airmail pages, carrying second-hand adventures and personal thoughts to faraway wives and girlfriends. One by one, the candles went out. One by one, the coughs were silenced beneath thick layers of down. Outside the dormitory whispers from the lodge proprietor's family were swallowed by the gentle crackle of their open hearth fire. The personality clash discovery of the day seemed unbelievable in the peaceful stillness of night.

Shorong Yul Lha, the God of Solu, was wrapped in a shroud of predawn snow. Dew clung to the vibrant green fields around Junbesi and puddles in the schoolyard became the target for well-aimed pebbles. After an early breakfast and redistribution of the porter loads, Jill and I wandered up to the new village temple. The morning sun, as it finally crept over the high fortress of hills, glowed against the painted sun-dried brick entrance to the Buddhist temple. In the centre of the elaborate tiered roofing, the light rays struck the cast gold 'wheel of life' and its two protecting deer. Pleated cotton trimming waved in the slight breeze above the third-floor windows. A line of sun-bleached prayer-flags stretched from the lower barred windows across the enclosed courtyard. A small child and a freckle-coloured rooster played on the long step in front of the locked building. Shafts of cobweb-thin cloud radiated out from the rooftop. We waited for a while, but no one came to open the temple doors, so we wandered on up the sloping hillside to the right of the village for a more overall view of the quaint Solu capital.

Even though we were last to leave Junbesi we regretted not being able to stay longer! If I were a saint and there had been a full moon last night, I would have tried pulling it even closer to the magical Sherpa settlement. The trail out of town crossed the Junbesi Khola and wound its way up through a magnificent stand of pines. A million golden splinters of light pierced the flank of the hillside as the sun burst through the trees. I felt fantastic! My cold was still hanging around, but my head was clear and confident. I knew I would return from this little jaunt, despite earlier uncertainties. I don't think I had ever felt so good in all my life! Optimism is not an illusion, it's a force, and some of it rubbed off onto Jill. We skipped along the ridge, gradually curving to meet the next valley, singing 'The Sound of Music' and other melodic headbangers.

Suddenly we both stopped dead in our tracks. The incredible Northern Himalayas had sprung up, without warning, in front of us. Bang, there they were—so close you could almost reach out and touch them. My pulse raced—this was God's own masterpiece of creation. The highest mountains in the world sat in a line, like

Living in the shadow of the magnificent Northern Himalayas.

apostles at da Vinci's *Last Supper,* sublime before the simple banquet of hills and valleys. Chomolungma lorded over the divine mountains, her dizzy head circled by a halo of clouds. Like a great work of art, it didn't matter how many times you had seen this vista reproduced on postcards and in books, the experience of seeing it *real* for the first time could not be equalled. There was no postage stamp on the back of this image; the mountains were rock, earth and snow, not brushstrokes on canvas or light on celluloid.

Equally real was the flimsy wooden shack to our immediate left. A mother sat with her back against the cardboard-thin wall, intently scanning her young son's head for nits. Two other children stared past us, disinterested in our loud, ecstatic approval of their backyard view. I couldn't believe their eyes were dulled with so much indifference. It was a perfect, warm sunny day on this prime piece of real estate and my mind had glossed over all the pitfalls of living in the shadow of the great Himalaya. How many freezing nights had hardened their souls? How many storms had ravaged their crops? How often had their dwelling collapsed beneath the powerful breath of the wind?

Later on that day, Jill and I stripped off and plunged into the numbing depths of the Ringmo River. We dried out and got sweaty again straight away climbing up to meet half a dozen of the guys at the 'Apple House'. The whitewashed chalet-style lodge could best be described as the Solu Khumbu's answer to the British country pub, and proprietor Dorge Pasang was jovial and patient, eager as a beaver to satisfy his clientele. He boasted the honour of being the only Sherpa lodge owner mentioned by name in the Lonely Planet *Trekking in the Nepal Himalaya* guidebook. His homegrown apple cider came in three strengths; juice, high-alcohol wine and 100 per cent proof *rakshi.*

The usual afternoon bank of clouds raced over the Apple House and hovered at around 3000 metres, on the Trakshindo Pass. 'I don't know …' Jon Muir said, simulating seriousness, 'good mountaineers aren't supposed to head out into that sort of weather.' He raised his glass and even his freckles started

shaking with laughter. 'I motion we make an emergency bivouac here in the cider house, boys!' Everyone agreed wholeheartedly, but after another hour of the brain-cell-slaying cider, the two Terrys, Chris, and Phil had had enough and set out to finish the day's walk to Numtala. Phil Pitham left behind the Tin Tin magazine he had been reading out aloud to everyone, so Jill and I finished the riveting tale while we waited for the plate of hot chips we had ordered when we first arrived at the Apple House.

They were worth waiting for, and fuelled our quick ascent to Trakshindo Pass. It was getting really cold, so we headed straight down the other side of the ridge to Trakshindo monastery. The monastery garden was perched on the side of a sheer cliff overhanging the valley. Looking over the edge, the enormous void below, as far and wide as the eye could see, was full of cloud. I felt like we had reached the end of the earth.

Ngawang Namkha Sherpa, a young monk educated by an American Buddhist nun in Kathmandu, came out of the thin mist encircling the monastery to greet us. He showed Jill and me around the main prayer room and we talked at length about Tibet and the Dalai Lama. After a while, has asked us if we wished to see upstairs. Naturally we said yes, and followed him up the steep, narrow stairway.

I could scarcely believe it. Foreigners are rarely shown the *tantric* room, normally reserved for private, fairly secretive practices and ceremonies. I had only once before been permitted into one; in Gyantse in Tibet. Ngawang opened the door and my eyes met those of a painted hellish beast, surrounded by an orgy of bizarre contorted naked bodies. Just below the ceiling a line of skulls formed a frieze around the room. The whole room swam in a sea of deliberately bloodthirsty, powerful images which served to remind all who entered of death and impermanence. From the room, ceremonies to wrathful deities were conducted and a set of cymbals and a small drum lay on the windowsill waiting to be played as offerings of music to the gods. Essentially there are four kinds of ceremony in Tibetan Buddhism—peaceful; increase (prayers which, for example, would improve the monastery's funds); power (political); and wrath. Because the symbolism is so emotive in the *tantric* room, it is open to misinterpretation. The first time I encountered it, unexplained, I was sure I had been targeted as a human sacrifice. Any minute now, I thought, some wierdo sect will crowd into the room and rape and torture me. An ancient chainmail suit lay lifelessly on a shelf below the Gyantse skull-motif band and I was convinced it was the armour of the last Western visitor—probably one of Younghusband's British soldiers, caught while fighting their way through to Lhasa in 1904.

Ngawang gave Jill and I an elaborate ink-block print of Buddha, flanked by two plump goddesses, floating against a background of stylised clouds. We couldn't stay longer because Jill had to fulfil her duty to the team, most of whom were probably already in Numtala asking Wanchu when their dinner would be ready. We headed down through another thicket of moss-covered giants, many playing host to pastel-coloured orchids or strangling figs.

Pockets of virgin forest were becoming fewer and smaller in this heavily trekked region of Nepal and as I passed by a trail-side stack of freshly cut green timber, I was reminded of the

Projects to build schools, health posts and suspension bridges (like this one spanning the Dudh Kosi River) were initiated by Sir Edmund Hillary after his successful Everest climb in 1953.

government's growing concern for their nation's forest resources. Despite their impregnable appearance, the Himalaya is a very fragile environment. While tourism and mountaineering have obviously helped the kingdom's economy and raised the standard of living in the Solu Khumbu, it has had a devastating effect on the high-altitude forests. After the 1953 Chomolungma expedition, Ed Hillary made an enormous effort to give something back to the Sherpa people he had befriended and admired. He initiated a series of extensive building projects to provide them with schools, bridges, water pipelines, health posts and hospitals. To facilitate operations an airstrip was built at Lukla, right in the

heart of the Solu Khumbu. But apart from flying in heavy equipment, tools and materials, it also gave easier access to the Chomolungma area and increasing numbers of tourists and trekkers accelerated the demand for firewood. With the closure of the Tibetan border in 1959, the Sherpas had lost their trading links and associated incomes, so they welcomed the opportunity to service the growing number of expeditions and trekkers. The tourists needed accommodation, teahouses and chang shops as well as food and warmth, and the ensuing building boom further depleted the forests. Firewood became a cash crop, and green wood was cut because it weighed more.

In response to the problem, Sir Ed helped to persuade the government to establish a national park, and when this was realised in 1973, a law was passed against cutting green wood in the park. It has never been an easy rule for rangers to enforce:

selling firewood to tourists and Sherpas to heat their homes and cook is big business and without alternative fuels—since these are prohibitively expensive—many Sherpas resent the no-cutting-green-trees law. Even if they are individually aware of the future problems, they still adhere to the practice because if they stopped selling firewood, someone else would take advantage and make the money instead. Outside the park, as we were now, there were still no hard-pressed restrictions, and indiscriminate wood chopping was leaving ugly scars on the land.

I still thought a lot could be done to save Nepal's forests by the people who come to admire what is left of them. It was estimated that each expedition used 120 kilograms of firewood per day, and since they stayed in the park for two months, that totalled 7.2 tonnes. Consequently, mountaineers were forced to carry their own fuel into the park. Perhaps trekkers could follow

*Terraced rice paddies cover every arable piece of land rising above
the Dudh Kosi River.*

Returning from a wedding in Khari Khola, attendants carry the dowry of a Sherpa bride to her new home.

this example and agree to support, through higher meal prices, the use of liquid fuel in lodges and teahouses. They could also show some sensitivity towards the environment by resisting the urge to have hot showers while out on the trail.

The next few days trekking brought us closer to the Sagarmatha National Park, via some of the most extensively cultivated land I had ever seen in Asia. Terraced rice paddies covered every feasible metre of land on both sides of the spectacular Dudh Kosi—the turbulent, turquoise river which dominates the Khumbu-Himal region. A small plot of bamboo and bananas at Juving broke the pattern of stepped fields briefly, and occasionally a monstrous, ganglionated rhododendron-shaded the track.

On the seventh day of the walk, heading down to the small riverside settlement of Surkhe, we passed a party of beautifully dressed villagers, weaving their way back along the track to Khari Khola. Chang (rice beer) laced the breaths of the wedding wassailers and their laughter bubbled like champagne into the crystal clear air. The women wore their best wrap-around dresses, called *chubas,* and colourful striped aprons. Turquoise, coral and silver jewellery swung from their necks half-hidden beneath stark white *katas,* or ceremonial scarves. The normally demure Sherpanis were as high as kites on booze and the euphoria of the day and one daring young lady brushed close to Chris Curry and grabbed him by the short and curlies. I still don't know who was more surprised, Chris or his assailant! The menfolk wore a variety of hats and comical grins and the bridegroom, waving a handsome yak's tail about, sported a tan Chinese satin overcoat.

After recovering from the surprise fondle, Chris detailed the courtship and wedding ritual to me, and explained the clan system which frameworks Sherpa social structure. There are twelve existing clans and since sexual relations between clan members are regarded as incestuous, all Sherpas marry outside their clan. The traditional marriage is arranged by the parents, and the long courtship process begins with a *pujah* in the man's house by the local village lama. Accompanied by his relatives, the prospective bridegroom (armed with a special brew of chang in hand) ventures to the woman's house to formally seek her parents' permission. The ceremony is called the *dem-chang,* meaning 'the beer of tying', and although the couple will now have a semi-marital relationship, the bride continues to live with her parents. Children born after the *dem-chang* are considered legitimate, even though the actual wedding—the *lhopsang pujah*—may not take place for several years. The exchange of cooked rice and chang indicative of the *lhopsang* had already happened; what we were witnessing was the final stage, the *nama titup,* where the husband takes his bride to their own home. After *katas* have been presented by the bridegroom to all the bride's family, they then give her a dowry of clothes, jewellery, household utensils and property and choose several girls to carry the presents to the groom's home. On the way, the groom's family members meet the procession at certain locations to welcome the new couple and regale them with more chang and offer still more *katas.* After bestowing good luck on the house, the two families and their friends get down to some *really* serious drinking and dancing. The party goes on for several days, and on the fifth or seventh day, the couple return to the bride's home to keep some good luck there.

After staying in Surkhe for the night, Chris, Jill, Bruce and I volunteered to take the mail up to Lukla. We were to collect anything that may have been flown in (care of Mountain Travel's Lukla Branch), then catch up to the rest of the gang somewhere on the direct route to Monjo, the first village of the Khumbu region, right near the entrance to the Sagarmatha National Park.

We set out after breakfast, climbed up the shaded track from Surkhe and reached Lukla just as the first of two planes nose-dived onto the precarious dirt and rubble airstrip. I couldn't believe my eyes. The runway was only 300 metres long and terminated with a sheer cliff at one end, and an enormous mountainside at the other. To make take-off and landing matters even hairier, the whole strip sloped on a 15-degree angle! There was something slightly twisted about the 'Welcome to Lukla' sign: it was painted on the mangled wing of a plane wreckage, lying alongside the runway. The second Twin Otter aircraft appeared as a white speck against the distant, steep valley side and in a matter of seconds it surged onto the airstrip like some awkward white swan. It screeched to a halt and the deafening engines beneath its ruffled wings slowly wound down. A siren sounded giving the local Luklanians a green light to cross the strip, which, of course, intersected the town's main thoroughfare.

The tourists tottering off the plane into the thinnish air were largely ignored by the townsfolk. It was market day, and they were all preoccupied with the thought of purchasing something (anything!) fresh. Eager housewives milled in the main street, waiting for the Kathmandu-consumables to be offloaded from the plane and men squatted in front of the makeshift stalls, eyeing the dismal selection of goods: handfuls of boiled sweets and torn boxes of Yak Filter cigarettes.

We swapped a healthy wad of outgoing mail for a pitiful selection of letters from home. Jill was disappointed that the second of her surprise Le Bistro chocolate cakes hadn't arrived. Somewhere out there a piggish pilot or postie was piling on the calories … To console ourselves, we followed Chris to his friend Dalpudi's home for tea.

I stared out at the mountains through our gentle hostess's window. We were heading into the big ones now; up, up and more up. I read somewhere that if you added all these 'up' bits together between Jiri and Base Camp, it totalled 9000 metres of elevation gain—a little more than the full height of Chomolungma itself. From Base Camp, the summit was a mere 3514 metres further to climb. No worries! It was so hard to imagine what it would be like on the mountain; so difficult to face its harsh

Sherpas and Sherpanis crowd the main street of Lukla waiting for fresh foods to arrive by plane from Kathmandu.

realities when it still felt so damn far away. We were on the expedition, but we weren't *there* yet. It was so pleasant just ambling along a winding track each day. The actual 'getting from A to B' was bound to be a hell of a lot nicer than 'being there'. It was so easy to lose yourself in the immediate landscape, the immediate uphill slog, and forget the ultimate objective altogether. The moment was all. It was a delight to feel the breeze cool the sweat on my forehead, to hear the song of a high-flying bird and smell the earth all around me. Life was about now, not yesterday or tomorrow. Today, here in the hills, was simple and uncomplicated by possessions and pretensions.

We eventually caught up to the rest of the guys at Choplung, all of a kilometre from the village of Surkhe. It was a glorious day, just perfect for enjoying a few beers in the sunshine. Min Moor, Mick Pezet and Bruce Farmer were determined to be last in to roost for the day, so stayed longer on the lodge 'verandah'. So far Jon Muir had had the honour; in fact he was making a point of always rocking in last. It was high time someone else won the cherished wooden spoon, and today would be the day!

When we finally moved away from Choplung, the track continued winding downhill to meet the mighty Dudh Kosi again, and by late afternoon we were at last entering the realm of Khumbu. The porters caught sight of Khumbila, and literally exploded with joy. Big Pasang went wilder than normal and began to *run,* his hefty kitchen load somehow lightened by the vision of the sacred, inviolable peak. A distant glimpse of the mountain was enough to fill our Sherpa staff with boundless pleasure; they were home again, in their own valleys, among their own gods. Framed by dark foliage, the postcard-perfect mountain was brought to life by the late afternoon sunlight. Chiffon clouds, like white ceremonial scarves, fell from the heavens and draped the bare grey shoulders of Khumbila, the home of the God of Khumbu. It was not at all difficult to understand and share in our porters' awe and joy.

With the image still strong in my mind, it was hard to make room for my first glimpse of Chomolungma the next day. I had set out early from Monjo alone, to photograph the mighty Khumbila at sunrise and attempt to beat Jim into Namche Bazaar. He overtook me after a pathetic half hour on the long steep climb zig-zagging up from the Dudh Kosi. I was exhausted just watching him sprint towards and past me and gave up trying to catch him when I reached the teahouse a little more that halfway up the hillside. Record-holders always jealously guard their titles; even Jon had outsmarted everyone in the race for last—he never even made it to Monjo!

The view from the teahouse was simply fantastic. Chomolungma loomed above the Nupste-Lhotse wall, her black summit exposing itself fully for the first time. A 100-kilometre per hour wind sent a long plume of snow particles and cloud streaming from her crown like a ghostly ponytail. I didn't feel intimidated by the mountain for it still seemed so far away. One by one the other team members reached the cleared viewing ridge and stopped to assess the goddess. Rheinberger arrived and was obviously surprised to see such little snow on the summit pyramid. He expressed concern over the condition of the Lhotse Face, claiming it would be like climbing a smooth sheet of glass unless a lot of snow fell and consolidated on the face sometime

Khumbila, the home of the God of Khumbu.

over the next few weeks. The prospect didn't do a lot towards erasing the quickly deepening worry lines creasing Austin's brow.

BJ plonked his pack next to Austin and tried not to let all the frowning ruffle his feathers. It was the first time I had seen BJ looking at something other than his beloved birdwatchers' manual. At the end of every day he always came into camp flapping excitedly about the rarity of some bird or another he and Paul Bayne had spotted.

Eventually I pulled myself away from the view and continued plodding up the hill towards Namche with Chris. Seeing Chomolungma had fired him up in much the same way Khumbila had ignited our porters, and he began telling me all about his early childhood in the Kenya highlands and more recent climbing experiences in the Khumbu. 'The hospital I was born in is now a mental hospital in Nairobi—I think that reflects on my current mental status ...' he began, blaming his roots for his mad obsession with mountains. 'From a hill close to where my family lived, we could see the snows of Mt Kenya and Kilimanjaro. My father always promised to take me up Kilimanjaro when I turned thirteen, but we migrated to Australia just before my thirteenth birthday, so I never had the chance.' Australia isn't big in the mountain department, so Chris had to be content with the more usual Aussie outdoor pursuits of sailing, rowing and surf lifesaving. He rowed for Western Australia and competed in the national championships for six years and at the same time studied to become a doctor. He went back to Kenya for a visit in 1978 and rekindled his love of mountains. 'I climbed Point Wanana and from then on, I've had this compulsion to go up hills anywhere I found them!' Chris said. 'I didn't know how to go about becoming a mountaineer, so in 1981 when I heard an Australian expedition to A'nyêmaqên was taking trekkers along, I signed up for the trek, with the sole intention of meeting some climbers.' Chris in fact met some of Australia's best climbers:

Tim Macartney-Snape, Lincoln Hall, Andy Henderson and Geof Bartram. He got on well with Geof, and when trekking with him a month later through Nepal, Geof asked Chris if he wanted to be included in his proposed expedition to climb 7145-metre Pumo Ri. 'Pumo Ri was overwhelmingly impressive,' Chris explained. 'It was totally beyond my imagination. I said, "Hell! I don't know one end of a crampon from the other!" and Geof said, "Well you've got two years to learn." ' And he did. He did a two-week course at the Mount Blanc massif in France, joined Geof in South America for four months climbing in Bolivia, Ecuador and Peru, did another course in Switzerland and (voila!) he summited Pumo Ri in 1984. Between then and now, Chris had topped a whole host of peaks, including Acongcagua in Argentina, McKinley in Alaska (twice), and in the USSR's little-explored Pamir Ranges.

As we rounded the last uphill corner and began the brief descent into Namche Bazaar, Chris told me about his exciting climbs in Russia. It was quite strange listening to mountaineering stories from another part of the world, trying to visualise ranges, camps, climbers and summits so different from the ones presently surrounding us. I was so surprised to see the giant horseshoe-shaped village of Namche suddenly smack bang before us. I was half expecting Moscow's Red Square to be there.

But Namche it was, the administrative centre of the Khumbu, and for us, a place to hang our hats for a few days and enjoy a scheduled break. Chris and I followed the parade of pink-packed climbers through the streets to a rooftop restaurant in the heart of town. We ordered beer and cheese sandwiches and they came with a replenishable side-order of good jokes. Our lodgings for the stopover were actually in Khunde, another hour-long climb up the slopes behind the bazaar. But no one had any intention of moving from the sun-drenched balcony; the beer was the best Nepal had to offer, the cheese sambos were better than anyone's mum could make and the jokes ... well the jokes were just the most absurd, hysterical and even witty round of gags I'd ever heard! It must have been something to do with the altitude.

4

Mountains, Monks and Monasteries

The view from the ridge above Khunde.

Chapter Four

Mountains, Monks and Monasteries

Far higher in the sky than imagination dared to suggest, a prodigious white fang—an excrescence from the jaw of the world—the summit of Everest appeared.

George Leigh Mallory,
quoted by Captain John Noel,
in *Through Tibet to Everest*

From the balcony we had a bird's eye view of the street, and subsequently the passing parade of pedestrians and porters. Dominating the endless procession were yaks and bow-legged bearers carting bulky loads of another expedition's equipment out of town, towards the Base Camp track. The long white plastic cartons and bright orange kitbags weighing down the entourage were all emblazoned with a curious emblem: a dark blue triangle screen-printed with a stylised globe and the words '1988 Chomolungma-Sagarmatha'. Beneath the logo, 'China-Japan-Nepal' revealed all: the often mentioned and frequently feared 'Tri-Nation Expedition' were on their way to *our* mountain.

Our own expedition organisers had first heard about the massively scaled Tri-Nation assault, when they received a letter from its leaders demanding $A20 000 for our anticipated use of *their* Icefall route. Although the Australian climbers were the first to secure permits for the standard 'Hillary route' on Chomolungma, the $A17 million Tri-Nation odyssey had apparently muscled for priority on the hill. For the first time ever, the Nepalese Government had miraculously dropped their 'one-route, one-expedition' rule and issued the same permit as ours to the Tri-Nationers.

Austin had ignored the letter, since the Australian Bicentennial Everest Expedition (ABEE) planned to reach Base Camp and start work on the Icefall a few weeks ahead of the Tri-Nation team. He was obviously intimidated by the power our contenders had, and had not ruled out the possibility of having to cough up the $20 000 regardless. He was nervous about meeting with the Tri-Nation leaders when they finally arrived at Base Camp, for any lack of co-operation would undoubtedly result in the ABEE being thrown off the mountain altogether. The sad thing was, we didn't have a spare $20 000, and quite obviously, the Tri-Nationers were far from short of dollars. Judging by the rumours and backed up by the labels on the boxes that were passing beneath us, theirs was a no-expenses-spared expedition, which boasted such luxuries as generators which would ensure a power supply to every tent, individual heaters and electric foot-warmers

Buddhist scriptures grace the boulders lining the track to Khunde, above Namche Bazaar.

and of course a satellite dish which would facilitate round-the-world live television broadcasts and telecommunications.

The Tri-Nation extravaganza was destined to be the largest, most elaborate, most expensive expedition in Chomolungma history. A total of 253 mountaineers, media men, high-altitude kit-carters and kitchen cookboys were involved in the project, which planned to put as many of its ninety climbers, and their accompanying television crews, as possible on the summit on 5 May 1988. Forty-five climbers (fifteen from each nation) would be attempting the mountain from the Tibetan side and a similar contingent would try to rendezvous with them via Nepal's Hillary route. They had raised the wages of porters in Sherpaland to ensure availability of strong backs and yaks to carry all their equipment to the southern Base Camp. Sonam was worried we wouldn't find enough Namche-based porters and yak-herders to take over from the ex-Jiri gang, who would be returning to their homes in the valleys below Namche. To make things a little easier Sonam had promised the porters a good bonus, if they continued carrying their loads beyond the normal changeover place in Namche, to Khunde. He was confident he could, given time, find enough men and beasts to fill our needs from the small settlements in and around the Kumjung-Khunde area.

As I watched Tri-Nation package number 1020 wobble past, I laughed at the 5 May intention of the expedition. For the main part, the Tri-Nation odyssey was being sponsored by a Japanese television network that was celebrating its thirtieth anniversary. In Japan, 5 May was a public holiday, so by scheduling the summit attempt for that day, the network could be assured of a maximum national audience ... and ratings. Only the Japanese had the audacity to name, with such adamant confidence, a summit day some three months in advance. Perhaps they had developed some new high-tech gadget which harnessed the unpredictable weather and bonsaied the wind.

The horseshoe-shaped village of Namche, above the Dudh Kosi Valley.

The sky above Namche on Friday, 4 March, was set for its forecast afternoon change. Chris suggested I get moving up to Khunde, in order to photograph the Solu and lower Khumbu Valley porters receiving their pay. Namche, which fills a natural amphitheatre high above the Bhote Kosi gorge, was still some 350 metres below the twin villages of Khunde and Kumjung. The greatest concentration of Sherpas in the Khumbu lived in the dual town, nestled in a broad, shallow trough beneath the southern slopes of Khumbila. I walked through Namche Bazaar and onto the trail leading up the steep-sided horseshoe with Terry McCullagh. By the time we reached the disused Syangboche Airstrip it was freezing cold and fog had well and truly masked the sun. We couldn't see more than a few metres in front of ourselves.

The Syangboche Airstrip was built in 1971 to service the Hotel Everest View. The whole idea reminded me of scenes I had witnessed in Lhasa; guests flying in to fill the four-star (comparatively speaking) 'Holiday Inn', only to suffer from failing to acclimatise. The Hotel Everest View, which sat some 3720 metres above sea-level, had flopped—despite their 'oxygen in every room' bonus offer. The two planes which were used to fly in the ignorant (and rich) clientele crashed in heavy fog in the late 1970s, and by 1981 the stately looking hotel had lost a great deal of its patronage and former appeal. The best building in the Khumbu started to sink to some pretty shabby depths. The wallpaper was peeling off and rising damp had rotted sections of the carpet and crept up the walls. Despite this, claims that it was still the best, and most expensive, lodging en route to Chomolungma, abounded. Terry and I didn't have time to search around for it in the steadily thickening fog. It was hardly worth going to see what remained of the 'Everest View' when there would be no view of Everest from its windows.

The boughs of the forest trees between the runway and Khunde were drooping with cobweb beards of lichen. The wispy ends of the slimy green whiskers nodded listlessly in the fog, moved by the weak, fetid breath of the air. The musty stench of decaying leaves and fresh yak dung wafted from the forest floor

Andrew Smith and Phil Pitham paying the porters for carrying the expedition supplies through to Khunde.

to meet the otherwise fragrant smoke of burning juniper. The whole scene was as if it had been lifted straight from the pages of Tolkien's *Lord of the Rings*. I had this bizarre feeling that something short with pointed ears and warts was going to hop out from behind a tree. I quickened my pace to catch up to Terry.

I followed his footsteps through a light cover of snow, weaving between the piled-stone walls that led from the forest boundary into the potato fields and front yards of Khunde. I could hear that the porter pay-off was in full swing, but the fog continued to obscure the action until we were right on top of it. Outside the big new timber-lined house which Sonam had secured for our base for a few days, Andrew and Phil were sitting at a small table with their cashbox, a stamp pad and porter register. The house belonged to one of Sonam's cousins, and after I'd thrown my pack just inside the doorway, I started taking pictures of the enigmatic porters queuing for their hard-earned rupees. In turn, each man stamped his inked thumb print alongside his name in the record book, received his wages, then turned to pay the union rep his fee. The rep's hand was out, waiting like the best of his kind in the West, for his share of the spoils.

It was warmer to watch the pay-off from the second floor of the new house. Austin was bobbing up and down, trying to look both cheerful and 'in charge' of his employees as they spiralled towards the pay clerk's desk. Again the women were made to wait until last, but amused the crowd of porters and spectators by flatly refusing to grease the union official's palm. They argued and laughed and fled off together towards Namche.

I went back down the narrow stairs and retrieved my kit. The ground floor of most Sherpa homes was for storage of fodder and firewood, and Sonam's cousin's house was no exception. It obviously doubled as a stable in winter, for hay was strewn on the earthen floor below the smooth wooden staircase. Upstairs, one large room was partitioned at both ends to form a kitchen and a chapel. The huge living room between had windows running along the extent of one wall and shelving on the other. A few wooden and spring bed frames filled the chapel room and I was in time to reserve the last one. Mike Rheinberger, Terry McCullagh and James Strohfeldt were busy sorting out dirty socks and sleeping bags on the other beds and Jim Truscott had the remaining floorspace covered in an instant.

It was funny watching Strohfeldt unpack his suitcase full of 'light' bedtime reading. You can always judge a man by the cover of his books: side by side, on top of two stacks of James' tomes, were *Finite Dimensional Vector Spaces* and the latest issue of *Playboy.*

I liked James a hell of a lot. He was, by admission, incredibly proud and arrogant. I remembered him telling me, 'But even though I'm arrogant, I'm pretty talented—anything I do I'm good at.' To say I admired his self-assurance and openness would be nothing short of an understatement. It was so refreshing to talk to someone like him. As he unpacked all the study notes and reference volumes he intended reading at Base Camp, the arts scholar majoring in mathematics and philosophy at the University of Melbourne attempted to explain what a nice guy like him was doing in a place like this.

'Anything I try to do becomes easy, so I look for something harder to do. If I am successful in doing it, it was too easy,' James articulated with a typically philosophical air of confusion. 'I always try to do things that are harder and harder; as soon as I achieve something, it becomes irrelevant because it was obviously too easy and achievable. So I look for something I may fail at, and give that a go.'

I wondered if James had ever indulged in feeling truly happy or elated by any of his many academic or sporting achievements. Surely qualifying as a doctor can't have been a forgettable pushover. 'I think the biggest satisfaction and achievement I've ever had was when I passed my level two ski instructors' course,' James replied. 'That meant far more to me than my medical degree because passing those exams was a foregone conclusion and the ski course—since I'd done very little skiing—was not. I had to concentrate a great deal harder to pass that, than in my medical exams.'

Despite James' present athletic build, he had only recently turned his hand to sport. Under his father's rigid guidance, there was nothing in his life but studying, until he left home and went to Uni. 'I started studying when I was three; top of the class in telling the time—all that sort of thing,' James revealed with a laugh, 'and it wasn't until third year Uni that I started looking around and realised there was more to life than books. My life since then has been one big search for all those other things to do, experiences to have, horizons to look over and things to try and achieve.' James, who had always been pretty weedy, got interested in sports, and to improve his condition and abilities, he started working out in the campus gym. 'I met Jim Van Gelder there— he was doing one finger chin ups … that was four years ago. He asked me to go rock-climbing with him. Two and a half years ago, he found out about an Army Alpine Association climbing expedition on Pisang Chulu in the Himalayas in late 1985, and we both signed up.' For both James and Van Gelder it was a spectacular introduction to mountaineering and they enjoyed it so much, they were hooked.

'So here I am on my way to Everest, two years later. I think that's called jumping in at the deep end,' James joked. Perhaps Chomolungma, against such limited experience was a touch ambitious for the average mind to contemplate. But James, of course, did not have an average mind. 'Risk?', he said, looking at me as if I should have known better than to ask such an inane

James Strohfeldt in Khunde.

question. 'It's worth risking your life to live it. It is much more important to live hard and die young, than not to have lived at all. I climb for experience. Your life is nothing more than the sum of your experiences, and the more intense they are, the more alive you feel. Climbing is pretty intense. James was emphatic that danger was not an essential ingredient in climbing or life, but when it did occur, it defined his life even more. 'It is contrast— a pile of rubbish defines beauty; living close to death defines life.' James doubted he would feel the need to climb another 8000-metre peak, since all the preparation and effort needed would take up his life to the exclusion of other things.

It obviously didn't matter if he summited Everest or not, since success would only automatically make the achievement irrelevant. His career as a doctor was already that—its only real asset was that the income it earned allowed James to maintain his lifestyle. 'I couldn't live in Melbourne and be a doctor without also going to university and studying something a little more esoteric,' he said. 'Going to uni is the mental equivalent of the physical thing which drives me to climb Everest.'

What was even more endearing about James was his attitude towards the 'Australian' part of the ABEE climb. So far I had the impression that everyone was just using the Bicentennial banner as a tool for sponsorship and as an excuse to climb. Money had been handed out to all sorts of organisations to support all sorts of activities in the Bicentennial year. The proposed objective to 'place the Australian flag on the top of the world as their contribution to the nation's two hundredth birthday', looked good on the proposal for a Bicentennial Authority grant and subsequent press releases, but meant zero to most expedition members. The only motive for most climbers was to get themselves, as individuals, onto the summit—to fulfil their own personal aspirations, not some pious nationalistic ideal. James was the only one to voice otherwise. 'There's a lot of antipathy towards big expeditions among climbers—most would say they preferred climbing in a small group of friends. But I don't mind

the big team thing. I like the representing Australia aspect of it—that really counts for a lot. Society needs achievement; it needs to be proud of itself,' James surmised. 'This trip, in particular, is more closely linked to society than most expeditions because it is part of a celebration of our country.'

Paul Bayne bounced into our chapel-cum-bedroom and asked if I wanted to play Scrabble with him and Jill. I could tell James was itching to continue organising his books and things, so I accepted the challenge and nestled into a corner of the wide windowsill in the main room, opposite Jill. We played on and on into the evening, breaking only for dinner. Chris and I had planned to venture out on a midnight foray to photograph moonlight on Chomolungma, so while waiting, Chris joined Jill, Paul and I in the battle of wits and words. At 1.00 a.m. it was clear the clouds had settled overhead for good and since we couldn't see the mountains, let alone any photogenic moon rays, our staying power dissolved. Chris and Paul, who had teamed up to challenge the fairer sex, won the final deciding round of Scrabble, and we all retired to our sleeping bags for a few hours kip.

Terry McCullagh joined Chris and I at the crack of dawn for our second premeditated photographic frenzy. It was Saturday, and down at Namche, somewhere in the pea-soup fog, stall holders would be setting up the weekly market. I still hadn't managed to shake off my cough and streaming nose, so I trailed behind the boys as they sped off down the hillside.

The marketplace sprawled along the 'street' leading into the horseshoe-shaped village. It looked totally different to the path we had entered Namche by the day before. At one end of the area, in isolation from the rest of the colourful market, swarthy skinned butchers squatted in the dust over huge bloody carcasses. Big blowflies and carnivorous crowds swarmed around the meat, buzzing with satisfaction. The odd live yak wandered through the less gruesome section of the market, disrupting makeshift stalls and shoppers. One overcurious bovine got his

horn stuck in an empty cardboard box and, suddenly enraged, upturned a huge pile of saris and instant noodles. No one in the bargain-hunting throng so much as blinked: I couldn't get myself and tripod to a relatively safer vantage point fast enough! I had heard about yaks goring people, and I had no intention of putting those rumours to the test.

As the fog lifted, image after image filled my lens—swirling in a violent blaze of colour. Flashing jewellery and flashing smiles, appeared between the dusty folds of ragged clothing. Many of the men wore tatty Gore-Tex jackets and solid leather boots: in their clothes could be traced almost every foreign expedition that had come to Nepal. The odd Westerner, fresh from a forest-fire shower, wandered through the scene. Bruce Farmer's gleaming pink face, framed by a new market-bought woollen beanie, shone like a wild poppy in a field of tornado-torn wheat. Jill and Wanchu were right behind him, doing some serious shopping to replenish their meat, rice and dhal supplies. I welcomed Jill's wave and call to join her for a hot cup of tea. The breeze was quite cold and I had started to freeze into a hunched position. I waved to Chris, who was perched on a huge boulder on the other side of the market cursing and swearing because his film had torn off inside the camera. He waved down to Terry McCullagh and we all dived into the sea of shoppers and somehow surfaced together at the far end of the market.

After a couple of tea rounds in Wanchu's sister-in-law's teashop, Jill went back into the market and Terry dragged Chris and I off to PK's—a well-known restaurant/guesthouse above a chocolate, nuts and change-money emporium in the middle of Namche. More than 80 per cent of the households in Namche benefit from money spent by mountaineers and trekkers, but PK's popularity ensures the owners a lion's share of the gross profits. A few of our expedition members had spent the night contributing to PK's coffers. Temporarily paralysed by the local

Saturday is market day in Namche Bazaar.

Lodges, restaurants, and souvenir shops line the narrow, dusty streets of Namche Bazaar.

beer, they had not been able to crawl their way up to Khunde and were now in various states of recovery in the corner of the restaurant. A toothy portrait of Jimmy and Roslyn Carter hung above their heads. It was signed 'To our friends … [the proprietors of PK's]' and Min Moor was boasting he had slept in the same room the ex-President and his wife had shared (no doubt with a dozen bodyguards) on their holiday trek to the Himalaya. Beneath the dynamic duo, a fading Robert Redford stood before a frosted Namche Bazaar. I stopped staring at the three rehearsed, celluloid smiles and Redford's designer ski-wear, and turned to face my less charismatic but definitely real team mates.

Chris, Rick and the two Terrys were recounting one climbing horror story after the other.

'Did ya hear about that guy decking out on a 1000 feet fall?'

'Yeah—splat! Geronimo!'

'Dead?'

'Are you kidding? Scrambled, mate!'

'What about the guy who cut his partner off his rope to save himself falling into the crevasse as well?'

'Man, what a decision!'

'Reckon! The guy who fell in broke his leg, and six days later, with no food or water, he had crawled along the bottom of the crevasse and found his way back to Base Camp.'

'Jesus! Imagine how the other bloke must have felt! Haunted, probably!'

'You better watch out in the Icefall mate,' Terry McCullagh directed at me, 'any one of those big ice seracs could fall on you … bang, you're gone! Dead. Bulldozer flat.' He looked down at PK's menu and teased, 'Do you wanna order a buckwheat pancake or what?'

It was comforting to know that Namche Bazaar was free of falling blocks of ice, or seracs. Having the cheesy Carters drop off the wall and clip the side of my conk was about the worst thing that could possibly happen to me in PK's. To hell with it— I ordered the pancake and laughed off the assumption that I could be transformed into a similar flattened state by an avalanche or 300-metre fall on Chomolungma.

When I was halfway through my honey-dripped breakfast, Terry Tremble passed me a pamphlet he had been looking at. Ned Gillette, a well-known American skier and mountaineer was on the cover. I had met Ned at National Geographic's Washington headquarters the year before. I turned the page of the brochure, which served to promote his many expeditions and major sponsors, and whamo! There was Ned, doing the splits over a great gaping crack in the ice. Something in my brain short-circuited. I had never seen a picture of a crevasse before, and this was about fifty times more frightening than I thought they would be—fifty times deeper and fifty times more intimidating. Words are one thing, but pictures are truth; they leave little to the imagination. The photograph of Ned leaping over a bottomless crevasse was not inspiring in the least; it was the sharpest slap in the face I'd had for a long time. What the hell had I let myself in for? I only cheered myself up by promising if I survived this expedition, I would never ever go on another.

More of the team arrived down from Khunde and in pub-crawl fashion, we moved onto another restaurant. By midday, the sun was giving its all so we migrated to the lodge with the outdoor balcony. The conversation eased onto more light-hearted topics and James initiated yet another joke-telling session. Laughter avalanched around my ears and momentarily buried the mountains of fear rising inside me.

The next morning I had planned to sleep in, but Jim shook me awake before dawn to inform me the sky was clear. 'Go on, get up and do your job!' he said, a little irritated I wasn't already outside fumbling through the frost with my lightmeter and tripod. He promptly wormed his way into his sleeping bag, rolled over and went back to sleep.

If I had to rise to the call of duty, I certainly wasn't going to do it alone. I dragged my two budding protégés out of bed, and within seconds Chris was flying out the door and down the track towards the Everest View Hotel. Terry had come down with some dreaded lergy, so he was as slow as I for a change. We staggered after Chris, short-cutting through the Government-financed Livestock Development Farm.

The yaks inside the farm were up and about, but only just. Rectangular imprints in the frost revealed where their fat bodies had slumbered overnight, slumped in long lines at regularly spaced intervals. The grassy pasture looked like an abandoned campsite from a boy scout jamboree.

As we crossed the field, we disturbed three spectacular Impeyan pheasants. They took off quickly and left Terry and I startled. The merest glimpse of these national birds of Nepal, scintillating in their nine iridescent colours, suddenly enlivened me. I put all my senses on alert, just in case the feathered beauties returned.

I forgot about hurrying towards the Everest View, for in the opposite direction (and downhill) the imminent sunrise had turned the Dudh Kosi valley into an magnificent picture. With subtle changes in hue, ridge after ridge, the valley unfolded into the distance in translucent shades of blue and lilac. A wash of pastel pink seemed to rise skyward from the monochromatic valley. The whole scene was as fragile as tissue, and blew away silently after just a few minutes. The watercolour valley was quickly painted over by the solid, oily brushstrokes of daylight. Its heavy olive green shadows and textured surfaces returned. While I watched the landscape complete its dramatic metamorphosis, clouds rolled up the river, rose and obscured the scene. The unseen artist had again curtained his miraculous canvas with yet another overcast day.

Back at the house, Jon Muir was getting ready to go for a walk up on the ridge-top above Khunde. He seemed uncharacteristically solemn beneath his black floppy felt hat, with its red chiffon scarf band. When I saw the new white kata clutched in his hand, the reason for his sadness and pensive mood became clear. On the ridge above Khunde stood a memorial cairn to his two climbing partners, Fred From and Craig Nottle. They had fallen to their deaths on Jon's 1984 Chomolungma Expedition, and the sobering memory of their accident was now as close to Jon's heart as the memorial was to Khunde. He slipped out the door without saying a word to anyone. It was obvious he wanted to be

On the ridge high above Khunde sits a sobering memorial to Craig Nottle and Fred From, two Australian climbers killed on Chomolungma in 1984.

alone, but I ran after him and offered to go along, if he needed a shoulder to lean on or someone to talk to. 'Na,' he said, squeezing my hand, 'I'm OK. I've got a couple of friends to talk to up there.' I went back to my sleeping bag and set up an all-day Scrabble competition with Jill, Paul and Zac.

James coerced me out of my warm cocoon later on in the afternoon and I followed him up to Khunde Hospital to visit the interns, Drs Simon MacLaurin and Marianne Wood. Built and funded by Hillary and the Himalayan Trust, the hospital was less than 100 metres behind Sonam's cousin's house. It had been snowing lightly since midday, and swirls of light powder snow quickly filled the folds and creases of my down jacket.

Outside Kathmandu there is only one doctor for every 100 000 people, so not surprisingly the Khunde Clinic had seen more action that most surgeries in the West. There is no such thing as a specialist, so the resident GPs are expected to wear all the medical caps and gowns known to mankind: they are mid-wives, surgeons, family planners, anaesthetists, pharmacologist, pathologists—the works. Simon and Marianne had served seven months of their voluntary two-year residency in Khunde and hoped to follow up their hectic term with a similar stint in Africa.

When James and I lumbered into the one-roomed surgery, Simon was sitting at his cluttered desk. He was frantically spinning an ancient looking device by hand, trying to centrifuge a urine sample and test it for TB. If he ever decided to give up medicine he could always get a job operating the coffee-grinder on Bondy's latest America's Cup challenger.

Marianne, who wore a long traditional Sherpa dress and striped apron, was trying to find a course of tablets for a patient, searching through a tatty cardboard box with 'mixed analgesics' pencilled on the side. One wall of the clinic was covered in shelves from floor to ceiling and cardboard boxes of every description held bandages, syringes, operating gowns, test tubes, pills, potions and 'sterile' packages of gauze and cotton wool. The 'use-by' dates on every item, drugs included, had expired—no doubt long before they even arrived in Nepal.

An archaic X-ray machine and a grubby, flat operating table and light sat in the middle of the linoleum-tiled floor. The poster above Simon's head graphically expounded the virtues of the holy condom, and a series of happy family-planning adver-tisements were set to pop out from their yellowed sticky-tape hinges and fall into the organised chaos of the desktop.

The hospital ran on donations from trekkers as well as funds from the Hillary Trust and Simon and Marianne received an allowance to cover their basic needs, but no wages. It's not every day you meet two professional doctors prepared to work seven days a week, often eighteen and sometimes twenty-hours a day. Rarer still are those who do it because they care about people; not money, sports cars and million-dollar mansions in Double Bay.

Simon and Marianne finished what they were doing, then welcomed James and I into their adjacent 'living room' for a cup of tea. It was an absolute pleasure to watch them opening their mail and food parcels from home. The 'postie' had arrived several days beforehand, but they hadn't, until now, found the

Ama Dablan towers above the twin villages of Khunde and Kumjung.

time to relax and absorb the latest family news from New Zealand. 'It's like Christmas!' Marianne said, unwrapping a packet of photographs. 'Oh look, more nephews and nieces!' she laughed, commenting on how the latest arrival looked like her own son, Dougal. Dougal was eighteen months old and sound asleep in another partitioned section of the living room. He was the only blonde in Khunde, and everyone in the area adored him.

Simon had dug out a few old medical journals and operating manuals for James, and these were piled on the coffee table, open at the 'amputation' chapters. James had offered to help the overworked doctors out, by amputating one of their patient's left leg. The old, frail Tibetan had contracted some disease in his shin bone thirty-five years ago, and had been in pain ever since. It had recently become so unbearable, he was contemplating suicide to end his misery. Simon and Marianne had been a little reluctant to perform the operation themselves because they lacked experience, so James' offer of assistance had come at exactly the right time. He had never performed an amputation alone, but had assisted orthopaedic surgeons on so many occasions he was confident he could pull if off. Chris Curry had offered to administer the anaesthetic.

While James studied the step-by-step photographic guide to felling human limbs, I listened to Marianne and Simon relate some of their everyday trials and tribulations. Late night emergencies were common and without a car to whiz them around the district, that usually meant hours and hours, even days, of walking through monsoon rain and winter snow to reach patients in need. 'I once trekked the equivalent of eight porter days in a single day of house calls,' Simon recalled. 'The day ended back in Khunde Hospital with a caesarian section on a fifty-year-old woman.'

'There was no light to operate by—the generator had broken down,' Marianne added. 'We had to work by torchlight. I was paranoid I'd left about half a dozen swabs inside the woman.' The baby was still-born, and the woman lost so much blood Simon doubted she'd live. Ten days later, she was strong enough to walk the four-hour trail back to her village.

Malnutrition and poor sanitation are the more usual causes of infant death. Statistically, one child out of every five born in Nepal dies within the first few weeks of life, and 35 out of every 1000 die between one and four years of age. Marianne did regular rounds in the immediate district to teach the local women about basic hygiene and diet, in an effort to reduce the alarming number of fatalities.

James had not simply brought me to the hospital to listen to medical horror stories. Inspired by my reaction to the photograph of Ned Gillette sprawled over the gaping crevasse, James wanted to see how I fared when exposed to some pretty wild pictures of the Khumbu Icefall on Chomolungma. He pulled a Canadian *Equinox* magazine from beneath the pile of dusty medical volumes and turned to a particularly graphic double page spread. On one side there was a picture of a corpse surrounded by mourning climbers at Base Camp and on the other, a hideous glimpse of a crevasse, spanned by a twisted ladder with a climber on it, as agile and as steady as a tight-rope walker. It blew me out. All the pictures blew me out. And reading snatches of the story had an even worse effect. Three Sherpas and one Canadian had

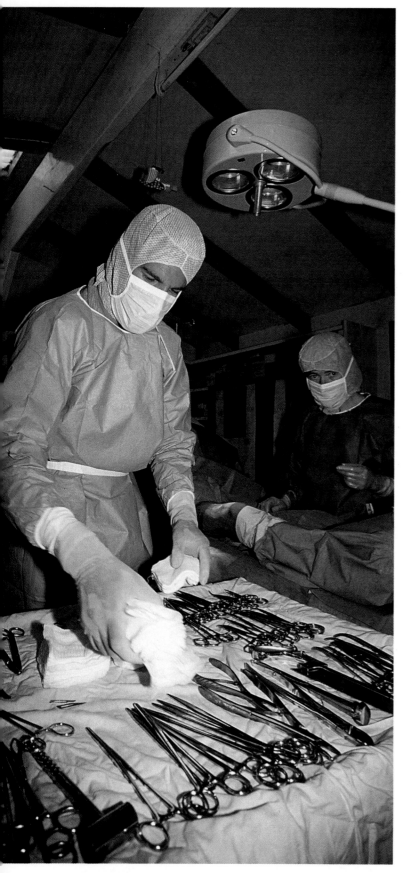

James Strohfeldt (left), assisted by Chris Curry and Khunde Hospital residents Marianne Wood (right) and Simon MacLaurin, amputated a Tibetan patient's leg.

died on the expedition. The descriptions and dimensions of the ice seracs and crevasses were stomach churning. I still have nightmares about the photographs. The only consoling thing about the story was the fact that the Canadian team's official photographer and journalist, Pat Morrow, had not only survived, but summited the Mother Goddess. Not that I was entertaining any delusions about my ability—on the contrary, I was starting to have second thoughts about going beyond Base Camp. 'No way, José ... you ain't getting me up there! Not for a million bucks!' I screamed, just as Pat, Zac and Austin entered the room. They had just finished one of their inner-sanctum meetings, chaired in an empty room in the small hospital ward.

'What's up Moo?' Austin asked, 'You aren't scared are you?'

'Who me?' I said, 'Too bloody right I am!' James laughed and re-immersed himself in his pre-op study. Zac asked how I was going to take the required spectacular photographs if I didn't go up into the Icefall. It was my duty to risk my life taking complimentary 'action-man' photographs of all the team members. I tried to avoid making eye contact with anyone—that was pretty easy since my eyes were riveted to the glossy magazine images—and said, 'Well what the hell do you think they invented the telephoto lens for?' I finished my tea, and raced away to save myself from being teased any further.

I was still entertaining the idea of shooting from the relative safety of Base Camp when I next saw Simon and Marianne, the following evening. It was Jon's twenty-seventh birthday and James was turning twenty-nine two days hence, so we were having a bit of a party on our last night in Khunde, and Austin had invited the two doctors and Dougal along. 'Changed your mind?' Simon asked me, over the merry din of laughter and clinking glasses. 'Change the subject?' I pleaded in return. Chris came to the rescue and butted in to ask if the amputation was still scheduled for the morning. They started talking doctor talk, so I excused myself and wandered over to Zac and Jill. They were chatting to our just-arrived number one liaison officer, Mohan Ali Singh. Mohan was a very handsome veteran of the First Ghurkha Rifles. He spoke textbook English with a slight Indian accent, and his squared jaw seemed to be clamped shut, even when he talked. Perhaps he was nervous—not so much about meeting us, as to what may be expected of him in light of the Tri-Nation Expedition issue. With a little whisky nudge Mohan relaxed and started telling us about his career and family. He had served in the Indian Army for ten years and fought in the war against China in Aksai Chin, and against the Pakistanis in 1965. He had reached the rank of sergeant, but now worked for the Nepal Police Force in Kathmandu. As a liaison officer, his main duty was to solve problems which the expedition confronted on the way to and at Chomolungma's Base Camp. Any disputes or undesirable incidents arising between any member of the expedition and local people, guides or porters, had to be settled by Mohan. If nothing flared up between the Tri-Nation and the ABEE, poor Mohan was going to have very little to do at Base Camp. The proud father of five children (the eldest was studying science at Kathmandu University) was about to walk his way into a three to four month battle with boredom. I hope he packed his Rubik's cube ...

While we stood discussing the dreaded Tri-Nation tragicomedy, Little Pasang came shuffling out of the kitchen with a bottle of beer, and presented it to Jon. There was so much joy in the giving, I was close to tears. So was Jon. Little Pasang was as bubbly as the amber fluid contained in the ceremonially decorated bottle. Fifty rupees worth of beer may not seem like much to the average well-heeled Westerner, but in terms of the Nepalese economy, it had cost Pasang more than a day's wage.

Jill had baked (in a saucepan) a real birthday cake with glacé cherries on top—and candles! Jon and James cut it, cheered on by a drunken, but rousing rendition of 'Happy Birthday'. Rosy cheeks glowed from every corner of the room. Everyone seemed to be having a good time; even Krondorf had found a new mate. Dougal, who had been dragging the floppy-eared mascot around all evening, had curled up with it on Simon's lap and fallen asleep.

The clanking of yak bells and thudding of hangovers woke us all at 6.30 a.m. the next morning. Sonam had not let us down— magically he had managed to pull seventy yaks and their herders out of the Khunde-Kumjung hat. While Little Pasang took strong coffee around to the groaning, disorientated climbers, Sonam and Phil Pitham weighed and distributed the barrels and kitbags fairly among the herders. Several dozen porters hung around outside the house, waiting to take any leftover or unyakable loads.

Chris and James were already up at the hospital, preparing for the big op. I found them on the verandah with the old man, unwrapping the filthy bandages from his diseased leg. The patient was so frightened he shook uncontrollably, so Chris jabbed him with some mild sort of sedative. I talked to him a bit in Tibetan and showed him a photograph of the Dalai Lama. He touched it to his head and started mumbling a few mantras.

James gave up the idea of scrubbing the old man's leg. It would take forever to remove the grime, built up over the years and encrusted in every pore of the Tibetan's wrinkled skin. He swabbed the leg instead, with copious quantities of rust-coloured betadine solution, then drew a 'cut here' line just above the knee. Chris covered the 'sterilised' leg in 'sterile' operating cloth and plastic and Simon helped him carry the man into the surgery.

I had no intention of watching and photographing beyond that point. I took a few shots of the team, and a couple of James with all his tools ready to make the first incision, then left. Min Moor was standing on a bench on the verandah, staring in through a small window. He didn't want to miss a thing, and had an extra roll of film just in case there was more than thirty-six frames worth of blood and gore. Jon was on the verandah too, fresh out of a solar-heated shower, trying to retrieve Krondorf from the vice-like grip of tiny Dougal. That dog was leaving a trail of broken hearts across Nepal. Every kid that shook paws with Krondorf didn't want to let go. He didn't have quite as much charisma as his master, but his furry face was a lot nicer to cuddle.

With Krondorf finally hanging from the backpack of his rightful owner and Dougal distracted by one of the hospital's Sherpa assistants, we quickly moved away from the verandah and back to Sonam's cousin's house. Everyone bar Rheinberger

Jon Muir's mascot, Krondorf, meets Ang Douli.

had left for Thyangboche. He was waiting for Jon, as they planned to visit a friend, Ang Douli, on their way out of the twin-village.

Ang Douli had put in several brief appearances during our stay in Khunde. She was the short, plump (for a Sherpa) wife of Mingma Tsering, the head man of Khunde and Hillary's personal sirdar since 1955. Mingma's main job was to employ local people to work on the various projects initiated and sponsored by the Hillary Trust.

Ang Douli greeted Mike, Jon, Krondorf and I at the door with a sensational smile and giggle. 'Me no happy. Not very happy today,' she said, bursting into a fit of laughter. It was hard to imagine what she would be like in a good mood. We followed her upstairs to the hearth and sat around dunking glucose biscuits in our tea. A framed photograph hanging on the smoke-blackened wall, below a frieze of finger-painted white dots and swastikas, caught my eye. It was a glossy print picturing Ed Hillary surrounded by numerous friends and associates on a 'This Is Your Life' television studio set. Ang Douli and Mingma were sitting in the front row, on either side of the celebrated honouree.

After a few cuppas, Ang Douli ushered us into the main room of her house to check out her son Temba's paintings. The shelves on the back wall of the room were chock-a-block with copper and brass utensils and chang bottles. At least half a dozen huge, copper water containers, decorated with a brass trim of good-luck swastikas, were glowing on the bottom shelf, warmly luminous in the dim light. It may seem strange for one family to have so many pots and pans, but in Sherpaland a family's wealth is reflected in the copper kitchenware. Ang Douli's display was no more or less excessive than owning two Rolls Royces and a gold Mercedes. Opposite the shelves, Temba was sitting on the wide windowsill in front of a traditional, cartoon-styled picture of the Khumbu Valley. He was just putting the finishing touches on the mountains surrounding Thyangboche Monastery. He smiled at us and mimed for me to take his photograph. Temba was a deaf mute, but his skilled gestures were simple to understand. He unrolled several finished and half-finished paintings and

Thyangboche Monastery on a clear, sun-filled day is often touted to be the most beautiful place on earth.

'asked' us if we were interested in purchasing anything from him. Ang Douli proudly told us that many people were buying her son's art, and all of the paintings Temba had just shown us were commissions from various trekkers and mountaineers.

I couldn't afford to place an order, but took a few pics of Temba in front of his latest masterpiece. The morning was starting to slip away from us, so we bade farewell and wandered past the last few houses of the village and back onto the well-worn trail to Thyangboche. As the crow flies, we were only 28 kilometres from Chomolungma Base Camp, but via the steep, switchbacking staircase of fitted stones smoothed by the passage of countless generations, the mountain was still five days beyond our reach.

Mike and Jon forged ahead, leaving me ambling behind a trail-filling caravan of four yaks and a scrawny looking dog. It was impossible to pass without risking a fall down the sheer-sided hill, so I walked with the Tibetan couple whooshing the beasts along until the track widened. Ama Dablan was so close, I could feel the breath of her avalanches. The knife-edged route Jon had applied to climb filled me with an even greater respect for his ability.

It was nice to be walking by myself for the first time—good to have a bit of space to think, feel and sing out of tune in. I crossed over the river and started climbing up the long, winding track towards the Khumbu's most famous monastery. Cloud

crept up the valley and by the time I reached Thyangboche, it was as cold as Khunde had been on first arrival.

On a clearer, warmer day I doubt I could disagree with the guidebooks, which touted Thyangboche as the most beautiful place on earth. The patron saint of the Sherpas, Lama Sangwa Dorje, was believed to have meditated on a rock where the monastery now sits, and Thyangboche takes its name from the heel imprint the mystical flying saint left behind in that rock; *thyang* being the Sherpa word for heel.

The monastery, so perfectly attuned to its surroundings it looks as if it just sprouted up from the earth, was founded around 1918, and took three years to build. The founder, Lama Chatang Chortar, died of shock in 1933 when an earthquake destroyed the original monastery. His reincarnation, or *Rimpoche,* Nawang Tenzing Zangbu, now governs and dwells in the fully restored ochre-red *rapjung* (celibate) monastery. Although he spent many years studying in Tibet, the *Rimpoche* is a Sherpa from Namche Bazaar, and consequently his people are very proud of him.

I did a quick circle around the external wall of the monastery, which resembled, on a smaller scale, several I had seen in Tibet. Inside, I knew the ground plan would be in keeping with the sacred mandala design—a diagram based on a series of homocentric squares, envisioned by Tibetan Buddhists as an aid to meditation—rather than the rectangular shape of Sherpa houses. I found the rest of the team, minus the doctors, in a large guesthouse opposite the monastery, wolfing down big bowls of noodles and hacking away at tough yak steaks. The eating room had huge picture windows which offered a 270-degree view of the world.

Around the monastery, like waves around a pebble dropped into a pond, were three concentric rings. The first comprised the monks' quarters, a school (offering optional religious instruction) and a rest house built by the *Rimpoche* for passing trekkers and visitors to Thyangboche. The area around the buildings was circled by a forest of stunted trees and juniper. Musk deer, thar and blood-pheasant roamed the forest, so tame they ignored passers by. The final ring surrounding Thyangboche was formed by the mountains themselves. Looking east, somewhere beneath the clouds, were Chomolungma and Ama Dablan. Turning south, Tamserku and Kangtaga rose high from the mountain ring, and obscured by the windowless wall of the guesthouse was Kwongde in the west. In the north, about to vanish in swirling cloud, Tawoche completed the majestic ring of mountains.

After spending the night in Mountain Travel's Thyangboche lodge, next door to the guesthouse with the big panoramic windows, we filed towards the monastery for a prearranged blessing of the expedition. It had snowed all night and Thyangboche thus transformed was a beautiful sight to behold. A light fall, as silent and gentle as sifted icing sugar, floated onto the milk-chocolate-iced monastery. It was bitterly cold waiting in the courtyard of the building, huddled together under a narrow eave just covering the long doorstep in front of the main entrance.

A monk, visible in silhouette in a small room built into one side of the enclosed courtyard, drummed a mournful beat and punctuated its rhythm with a deep tolling of bells. 'Shit! It sounds like we're lined up for execution, not a bloody blessing!' Jim Truscott jeered. As if on cue, a novice monk came and rescued us from the intimidating din and led us out of the cold upstairs to the monastery's library.

More than 300 sets of scriptures, printed in Tullung Chokpu near Lhasa, filled the pigeon-holed back wall of the cavernous room.

There were no lights—not even butter candles—to see by, but after about half an hour it was obvious a very important element was missing from the meeting room—the Rimpoche. The blessing was a total non-event without him, since his novices were not too sure what to do in his absence.

Sonam gave a kata to Austin to place on the statue containing the ashes of the monastery's founder and the rest of us stood around and watched. No one knew whether they were supposed to look impressed, mystified, pissed-off or just plain stupid. One by one we trickled out of the room and back on the snow-covered trail to Chomolungma. A young monk promised (after Austin had contributed to the community coffers) to pray for the expedition's safety every day until our return to Thyangboche. Sonam thanked him on our behalf, but was not satisfied the expedition had been properly blessed. He assured Austin the head lama of Pangboche, the next monastery en route, would be available to perform the ritual.

Mick Pezet and I were the last to leave the library and the young prayer-promising monk asked us if we wanted to see inside the *lha-kang*, or main hall. Butter candles flickered on the shrine at the back of the room, opposite the heavy curtained

Crossing the suspension bridge spanning the Imja Khola, en route to Pangboche.

doorway, There was just enough light to make out a dozen monks, sitting in two rows between the door and the altar, facing into the centre of the *lha-kang*. Only their hands and faces were visible, since their dark maroon robes had become one with the shadows. They were having a break from their chanting and the room was silent, save for the occasional slurping of tea.

Mick looked a bit stunned by the austerity of the scene and confided he felt like an intruder; like he had strayed into somewhere he had no right to be. I didn't feel at all alienated, but since we were expected to hurry to Pangboche for the anticipated 'new and improved' blessing, I followed him out of the *lha-kang* and into the snow.

Trekking the course between the two monasteries was like walking through an English Christmas card. Despite being Australian, falling snow always reminded me of the festive season. The yaks were Nepal's answer to the 'dashing through the snow' reindeer, and dripping juniper bushes and birch trees were sound substitutes for snow-trimmed firs. The sound of a clanking yak bell became my 'star in the east' as the snowfall thickened and limited visibility.

I caught up with Chris, Mick, BJ and Paul Bayne at the spectacular suspension bridge spanning the crashing, icy waters of the Imja Khola. Traffic had jammed at the bridge since the yaks were reluctant to cross. Half a dozen of them were nervously contemplating moving, and Chris and Paul were poised to photograph the imminent bovine bolt. I wandered into the middle of the bridge to bang off some shots of the thunderous river, but one great lumbering beast charged after me and nudged me across to the other side of the river gorge. Since I wasn't about to turn around and run head-on into the yak-pack, I contented myself with taking photographs of the Imja Khola from the bank.

As soon as I took my gloves off to work the shutter, my hands burned with the cold. My lens fogged and as the snow fell and melted, water droplets threatened to seep inside my camera body. I managed three shots before my snap-frozen fingers protested and threatened strike action. I chucked my soggy Olympus back in my pack and didn't attempt to dry it down or take any more pictures until we reached Pangboche.

Just inside the monastery's muddy courtyard, I pulled off my wet gloves and anorak and fumbled around for a new roll of film and lens tissues. Chris gave his camera a wipe, then the slow steady beat of a large skin-covered drum, the harsh hiss of angry cymbals and the hollow note of a conch shell lured us inside.

The impromptu blessing ended with the appearance of the holy donation box and mythical yeti leftovers. It was hard to believe the skull and hand skeleton were real, but harder still to suggest Pangboche's monks were nothing more than a band of clever confidence tricksters. Genuine or otherwise, it was a hell of a novel (and successful!) way for a charity to rake in dollars (US greenbacks preferred).

Most of the team had drifted away from the monastery and returned to the track to Periche when one of the older monks offered around the chang and tea. Chris and I accepted, and while we slurped away, another monk fished around between the maroon folds of his robe and produced a brochure for us to read. I thought mounting expeditions to climb big mountains was pretty bizarre, but this pamphlet really took the cake! In true Loch Ness style, a recent international expedition planned to search for the fabled red-headed yeti.

In 1951 the famous mountaineer, Eric Shipton, found and photographed a trail of wide, oval shaped, big-toed, human-looking footprints in the snow of the Melungste Glacier. The photographs satisfied even the most sceptical scientists of the day, and ever since then, people from all over the world have

Chris Curry jumps for joy on the ridge above Periche.

believed Nepal's 'abominable snowman' still exists. In 1954 London's *Daily Mail* mounted the first 'find the yeti' hunt, and in 1960 Sir Edmund Hillary himself led an expedition into yeti country, equipped with all the latest scientific instruments and sighting devices they could lay their hands on. They took a scalp, similar to the iron-hard dome of leather and red-bristles we had just been shown, from the monastery of Kumjung and had it examined in Chicago, Paris and London. It was declared to be a 200-year-old artifact made from the hide of a wild Himalayan goat, but the revelation did little to dissuade the masses.

The Pangboche skull was analysed in Europe in the early 1970s; some claimed it to be genuine, but the majority declared it a blatant fake. But further footprints around the Japanese Expedition Base Camp in 1974, the Polish Camp in 1980 and more recently an actual sighting of a beast by Reinhold Messner, have ensured the yeti myth lives on. God knows what the monks at Pangboche monastery would do for a quid if it didn't.

When Chris and I finally left the gloomy second floor library room of the monastery, we were delighted to find the monks' prayers had blessed the weather as well as our expedition. It had stopped snowing, and the sun was shining down on the glaring white landscape. We caught up to BJ and Paul Bayne, who had stopped to change back into their tee-shirts and shorts.

Paul was his usual champagne self, bubbling over with joy. He tried to teach me how to walk without slipping and tripping on the icy snow, but I wasn't much of a pupil. I eyed him jealously, as he danced effortlessly down the track. Slowly I skidded between his footsteps, convinced I would tumble to my death on the trail long before I even reached the wretched Chomolungma and her dreaded Icefall.

Small wonder Paul was so agile and confident on snow and ice: he lived, year round, surrounded by the stuff. Originally from Sydney's Whale Beach, Paul had been climbing and skiing full-time overseas for thirteen years—ever since he finished school and opted out of the academically professional life he was apparently destined to pursue. Like James, he was not known for his sporting prowess, but seeing Mt Cook in New Zealand for the first time changed all that quite dramatically. He stuck out one year of his science, chemistry and physics studies and then flew back to Mt Cook to live for good. He got a job in the local hotel and in his spare time learnt how to ski and climb. His family weren't too thrilled about him chucking in his courses, so he eventually wandered back to Australia to finish his degree. He knew that he would never use it, but he did it to kind of justify the fact that he was climbing from *choice*, and not any other reason. He went back to Cook and started guiding, and now works the season in both New Zealand and Colorado in the US.

Paul had already spent more time on crampons and skis than an average ace mountaineer would in an average lifetime. But despite that, this was his very first trip to the Himalayas and so far the ridge above Khunde was the highest he had ever been. I caught up to him where he and BJ stopped for a cup of tea and asked him why he climbed, and what he thought his chances would be on Chomolungma.

'Awww … geez … mountains are a really really nice place to be; really *wild*,' Paul began, 'There's a bit of magic up there— for me mountaineering is about being in incredibly wild, beautiful

Snow covers the flat, wide valley surrounding Periche.

places. The magic sunsets … just being there at the right time, in the right place. It's really nice being totally in control and even risking that control a little bit. When the stakes are high, it's a satisfying feeling, knowing that you're running the show. Being in a situation where you have to force yourself to keep your concentration up—knowing you can—knowing the stakes are high, but knowing you can do it.' Paul admitted he knew Chomolungma was within his capabilities. He wasn't worried about altitude—it would just increase the pain and exhaustion factor, not decrease his determination. 'As far as I'm concerned,' he said with fiery passion, 'I'm only here to reach the top. It's summit at all costs, definitely, and I'm not going home unless I've done the damn thing.'

Fortunately, Paul did not have such unshakeable, high-risk objectives when guiding climbs and skiing trips in New Zealand. He didn't do that to prove something to himself, rather to give something to others. 'It's different,' he assured me. 'I take people to places they would never get to without me or another guide. There are doctors, lawyers and professional people who have very little time off, but still have the capacity to appreciate the magic of these places. You can give these people an experience they couldn't otherwise have, without giving up their own careers. The buzz you can give people! They are so high, it rubs off—you really feel like you've given them something, and that it will rub off on others when they get back home.'

A huge smile swept across the thirty-two-year-old's pixie-featured face. 'I'm only going to have one shot at this—at Everest—and I'll make it', he said, some of his sunny, if premature, confidence rubbing off on us. The four of us—Paul, BJ, Chris and I—stepped boldly out into the sunshine and marched, without a single slip, into Periche.

Chris and I dumped our packs in the dormitory of 'Nima Tsering's Himalayan Hotel', and confident of a classic sunset, we quickly climbed the long ridge behind Periche, separating it from the Imja Khola valley and the settlement of Dingboche. The view as we ascended was just magnificent. The small stone dwellings of Periche hugged the base of the ridge and wobbly stone walls cobwebbed from it, partitioning the front lawns and fields of the village's land-owners. Yaks, like stray poppy seeds on a starched white tablecloth, stood motionless on the snow-covered tableau. Our expedition gear lay like crumbs, swept into vague piles between the yaks. In the middle of the valley, just short of the shadow cast by the craggy peaks of Tawoche and Lobuje, a narrow glacial stream twisted and glistened like a pure gold chain, falling from the geisha-white neck of the valley.

By the time we reached the top of the ridge, low cloud had completely concealed Dingboche and all the mountains behind it. The summits of Makalu and Ama Dablan vanished, just as two doctors from Periche's first-aid post for the Himalayan Rescue Association appeared. Chris had met David and Lynley Cook during the course of his Pumo Ri expedition and hastily introduced them to me, before they flew off down the track for 'home'. The New Zealand-born duo had been in Dingboche lecturing to trekkers about the ravages of acute mountain (high-altitude) sickness. They didn't think much of our chances for a sunset photo, but Chris remained optimistic. 'You just never know

around here what will happen,' he called after the sensible, retreating pair. 'If you don't freeze to death, drop in for a cup of tea on your way down,' Lynley called. David's reply was lost on the wind that had whipped up with the cloud.

Determined the ridge was the elusive 'right place', and 5.00 p.m. on 9 March was the 'right time', Chris and I sheltered behind a memorial to some Spanish woman called Angela and waited for the sky to clear and turn postcard pink. It didn't. We raced off the ridge at 5.30 p.m., welcomed the doctors' invitation and subsequently thawed out by their pot-bellied stove.

Our persistence was rewarded the following evening near Lobuje—the next sizeable collection of lodges on the Base Camp route, tucked in a sheltered corner at the foot of the Lobuje Glacier. Chris and I dragged our tripods up to a high ridge, a few kilometres away from the village. At 5500 metres we had a spectacular panoramic view of Nupste, the Icefall, where Base Camp was likely to be, Changste in Tibet, and before it, the Lho Lha, Lingtren and Pumo Ri. It was the same ridge Geof Bartram had taken Chris to, for his first long look at Pumo Ri. The scene had been spared of cloud, but not the western horizon. Disappointed, we watched the sun sink into a thick smudge of grey, and shadows slowly creep towards the summits of the big mountains. I followed Chris, who had given up and started back for Lobuje.

Suddenly, a shaft of light slipped between the clouds and struck a very distant Ama Dablan. She blushed, and as I turned my head politely, I caught Nupste off guard, and similarly embarrassed her. I didn't know where to aim my camera first. The clouds around Ama Dablan turned dark grey, then orange, and finally pastel pink. Nupste, not to be outdone, turned pink and lilac. With each passing second, her glowing summit grew more and more intense: orange and gold with touches of pink, crowned by the bluest sky I had ever seen. I was breathless, and not just because of the altitude.

After four minutes the show was over and darkness fell like a heavy cloak around our shoulders. We raced away and back to Lobuje, high on the Himalaya and ecstatic over capturing a fickle glimpse—not to mention photographs—of her wondrous evening light show. At last! An image worth writing home about!

We were nearly there. Just another day to reach Gorek Shep, and one last push up the glacier to Base Camp. I had seen its barren, desolate extent from the ridge. Everyone was excited; you could feel it. The fun was coming to an end, and the serious business of climbing was about to take hold. The mood was not depressed, but electric. Even Jim was starting to smile and show some enthusiasm. Bruce Farmer had gone on ahead of the crowd, and radioed a report back to say everything was fine at Base. Peter Allen and Norm Crookston had secured the favoured site in the area and Peter Lambert and Charlie Hart had helped them prepare platforms for individual tents and erect the mess. Carol, Van Gelder and Ali Shah were putting the finishing touches to their research station and, according to a general consensus, all Base Camp needed to be a complete home was the culinary expertise of one Corporal Jill Trenam.

A sight to write home about—the summit of Nuptse bathed in the orange and pink hues of sunset.

A climber enters the spectacular yet treacherous realm of Chomo-lungma's Icefall.

5
Into the Icefall

Chapter Five

Into the Icefall

Climbing the Icefall is a cross between a mediaeval assault on a fortress and crossing a dangerous minefield.

Chris Bonington,
writing of the 1975 South-West Face Expedition

Chomolungma, sensing our arrival at Base Camp, rolled out the red carpet. The wind clapped about our ears and a crowd of clouds raced to fill the dress circle. They started heckling, showering ice popcorn down on our frenzied crew as they struggled to put all the expedition props in place. Right of centre stage the peak of Nupste roared with laughter and an avalanche, frothing like champagne, dribbled down her enormous wrinkled chin. This was going to be one hell of a cold, miserable performance.

Norm, the Base Camp manager, screamed instructions to the cast: 'Move all those kitbags up to the sundeck before it really starts snowing!'

'Sundeck?' I yelled back into the cheering wind, 'Who, what and *where*?'

Norm tossed his head, motioning towards a small platform he and Peter Allen had levelled and fenced off with the wooden oxygen cylinder cases, right alongside the 'kitchen'. Snow swirled around a lifeless pile of equipment lying beneath a heavy plastic tarpaulin. It didn't look like a sundeck to me; more like an open-air mortuary, complete with deep-freeze facilities. Austin threw me a padlocked bag of climbing gear and I dragged the dead weight up to the 'slab'.

It was exhausting business, unloading yaks at an altitude of 5300 metres, and, after moving two kitbags a distance of 20 metres, I had well and truly had it. I ducked into the kitchen to escape the chaos, wind and driving snow.

The stone-walled hut was the legacy of Jon and Mike's expedition the previous year. The five-member climbing party and their Sherpa Base Camp staff had laboriously piled huge moraine rocks together to make a solid shelter for their cookhouse-cum-mess-tent. Norm had re-roofed it with a stained canvas tarp, lined the inside with thick black plastic and decreed it off limits to everyone bar the cooks and their kitchenhands. A narrow rock bench for sitting and piling things on ran around three sides of the tiny hut and a knee-high pile of rocks formed a crude table in the middle of the floor for all the brass stoves and their gas cylinders.

I wasn't the only one defying orders and escaping the yak-unloading task. Jon and Little Pasang had wedged themselves into a warm corner and were poring over a full-colour porn magazine brimming with blondes, breasts and bottoms. Three more editions lay in a torn manila envelope on Pasang's lap. Jon was in hysterics and poor Pasang looked like he was about to pass out. Censorship laws are so strict in Nepal even *National Geographic* bosoms fall beneath Customs' black Texta patches. This was probably Pasang's first unedited exposure to the naked Western woman, and he was deliriously impressed. Conscious of his country's stand on the issue though, he had blackened the nipples of a pull-out poster model, before taping her to the wall just above his head.

I joked with Jon and warmed my frozen hands in front of a burner heating up a big pot of sweet Sherpa tea. By the time I'd thawed out, the last of the yak herders had fled down-valley with their beasts, leaving their burdens at the mercy of thick, falling snow. Norm and his helpers had turned their energetic attentions to the mess tent; it was heaving and swaying violently in the wind. When they had it anchored a little more securely they were clearly in need of a hot drink. While Pasang tracked down the cups, Jon found the fold-up chairs and tables and, with the others, we transformed the big top into a serviceable, though spartan, 'dining room'.

I took the opportunity to introduce myself properly to Norm. He and Assistant Manager Peter Allen, who I knew from the New Zealand Expedition to Chomolungma in 1985, had left Sydney a few weeks ahead of the main group in order to prepare the site for our Base Camp. They had done an amazing amount of work, moving boulders and large stones and levelling platforms with their ice-axes for the office, equipment store, pantry and mess tents. With the additional help of our two-man advance

Arriving in a gusty snow storm, expedition members batten down the hatches on the Base Camp mess tent earlier erected by Norm Crookston's Advance Party.

party, Pete 'Lambo' Lambert and Charlie Hart, they had started to clear smaller spaces on the glacier for the team's personal tentage.

The medical research team had arrived earlier too, and Carol was floating around begging blood from her now reluctant volunteers. Thick, flowing red hair framed her perfectly made-up face; she was enviably clean and her slight body, clad in aerobic tights, belied her professional intentions. She looked totally out of place—like a debutante in a football scrum—and even the biggest, roughest-cut guys on our team were falling for her; her success rate for inducing them to faint at the sight of their own blood was a staggering 80 per cent! To them, anything was better than a session with the 'vampire'; even pitching tents in a howling gale and blizzard. Everyone fled to their pre-picked platforms and battled to get their individual 'home away from home' shelters erected before nightfall.

It was so cold that night I could hardly sleep. The wind was a pro-fighter and my tent, a punching bag. An avalanche peeled off the side of Nupste or the Lho La nearly every half hour and kept me awake with its alarming roar.

Poor Chris had had to go back to Gorek Shep to help BJ, who'd apparently come down with a pretty bad bout of stomach cramps, fever and diarrhoea. At least his altruism would have been rewarded with a relatively comfortable bed in a relatively warm, windproof lodge.

Zac's thermometer had frozen at –20°C during the night and daylight had done little to shift it. If anything, the weather had worsened. We huddled together in the mess tent until breakfast flowed into morning tea. Norm laid down the laws regarding water collection, bathing, eating, calls of nature and borrowing of equipment, tempering his military-style delivery for those of us still unused to receiving commands. When the wind died down a bit we took up the task of hacking out additional tent sites in readiness for the rest of the team. They were expected to arrive at Base Camp sometime in the afternoon, weather permitting. How wise they were to have stayed that extra day at Lobuje …

By 4.00 p.m. most of them had straggled in, in varying states of weariness and health. BJ still looked pretty weak and added his name to the Base Camp casualty list. Carol was already nursing Jim Truscott for a sinus infection and fever, Wanchu and Saila had severe altitude headaches, Mohan had arrived looking like death and Norm had gone down the glacier with a flask of tea to resuscitate Jill. The rest of us had rib-cracking coughs, running noses, nausea or a combination thereof, but were not sufficiently ill to be declared 'unfit for work'. Collectively we looked ready to check into a seaside health farm for a few months, not a Base Camp at the foot of the highest mountain in the world.

Austin and I pitched Jill's tent near the sundeck. Jon and Mike were shielding themselves behind the oxygen boxes, peering over the top of them, like soldiers in a bunker, towards the enemy: the Icefall. Falling curtains of snow had kept it out of sight for the past twenty-four hours and a general preoccupation with Base Camp duties ensured it remained out of mind for that time as well. But now it was there, dominating the whole icy,

The Icefall, a labyrinth of huge ice blocks and bottomless crevasses.

white scene. Austin looked over to the two old Icefall soldiers, deep in discussion and taking turns to view their *bête noire* through the binoculars.

'How's it look then?' he asked, a little hesitantly. There was no way of knowing in advance if this, the greatest single obstacle on the Southern approach to the mountain, would be better or worse than the previous season.

'Not too bad, not too bad,' Mike retorted, reassuring himself as well as our anxious leader.

They were empty words though; the Icefall is incapable of being anything but *dangerous*.

Jon, who had already been through the notorious maze of ice twenty-eight times, made no bones about his fear for the place. 'If it was on any other mountain, there's no way I'd climb it!' he said as he roughly scanned his '87 expedition route up to the lip of the Western Cwm. 'It's a *bad* place …' he mused, laughing nervously. 'Be ready to dance up there when something moves under your feet!'

The whole Icefall is in constant motion. Technically speaking, it is part of a huge glacier bed—a moving river of ice—which inches downwards through the Western Cwm and spills over the lip of the narrow valley. Like a waterfall in slow motion, it tumbles over 600 metres to the main valley floor of the Solu Khumbu. As it moves over the lip, the frozen river splits and cracks, forming huge ice-blocks the size of big department stores. As pressure forces them forward, they peel away from the cliff, lose their balance, fracture further and tumble. Everything in the Icefall keeps shifting, crumbling and shattering. Ice spires the size of cathedrals could topple at any moment, the deep chasms between the icy-city buildings could widen or close without warning and snow bridges could collapse. For climbers in the wrong place at the wrong time any of these movements could be fatal. The Icefall is a deathtrap which doesn't discriminate between experienced climbers and novices. Anyone entering it is at risk. It makes Russian roulette look like child's play.

The first climber to see the Icefall was good old 'Because it's there!' Mallory, in 1921. Trying to find a route into the Western Cwm from the Tibetan side, he climbed the Lo Lha pass between Lingtren and the West Shoulder of Chomolungma and looked down on the Icefall. He was suitably impressed and did not think there was a likely chance it could be climbed. The leader of the 1950 Reconnaissance Expedition in Nepal looked up at it from where we were now and confirmed Mallory's suspicions.

The following year the Brits came, saw and eventually conquered the obstacle. The leader of the expedition, Shipton, aborted the team's first attempt at pushing a route through the Icefall. He realised it would be impossible to climb the mountain without Sherpas and the thought of putting their lives at risk in the Icefall for his team's summit aspirations and glory, was a totally repugnant one. It was the personal decision of a climber to weigh the risks against his goal. But was he justified in putting his porters' lives in danger as well? Hillary thought so, and later wrote:

Shipton was far from happy about subjecting Sherpas to such a route—it hardly worked in with the deep-seated British tradition of responsibility and fair play. But in my heart I knew the only way to attempt this mountain was to modify the old standards of safety and justifiable risk, and to meet the dangers as they came; to drive through regardless.

On the 28 October 1951, he, his team mates and three Sherpas stood on the lip of the Western Cwm. They had bridged their way over and through the icy moat barring the southern gateway to the Goddess' 'castle'.

With the Icefall conquered and the spell of the unknown broken, a huge psychological barrier was removed. The moral question of placing Sherpas' lives at risk was left unanswered; the precedent had been set and the use of Sherpas for Icefall load-carrying and therefore risk-taking was very quickly taken for granted in expedition circles. Hunt, the leader of the 1953 triumph justified the situation saying, 'Our energy had to be spared as far as possible for the tasks which would fall to each of us in the assault.' Up until now, that attitude had been adopted by all large-scale expeditions and, as a result, more than thirty Sherpa porters have been killed just 'doing their job' for the rich glory-seeking sahibs.

For the first time in history our expedition planned to challenge the thirty-five-year-old philosophy. We would climb Chomolungma without the aid of Sherpas. We would carry every last little bit of equipment we needed on the mountain through the Icefall ourselves. We were breaking with tradition and gearing up to break our backs for the privilege. Far from feeling rejected and out of pocket, the Sherpas respected our

The lama from Pangboche blesses the Icefall in a traditional Buddhist ceremony.

stand; there was plenty of safer work carrying loads through the hills for trekking groups, and for the masochistic there was always the great Tri-Nation Expedition …

Despite our all-Australian intentions, we adhered to the local custom of having the expedition blessed en route, and now we were at the mountain it was imperative to stay clear of the Icefall until it, too, was subjected to ceremony. Sonam, our sirdar and veteran of no less than thirty-seven expeditions, had been emphatic about the Sherpas' superstitions linked to Chomolungma, and had made all the arrangements for a monk from Pangboche monastery to attend to the blessing. He arrived in a cloud of wind-driven snow on Monday morning, our third day at Base camp, with two yaks in tow, and a smile as wide as the Icefall itself on his face.

Everyone put in an appearance for the ceremony—sceptics included. Tony Delaney, the expedition doctor, was yet to materialise and Terry Tremble was still on his way up from Lobuje, but the rest of the team, including the sickies, gathered around the stone altar in the centre of Base Camp.

Sonam, Wanchu and the cookboys had been busy all morning, preparing things for the ritual. They had fashioned a pulpit from three wooden oxygen cases, and arranged on it all that needed to be offered by the monk to the gods; samples of everything we would drink on the expedition, and plates of rice, *zumpa* (the barley flour staple of the Sherpas) biscuits, cake, nuts and sweet muesli bars. A high-altitude ration pack was positioned in front of it for the monk to sit on, and a sack full of brand new coloured prayer-flags was opened in readiness. Three porter baskets full of fresh juniper were put up near the altar and a pole for the flags erected behind it. Chairs from the mess tent were placed in a

semi-circle behind the monk's spot, facing the altar. The upper echelon (the leaders) took these positions and the rest of us—the 'Chook Union' as we called ourselves—sat down on tarpaulins stretched out on either side in the snow. The smiling monk sat down and, holding a worn set of scriptures for reference, started chanting.

Little Pasang lit the juniper and its pungent aroma brought a nostalgic tear to my eye. This was the smell of Tibet. There was nothing superstitious about the calming effect of the monks relentless, if monotonous, chant; there was nothing questionable about the juniper or prayer-flags. This was the Tibet that had so protected me on my journey a few years ago. Mike and Jon took it all as seriously as I, and we exchanged nods and smiles as if sharing a secret elite understanding of things. To the uninitiated, it was, above all else, a fascinating start to an expedition. When the clouds suddenly parted and the wind dropped, letting sunshine and warmth flood the scene, even the most ardent cynics attributed the change to the monk and saw it as being both fascinating *and* auspicious. With enthusiasm, they listened to the incantation and followed the monk's instructions to a tee.

Big Pasang came out of the kitchen with a tray of cups and, screaming like a chai (tea) woman at a New Delhi railway station, offered tea to everyone. The monk kept on chanting and took up the jug of chang, dipped a twig of juniper in it and sprayed it towards the altar. He repeated the ritual offering with the milk, orange Tang, water and finally Dewar's whisky and, after each blessing, we were asked to take a hefty swig of the fluids. Drinking chang then milk then orange juice, more chang, tea and whisky willingly, in that order, was proof of the team's new respect for Buddhism.

A huge avalanche crashed down the side of Nupste just as Sonam was about to pass around the blessed plate of rice. All heads turned at once to watch the debris rolling towards the glacier. The monk was peering at it through his sixties-style sunglasses and, needless to say, he hadn't missed a beat of his chant. I wondered if he used circular-breathing, like a didgeridoo player, to keep up the unbroken meter. Preoccupied with the avalanche, Austin misunderstood Sonam's conveyance to toss a few grains of the uncooked rice towards the altar: he ate them instead.

Everyone's spirits were well and truly uplifted, as much through the chang as the clear skies and good vibes. There is nothing sombre about such ceremonies, unlike its counter religions, Buddhism lets you laugh and party during a sermon. The guys liked that, and a happy feeling lingered long after the monk had finished the proceedings. The big black choughs and pale pink rose finches who had earlier appeared to help the gods eat their offerings, hung around for a while as well, hopping around the smouldering juniper, hunting out the smallest crumbs. This was the first time we'd seen birds at Base Camp, and again the monk was believed to be responsible. An unusually marked chough with a pink piece of cloth tied around its neck was said to belong to the holy man.

The bright prayer-flags had gone up without too much trouble and the cookboys had tied additional *katas* to the lines. The white, yellow, red, green and blue flags printed with various Buddhist mantras reflected the Buddhist states of mind: form, feeling, recognition, karmic formation and consciousness. At a higher level, the colours stood for the five Buddhist wisdoms: the abilities to reflect what the mind sees, to compare, to differentiate, to accomplish and, finally, the perception of truth—Buddha-hood. At a purely practical level, however, they flapped in the wind and were supposed to send the printed prayers flying up to the heavens. The *katas* or white ceremonial scarves were given as a mark of respect and thanks to the gods.

During the last phase of the long religious rite, Sonam had given everyone a protection cord—five coloured strings tied together and blessed—to place around their necks and wear for the duration of the expedition. A few grains of special yellow rice were handed out, tied in a tiny piece of scarf or handkerchief and attached to the cord, to ensure safety in the path of an avalanche. Terry Tremble turned up just in time to receive one and bid farewell to the monk.

As the monk was leaving I caught up to him and thanked him in Tibetan for the ceremony. He prophecised snow would fall on 8 April, one month hence, and told me he had a good, very strong feeling about our expedition. He had a good strong feeling in his pocket from our expedition as well: a 1500-rupee ($A75) 'donation' for his monastery. He turned and beamed another of his magnificent smiles at me, looked up at his bird hovering overhead and, chanting again, continued down the valley. Big Pasang followed him; his duties on the expedition were finished now that Base Camp had been established and Wanchu and Saila were on the road to recovery.

Mohan still wasn't doing the best; he'd gone down to Gorek Shep the day before and Terry had arrived with a pretty bad report on his condition. After lunch Chris and Bruce left camp to go to his aid and, if necessary, take him down to Periche. I lay on the sundeck watching thin wispy clouds twist, turn and tumble themselves across the glorious blue sky.

It was like being part of some weird time-lapse film. The clouds tore up from the valley and threw themselves into the Western Cwm one after the other, as if travelling on an invisible conveyor belt. Late afternoon brought even more sensational effects to the aerial stage. Flames of sunset licked the sides of Pumo Ri and huge pink clouds of smoke rose from her summit and blew into the Cwm's cauldron. The sun had set quickly and only the top of the Lhotse Face was haloed in light. With the rays went all warmth, so I hastily retreated to the mess tent for another of Jill's superb dinners.

After dessert Austin broke the news everyone had been hanging out to hear. The team leaders, Pat Cullinan, Zac Zaharias, Mike Rheinberger and Lambo Lambert, had picked their players. Mike headed 'Dad's Army': Jon Muir, Jim Truscott, Phil Pitham and James Strohfeldt; 'Zac's Yaks' included Bruce Farmer, Terry McCullagh and Jim Van Gelder; 'Lambert's Layabouts' were Chris Curry, Andrew Smith, and BJ Agnew; and the others, Paul Bayne, Terry Tremble, Mick Pezet and Min Moor found themselves in the 'Pat's Rats' (initially 'Cullinan's Commandos') team. There were a few unhappy faces: Terry McCullagh fumed for a good twenty-four hours before accepting his fate. But, by and large, people were pleased with the selections. I was amazed the guys hadn't shown more maturity and settled their differences before the expedition left Sydney: the personality clashes within

the military side of the team were deep-seated, and even to my inexperienced mind, they seemed a dangerous element to have lurking up there on the hill. The happy, carefree days of the walk-in were clearly over. It was time for the serious business of planning, politicking, more planning and, of course, climbing. There's nothing more effective than a big expedition to bring out the Jekyll and Hyde in everyone—it would be naive to anticipate differently. Climbing puts people out on a limb; physically, emotionally and psychologically it stretches them to the limit. Chomolungma, the highest mountain in the world, pulls a little further still.

Over the next day and a half, we managed to avoid what we all detested the most: our mutual enemy, the Icefall. Pat demonstrated how to use the oxygen cylinders and regulators and Jon and I filmed and sent out our first ABC news broadcast. Lessons were given in how to assemble the Icefall ladders, how to use the Philips high-frequency radio sets, how to rescue someone from a crevasse the Paul Bayne way and how to outshine your opponents in Bicentennial Trivial Pursuit. A whole afternoon was spent playing 'hunt the avalanche transceiver'. Heaven help anyone relying on me to find and dig them out …

Eventually we exhausted the list, and Dad's Army prepared for a late afternoon foray into the Icefall. Given Mike and Jon's experience, their team was the obvious choice for the task of finding and marking a route through the ice labyrinth. They set out with backpacks full of cane wands, confident and no doubt glad to be making a start on the hill.

I ambled over to the Icefall, dragging my tripod and fat 300 millimetre lens behind me. It was impossible to keep up with the guys; they were already powering through the lower reaches of the enemy's fortress when I arrived exhausted at the foot of it. It took me half an hour to walk—ah, let's be honest … stumble—from Base Camp to the rock obelisk we'd nick-named Nelson's Column at the bottom of the Icefall. After catching my breath, I settled down on a boulder and focused on the scene before me.

The view from Base Camp revealed nothing of the awesome scale of the Icefall. From directly below, the frozen river was so imposing and steep, so wide and fragmented, it just never seemed to end. Dad's Army were mere specks—fly dirt on a white-washed skyscraper. They disappeared into the shelled ice-city, Lingtren rumbled and another rock avalanche pelted down her side.

Again I was gripped with fear; the Icefall was a killer and I had agreed to be a potential victim. I was out of my mind. All this for a few photographs … I loved challenge; loved to venture to wild places which existed beyond and without humans' control—to places which permitted me on nature's terms only. I loved to be reminded of my total insignificance in the *real* world; that which lies a light year and a day from the artificial, material one I grew up in. But this time … well, maybe I'd gone too far. To accept the conditions laid down by the Icefall was suicidal.

Sunset-pink clouds rise like smoke from the summit of Pumo Ri.

Aussie climbers and Tri-Nation Expedition Sherpas ferrying equipment and supplies through the Icefall. (Andrew Smith)

I tried to rationalise the danger, quickly adopting the 'Well, it won't happen to me' defence. I was only going to go through the Icefall twice; once up and once down; so my chances of getting creamed up there were surely less than those of my load-carrying team mates. But history served me a rude reminder. The only Australian ever killed in the Icefall was Tony Tighe, a novice like myself, on Chris Bonington's 1972 South-West Face Expedition. He had been trekking around Nepal and had joined Bonington's party as a volunteer Base Camp helper. During the course of the climb, he decided he wanted to see the South-West Face for himself, and on the very last day of the expedition, he received permission to help the Sherpas clear Advance Base Camp in the Western Cwm. But he never made it that far. He was crushed beneath an ice serac collapse in the Icefall, and they never recovered his body. That wasn't an easy piece of fate to swallow at all. The realities of this place were best stored at the back of one's mind.

But oh, the sheer beauty of the place! No one had ever mentioned it in books, articles or interviews. It was one of the most hauntingly beautiful landscapes I'd ever seen. Once inside it, once moving among its white sculptured forms, I completely forgot about its dangers and casualties. I couldn't get enough of it; the Icefall was a sorcerer, and I was spellbound by its magic. The guys kept warning me about the dangers higher up: 'Ha! Wait till you see the hideous hanging seracs and the terrible tottering towers! You won't think so much of the place then!' James assured me. I couldn't wait; and when I saw them, I just loved the Icefall even more. Perpetuating a long mountaineering and rock-climbing tradition, the most outstanding features in the Icefall had been given gruesome names; by the sound of things it was going to get pretty spectacular higher up!

On a clear windless day it was the most breathtaking, unearthly place on the globe. The silence, the power, the joy of discovering you can actually feel comfortable and efficient in a pair of cumbersome plastic-spiked boots; it was all fantastic. There wasn't time or reason to contemplate the dangers; my feet were on the shaky Icefall blocks, but my head was way up high in the clouds, out of harm's way.

After their afternoon of trail-blazing Dad's Army ventured back to Base Camp. James Strohfeldt later wrote of his experience in the Icefall:

To our team, Dad's Army, fell the task of picking a route through the Icefall, up 600 metres to Camp One. It was a thrilling few days as we bobbed and weaved our way over slots, under seracs and between huge boulders of ice. I recall the day Mike and I pushed the route through a particularly notorious section called the Traverse. There are two salient memories: one of the excitement and one of coming to terms with the danger.

We reached our high point, masked by a sheaf of bamboo wands, before the sun had hit the blue and grey ice. It was cold. We had scouted a plausible option by binoculars from Base Camp, so we headed off in that direction. We were like ants trying to cross a page of a horror story written in Braille. Up a 2-metre block, step onto another, down the other side, step onto a 2-metre boulder, it topples and the whole kaboodle

settles, gulp, step over a 15-metre crevasse onto another boulder. It was absorbing, exhilarating work, but we soon reached an obstacle bigger than both of us. A huge blue-black crevasse 20 metres wide, with faded ropes stretched taut across its expanse, a legacy of a previous expedition's route. No future there, so we traversed back to our starting point and crept off in a new direction.

Everything was horribly loose. Intermittently a downward glance would reveal that the iceblock I was on had no foundation, but just rested on other equally dubious pieces of ice. I just hoped the energy here stayed potential. Hauling and offsetting on our ice-tools, we in time passed through a tunnel of blue water ice, rounded a room-sized block and emerged onto the start of flatter ground. That was the first of some thirty crossings of the traverse for us.

I remember also how easy the danger was to come to terms with—at least at one level. The Icefall had to be passed in order to climb the mountain, so we simply had to do it as often as necessary. Make it as safe as possible, pause, then run under a serac; clip onto the fixed rope to jump a crevasse; knock the snow off one's crampons to balance across an aluminium bridge; leave the rest to fate! The Icefall never got boring. It flowed and fluxed, sometimes whole sections buckling and heaving overnight, tearing aluminium ladders to pieces and stretching ropes whip tight. Sometimes it was knee deep in new snow, in others blunt crampons would skid and screech on the hard ice. It was never safe; but it was always one hell of a place to be.

The guys were doing well preparing the route. Following in Dad's Army's exploratory footsteps were Pat's Rats, Zac's Yaks and Lambert's Layabouts, carrying ladders, building bridges and fixing several kilometres of rope to make the thoroughfare less debilitating. The 4 a.m. starts carrying 15–20-kilogram packs full of hardware were nobody's idea of fun, but it had to be done. Austin and his Inner Sanctum (the team leaders) wanted the route through to Camp One established before the Tri-Nation Expedition arrived, presumably at the end of the month. A temporary camp (called Camp 0.9) was placed near the foot of the last obstacle in the Icefall—the 15-metre high headwalls on the lip of the Cwm—and several days later, on 21 March, Lambo and his Layabouts located the permanent Camp One.

Discontentment was starting to breed among the members of the Chook Union (the rank and file). Some felt the team's progress was far too slow; others needed more rest days to recuperate from the draining labour and load-carrying. The packed lunches weren't big enough and there weren't any sweets and chocolates to pacify the weary workers when they returned to Base Camp after a hard day in the Icefall. When the expedition's first official Supporters' Trek arrived in the afternoon of the twenty-first, I welcomed the opportunity to escape from the tensions and politicking and headed off with Peter, Bruce and the new crowd to climb Island Peak. Bruce's wife, Rosemary, was in the trekking party, so at least one man was happy with his lot.

Paul Bayne takes a flying leap across a crevasse in the Icefall.

6
The Ambassador Comes to Tea

Chapter Six

The Ambassador Comes to Tea

Both man and mountain have emerged from the same Earth, and therefore have something in common between them.

Sir Francis Younghusband,
in *The Epic of Mount Everest*

Di Johnstone, Australian Ambassador to Nepal.

Bruce and Peter flew down the glacier and I ambled behind the main body of trekkers. It was difficult to orientate myself in the sea of frozen ice-fins between Base Camp and Gorek Shep. Everything looked different back-to-front and the track was less obvious than it had been on entering Base Camp several weeks earlier. Actually, there isn't a track, in the real sense of the word. The glacial moraine stones underfoot on the said route are no different in colour and texture from the glacial moraine stones surrounding it. What makes this track a track, is simply the fresh yak dung, deposited like milestone markers along the glacier. Random piles of stones acted as cairns, but because we were now walking down valley and not up, they blended in imperceptibly with the moraine.

The ice-fins were daunting sculptures erupting from the moraine—huge blocks as high as 15 metres, thrust upwards by pressures within the glacier itself. They formed a spectacular landscape of frozen waves, with each crest textured by sun, wind and time. Because of the dismal weather that had accompanied our arrival at Base Camp I hadn't taken many photographs of the glacier. I was determined to use this second trip and opportune sunshine to knock off a few rolls of film, even if it meant missing lunch. Nupste and Pumo Ri made perfect backdrops and my shutter finger was determined to 'hang in there' as long as the clear skies did. I didn't catch up to the others until Lobuje.

Bruce and Rosemary had secured themselves a tent-site somewhere in the jumbled canvas and Gore-Tex city that had sprouted on the dusty space in front of the Above the Clouds lodge. I lobbed inside the cosy kitchen of the small dormitory-style guesthouse and found Peter, enjoying a cup of hot lemon with the *didi* who ran the joint. (*Didi* literally means 'older sister', but is popularly used for any female who's Christian name you either don't know or can't remember.) He had secured us the two spare benches in the storeroom separating the kitchen-cum-family-living room from the main dormitory.

I poked my nose into the dorm to see who was aboard the double-decker sleeping platform. It was almost entirely populated by Japanese and Sherpas, all wearing brand new down jackets emblazoned with the familiar Tri-Nation Expedition emblem. They'd finally arrived! I leaped over to introduce myself to a handsome young-looking Japanese chap, studiously making notes on a small pad. It just so happened to be the climbing leader, Gota Isono.

We talked small talk for a while, about where Gota lived and my own impressions of, and experience, in his motherland. I was a bit rusty on the lingo, and when I faltered, Gota corrected me or reanswered my questions in English.

When Gota started asking questions about the progress of our expedition, I grabbed Peter and Bruce and introduced them to the leader. Several more introductions followed between our token Australian delegation and the Japanese and Nepalese climbing contingent. Bruce realised he had met Gota in 1981 at a function hosted by the Japanese Alpine Club. Bruce and his expedition team mates had a stopover in Japan en route to China (where they planned to climb Molamenqing) and were accorded the generous hospitality of the Tokyo-based mountaineering club.

Narayan Shresta, one of the Nepalese climbers, was also familiar to not only Bruce, but all three of us. I'd never personally met him until now, but had read about him in Lincoln Hall's book, *White Limbo*. He had climbed with Tim Macartney-Snape and the gang on the Australian Chomolungma Expedition in 1984. He shook my hand and cheekily drawled in his best Australian accent, 'How ya goin', honey?' 'Beautiful mountains, eh?' he added, stressing his mastery over our national nasal twang. He had taught the Japanese climbers how to say 'today' the great Aussie way. The photographer from the expedition was sitting on the lower deck of the sleeping platforms playing cards, and on hearing Narayan, began reciting: 'To-die, good-die, Mon-die, Tues-die …' Two of his poker-faced opponents cracked up, and animatedly went on to explain the significance of the pun 'to-die' to those who had not grasped it.

Gota took notes while Peter and Bruce filled him in on the condition of the Icefall and our route through it. Other than that, the meeting was totally informal and relaxed. The 'First Encounter of the Tri-Nation Kind' had gone smoothly, and now the ice had been broken, it would be a lot easier for both the expeditions to sail towards each other without fear of a disastrous collision. Bruce left the dorm after an hour to write a letter to Austin about the meeting, and organised a runner to deliver it to him the following day. Since the Tri-Nation team intended spending another night at Lobuje and one at Gorek Shep, the letter would arrive well in advance of them. Just in case that plan fouled up, I gave Gota a huge bag full of ice-breaking sweets I'd purchased on behalf of the ABEE, and asked him to hand-deliver them to Austin.

After dinner, the trekkers retired and Peter wandered into the middle room to read. I took up an invitation to play cards with the Japanese climbers, who were gambling thousands of rupees on a game of chance. I started off with 50 'borrowed' rupees, played by torchlight for a marathon two hours, and walked away with over 300 rupees. My financier was also happy with his share— a 250 rupee profit. I wasn't a bad investment after all. I hoped to God the other card-sharps weren't too disgruntled by my small winnings; it would be a shame to learn I'd unwittingly undone

Ice peaks between Base Camp and Gorek Shep form an unusual and imposing gallery of sculptures on the glacial moraine.

what appeared to be the first happy knot tied between our two expeditions.

In the early hours of the morning, an incredible wind picked up. The fairly solid buildings of Lobuje seemed poised to blow way. Dust and snow swirled violently up from the ground and the wind blasted the fixed wooden shutters on the dormitory windows from their hinges. The gale was howling in from Tibet, screaming over the Lo Lha and straight down the Khumbu glacier. We were experiencing the tail-end of its force.

At about 7.30 a.m. Gota radioed the Japanese Base Camp and I listened in to the crackled high-frequency damage report. Every tent their advance party of Sherpa attendants had erected had blown down. The Tri-Nation camp had been flattened— literally. Our own tents suffered a similar fate, and any that hadn't simply exploded or blown away were intentionally de-poled to prevent them from doing so.

Later on we received a fuller analysis of the wreckage. Base Camp had unfortunately received the full brunt of the cyclonic wind. Andrew Smith recorded the disaster in his diary:

I made my way into the wind to Phil, who had just collapsed his tent. We both turned just in time to see Zac's tent ripped from the ground and flung across the main camping area. It disappeared over the ridge. I ran after it, and passing Min's tent, heard some muffled yells. A pole from one of the large Japanese tents had speared into his, ripped the fabric, broken

Fluted ice-walls flanking Amphu Lapcha, near the support trekkers' Island Peak Base Camp.

one of his poles and almost gouged his eye out. Over the ridge I found two half-empty kitbags, Zac's tent impaled on a rock and gear strewn all over the snow, including a vast number of film canisters and Zac's camera, which I grabbed just as it was about to disappear down a slot [crevasse]. I found my Bonington book—it was ripped in two. Lambo's tent was damaged, Norm's was literally torn apart and Mike Rheinberger's was inverted—with him in it. He looked like a bemused, upturned tortoise. We deliberately collapsed the few tents left standing, to prevent further damage.

The only casualty from the frenzied wind storm was poor Phil. Somehow he managed to get so dangerously cold he lost all feeling in his feet and hands. He went into the cookhouse to thaw out, but a rock fell out of the wall and hit him on the back of the neck. It took Chris Curry (who had slept right through the whole blustery blight) and James Strohfeldt a couple of hours to warm Phil's appendages back into action.

While our team mates spent the day mopping up after the disaster, Bruce, Peter and I happily continued along with the trekking group towards Island Peak. One of Peter's good friends from Melbourne, Kieran Sell, was in the supporters' party, and planned to stay with us at Base Camp for a few weeks after the trek. Peter was leaving the expedition on 11 April because of work and family commitments, and had mapped out an interesting

'après-Everest' hiking course through some of the less frequently visited regions of the Khumbu. Charlie Hart had enthusiastically accepted Peter's offer to join him and Kieran on the walk, since he, too, had to return to Oz early for 'business as usual'.

The trekking group were well strung out along the trail to Island Peak. Peter and Kieran were usually out in front, Bruce and Rosemary somewhere in the middle together, and I tagged along at the end with whoever had the best selection of Mars Bars and sweets.

We reached the base of the 6189-metre 'Island' on 25 March. The Peak was nestled in the middle of a natural amphitheatre created by the great south face of Lhotse, Amphu Lapcha, and the east face of Ama Dablan. Its beauty palled considerably against the spectacular backdrop of immense fluted ice-walls flanking Amphu Lapcha. Our mountain was a rough, peeling scab on the otherwise perfect face of the earth. The scant winter snowfalls appeared to have missed Island Peak altogether; the only white patch glaring from the side of the mountain was a small but impressive icefall.

We made camp directly below the Island, facing a huge ridge of moraine which blocked our immediate view of the Imja Glacier and lake in front of Amphu Lapcha. A few of the trekkers were having trouble with the altitude so they stayed down-valley at Periche. Of those remaining, at least half were getting quite worked up about the climb. Island Peak was, in a sense, their own personal 'Everest', so I shouldn't have been surprised to see the competitive ego-tripping side of their natures surfacing. While they fussed around sorting equipment and clothing into 'leave at

Dawn over our Island Peak Base Camp.

Base Camp' and 'up the mountain' piles, Bruce, Peter, Kieran and the trek's group leader Steve McDowell checked over the ropes and harnesses and made sure the points on everyone's crampons were filed sharp.

I slept alone in one of the tiny Macpac tents semi-designed by Mike Rheinberger for use at the highest camps on Chomolungma. How he envisaged fitting two great burly men into it was beyond me. I couldn't even roll over in it. I tried to visualise BJ and Lambo wedged inside it, sheltering from a storm above the South Col, attempting to cook breakfast for themselves ... Oh to have a remote control camera around the neck of the proverbial fly on the wall!

In the morning I managed to wriggle my arms out of their mummified position and unzip the arched doorway of the tunnel-like tent. I rubbed the sleep out of my eyes and peered into a magnificent Saturday morning sky. Pink and yellow hues danced above the horizon. As the sun rose, the clouds were like an oily bubble, reflecting light in swirling, bizarre colours across the sky. It was beautiful. More beautiful than any dawn I could remember. The colours lasted for over half an hour then slowly dissolved beneath the harsh, brighter rays of the day. Peter interpreted the spectacular display: for all its beauty, it indicated bad weather. A storm would probably pass through the next day.

And it did. The close to perfect conditions for our climb up the loose rubble and rock slopes to the designated High Camp location deteriorated overnight. By the time we reached 6000 metres the weather had clagged out completely. Peter, Bruce and Steve still believed they could go for it, so they battled on against the wind with some of the more intrepid trekkers. I was about 100 metres below, preparing to help two numb-toed and disillusioned ABEE supporters back to the ridge-top camp at 5700 metres, when the leaders roped their charges together and led them onto the mountain-top glacier. I watched them disappear into heavy fog, then moved quickly back to camp. I glanced at another bank of cloud racing towards the peak and only just managed to make it into our cookboy's flimsy canvas tent before it started snowing.

The half-dozen 'would-be-if-they-could-be mountaineers' who had retreated from the summit bid, crowded into the warm cookhouse. Apart from one young supporter, Rodger Henning-Smith, who had the admirable ability to find joy in anything he tried, irrespective of 'failure', the trekkers were angry and upset. They felt that Steve was responsible for making them abort their one and only chance to top out; their one and only chance to prove they were real men. Whingeing like spoilt children, they complained they hadn't been given the right advice about footwear, and Steve had ordered them off the mountain because he thought their boots, given the terrible conditions of the day, were inadequate. 'It's Steve's fault! Wait 'til I get back to Sydney! I could have made it if it wasn't for him!' one of the more vocal, vindictive members screamed.

It's too bad people can't accept nature; can't accept they must play the game on her terms. Some of the trekkers were too busy complaining and trying to pacify their egos, to realise their efforts were an incredible achievement in themselves. Not one of them had ever climbed anywhere near as high as 6000 metres before. They were too preoccupied with 'failure' to recognise success, or, for that matter, remember the glorious vistas over the Imja Khola Valley from High Camp. No one reflected on the purity of the air, the silence of the early morning nor the awesome, exhilarating beauty of the surrounding environment. All they did was sit and whinge.

When Peter and the rest of the troop returned an hour later, the weather was abysmal. They had abandoned their attempt less than 100 vertical metres from the summit because of fog and cold. They couldn't see more than a metre in front of themselves so wisely they turned around, de-cramponed their boots and raced back down the rocky slope. The porters had taken the tents and packs all the way down to the base of Island Peak, so there was little point in remaining on the 5700-metre ridge.

Mark Nordern and Robbie Parker, two of the non-complainers who had roped up and crossed the glacier, joined Rodger and I in a joke-cracking session as we skidded and slipped our way off the mountain. It was so cold that most of the men had icicles hanging in their beards and moustaches. My glasses kept fogging up, and since it was a pain in the arse to stop every five minutes to de-glove, de-hood, de-balaclava and finally de-Bollé myself

and clean them, I left them misted and trusted the others to be my temporary seeing-eye dogs.

We stopped at the bottom of the mountain and re-organised our packs for the porters. Steve had decided to press on down the valley to Chukhung or Dingboche. It was warmer moving around, so everyone agreed. We grouped up again and continued battling our way through the wind and driving snow.

Rodger, Robbie Parker and I paused at the area which until recently had served as Island Peak's official Base Camp. One night in October 1987 an avalanche rolled off the mountain and blanketed the site, crushing four unsuspecting trekkers, asleep in their tents. I watched the wind spiralling snow around the exposed, tatty ruins of their ill-fated camp. The bodies had been buried beneath a memorial, which acknowledged the deaths of its builder's wife, friend and two Tamang guides. What remained of the wreckage had been left to the ravages of wind and weather. A single size 8 sandshoe and a thong lay forgotten near the last few threads of an orange tent. The yellowed pages of a thick science fiction book had frozen together and become one with the crusty, dried mud. The whole scene filled me with a sense of hopelessness and despair. We hadn't reached the top of the mountain, but at least we were walking away with our lives.

Chukhung wasn't exactly the most picturesque place on earth when cloud and snow obscured its surrounds from view. The four-house summer settlement was abandoned, save for one lodge, and since the snow had turned its bare courtyard into a quagmire, we opted to walk right through to Dingboche.

It stopped snowing and the clouds actually parted when we neared the end of the Imja Khola Valley, and the sight of Ang's (the trekking group's sirdar) parent's house was a welcome one indeed. The porters had beaten us into camp and the cookboys were busy pitching our dome tents. I dumped my camera and pack into mine, then wandered over to the thin canvas mess tent to play cards with a few of the trekkers. I looked back up the valley towards Island Peak. Blue sky crowned the summit. Too bad we hadn't stayed an extra day ... *C'est la vie*, as Jon Muir would say.

One of the older Sherpas—a porter who had lost all his fingers from frostbite—came into the mess and tapped his leathery deformed stumps on my shoulder and beckoned me to follow him. We moved back onto the trail, then up onto the gentle slope above it. The old man pointed to a field just a few hundred metres down valley, near the bottom of the ridge separating Dingboche from Periche. Tents identical to ours dotted a farmer's empty potato patch. '*Dui trek; Dui trek,*' the disfigured man said. *Dui* means 'two' in Nepalese. The Number Two Supporters' Trek was also in Dingboche, obviously en route to Base Camp.

I raced back to tell Peter, and together we ventured down to greet the group. John Peryman, the illustrious expedition chairperson and chief fund-raiser was in the rank of supporters, and hopefully he was bearing a case of whisky, donated to the expedition by one of our many sponsors. More importantly, we anticipated that our ambassador, Di Johnstone, had been able to find time off from her hectic schedule to join this second

Despondent trekkers returning to Chukhung from an unsuccessful attempt to climb Island Peak.

'official' Supporters' Trek to Base Camp. For the first time in weeks Peter and I felt conscious of our appearance. 'We've got to look our best for the ambassador—we don't want her thinking we're a couple of ratbags,' Peter said. 'Not yet, anyway,' I joked. 'Not until Peryman's handed over the whisky and we've finished all the champagne!' We checked each other over and rubbed away at the really grimy spots on our faces with spit.

Nick Deacock, who was leading the Number Two Team of supporters, welcomed us into his group's mess tent, and introduced us to the few people in the tent. Peryman came in and showered me with his usual array of compliments, calling me 'pox-face' and 'toots' in front of everyone. I felt like kneeing him in the groin for talking to me as if I was some Kings Cross floozy. But I smiled politely and pretended his insults were just water off a duck's back. He did, after all, have the whisky … and Peter dived right in and asked him for it, right on cue.

Peryman looked amazed and stunned. Hadn't we received the second case? Peter and I looked at each other and groaned. We hadn't even 'received' the first. Somewhere in the endless network of systems which had been devised to ensure all our food, equipment and personal belongings made it to Nepal and ultimately Base Camp, a case of Dewar's whisky had gone missing. Not a single Arnott's cookie nor John West sardine had been misplaced; just a whole damn crate of soul-fuel. The sponsors had very kindly replaced it with a second supply, which everyone at Base Camp assumed would arrive with the Number Two Supporters' Trek. Peter and I were not amused. The boys at Base Camp would be livid.

Nick kindly offered to donate his own bottle of whisky to the expedition. Di Johnstone entered the tent, much to Peryman's relief, and after a very friendly reunion, cheered us a little by telling us her personal porter had two bottles of champagne in his load.

Di looked radiant; the walk-in certainly hadn't done her any harm. She was anxious to hear news of our progress on the mighty Goddess, and listened with genuine interest as Peter offered our latest, but now outdated, report. We presumed the boys would have finished the route through to Camp One and established a good stock of food and equipment there. If things had gone smoothly, they would probably be consolidating the route from Camp One, through the Western Cwm, to the bottom of the Lhotse Face, in readiness for load-carrying to Camp Two.

Di's livewire sister, Sandi, joined us in the tent, followed by a laughing pair named Deirdre and Sue. They looked like they'd stepped out of a fashion magazine, not the middle of a steep Nepalese valley. There was something rather incongruous about lipstick, nail varnish and eyeshadow in the hills, but these self-effacing humourists were otherwise perfectly attuned to the environment. It was great to be in the company of so many women for a change! It was greater still to be in a group who didn't even know how to whinge—about anything! They liked the food, they liked their leader, and they were not encumbered with climbing aspirations. They had come to the mountains to give moral and financial support to our 'lads on the hill', and were having a damn good time doing it too!

The next morning we bade farewell to the ABEE Number One Supporters' Trek, and welcomed the opportunity to accompany

Vista from the ridge above Dingboche.

the new crowd into Base Camp. Even Bruce, who had had to part from his wife, couldn't help but revel in their joyous sense of fun and mayhem. All the way from Dingboche to the evening's hitching post at Lobuje, the Number Two Team horsed around. Snowball fights and friendly slinging matches whiled away the hours, and although the ever-increasing altitude slowed the pace of the walking the next day, it did little to stifle the jokes. It was a mean haul up to Gorek Shep, but the Number Two Team handled it in style.

On route to Gorek Shep, we ran into Charlie Hart, Mohan and Mahander (the second liaison officer who had arrived at Base Camp during our absence). Mohan was fighting fit, having recovered well from his bout of Acute Mountain Sickness (AMS), but Mahander looked weak and pale. Charlie looked uncharacteristically annoyed, so Bruce and I sat down on a rock with him and Mohan to find out what was up, and catch up on all the latest gossip.

Mohan explained that Mahander was suffering from the dreaded AMS, but Charlie confided that his apparent health problems were far more serious than that. Two days previously, Mahander had taken a bit of a weird turn; something in the order of a Grand Mal seizure. The various doctors believed he had had an epileptic fit, but Mahander pleaded innocence. Going along with the AMS line, he had agreed to go down to Thyangboche, but Charlie and Mohan had been given orders to accompany Mahander to Lukla and see he boarded the first available plane back to Kathmandu. They carried a letter explaining what had happened at Base Camp for Mahander's superiors, and suggested the sickly, skinny LO (liaison officer) undergo a full medical check-up. Since everyone else was in full swing on the mountain, Charlie had reluctantly agreed to help Mohan coax Mahander down to Lukla.

Mahander's employers, the Ministry of Communication, would undoubtedly send a replacement LO, even though there was scarcely need for one. Mohan alone had little to do, since according to Charlie, everything at Base Camp was running very smoothly indeed. The ABEE were getting on famously with the Tri-Nation Expedition and the matter of the $A20 000 hadn't even been mentioned. Austin's innumerable sleepless nights, his worrying and scheming and his 'strategy' discussions with Sonam, had all proved a waste of time. The initial 'formal' meeting between Austin, Gota Isono and Mr Asawa (the overall Tri-Nation Expedition leader) had taken place yesterday morning, 28 March, and mutually satisfying arrangements regarding the maintenance of the Icefall route, and co-operation higher up the mountain, had been reached without a single drama.

While Base Camp enjoyed a peaceful 'intermission' of congenial discussion, plenty of live action-packed theatre (a touch vaudevillean!) was happening on the hill. Mohan started to relate

The two official Supporters' Trek teams meet up in Dingboche.

a spooky Icefall story starring Mr Icefall himself, Jon Muir. Apparently Jon was descending the route at his usual Olympian pace and hadn't bothered to clip his harness karabiner to the fixed rope. The rope ran the full length of the Icefall and was anchored every 50 metres or so by means of aluminium sections called snow-stakes, which were hammered well into the hard ice. The rope marked the location of the route, but was primarily for safety: if you were clipped to the rope and fell, presumably you wouldn't fall more than 50 metres. If you were not clipped to the rope … well … it usually meant 'Goodbye Charlie'.

Mohan explained that Jon had casually stepped onto a huge block of ice bridging a bottomless crevasse. 'The whole thing went whoosh! It collapsed beneath his feet and fell into the crevasse!' Mohan detailed, heightening the drama with very graphic hand movements. Our animated LO paused then, to catch his breath and clear his throat, unintentionally leaving us on tenterhooks. My head filled with visions of Jon, dressed as Alice in Wonderland, hurling down an endless, icy tunnel. There were no white rabbits or Cheshire cats—only blood and broken

bones. Mohan saw the panic in my eyes and quickly went on with the story to put an end to my gruesome assumptions. 'He is OK Miss Sorrel, OK. The rope was twisted around his arm.' Jon only fell about 10 metres, then managed to curl his fingers around the rope and grip tightly, to stop the line simply slipping through his hand. Talk about lucky. He managed to climb out of the crevasse by spreading his legs apart, with one foot on either wall of the icy bottomless gorge. He kicked his crampon points into the hard ice, one foot at a time, balancing his upper torso by pulling on the rope with one hand and anchoring his ice-axe into the wall with the other. He eventually hauled himself over the lip of the crevasse and wandered, as white and spooked as a ghost, back to Base Camp.

Charlie took up the tale, adding that despite the fall, Jon was back to his normal irreverent, laughing self, and the expedition was gradually progressing onward and upward without too many major hiccups. Just before setting out from Base Camp with the two liaison officers, Charlie had heard a report over the radio that stated Pat's team had finished consolidating the route to Camp One, and Chris Curry and BJ had finished exploring the Western Cwm. They had at last found a relatively safe, but very long route through to a suitable Camp Two site.

In relation to other large-scale expeditions, our 'progress' seemed painfully slow. But then, without Sherpas to carry loads and anchor ropes, what else could one expect? The Tri-Nation team were yet to make their first full journey through the Icefall to establish their own first camp, so we were still way out in front. Austin envisaged having the route fixed all the way to Camp Three on the Lhotse Face, before the Tri-Nationers caught up (and no doubt overtook) our expedition.

Mohan and Charlie stood up to leave. It was getting late in the day and they weren't supposed to let Mahander out of sight. Bruce and I said our goodbyes and carried on through to Gorek Shep.

Peter was anxious to get back to Base Camp, so when we arrived at the two-house outpost, Bruce teamed up with him, and together they sprinted on up the Khumbu Glacier. I tossed my pack against a rock and slumped down on the picnic cloth, laid for the trekkers afternoon tea.

Nick Deacock made me a cup of coffee, and started talking about a drunk Sherpa we had passed on the track about 100 metres before Gorek Shep. 'That was Sundare—the man who has climbed Everest four times. He's an alcoholic,' Nick said, very matter-of-factly. I had heard our expedition climbers talking about him before, but I never assumed his drinking problem was as bad as it now appeared. He was virtually unconscious on the track, barely able to loll his head from side to side. Sundare was pencilled in to make two climbs this season—one on Pumo Ri with an Indonesian team and the other on Chomolungma, with the Tri-Nation Expedition. Both trips were now under way, but poor Sundare had a lot of sobering up to do before he could join either climb.

I finished my coffee then set out to watch the sunset from Kala Pattar, a 5530-metre ridge behind Gorek Shep that was famous for its great views of the surrounding mountains. I was stunned to see the whole summit pyramid of Chomolungma completely devoid of snow. The whole enormous south face was nothing but bare, black rock, which shone like ebony in the fading daylight. The layers of sedimentary rock caught the colour of the last few rays of the sun and turned the Mother Goddess's crown a glittering gold. It was so stunning, I was left speechless. I had been in the right place at the right time *again,* and I just couldn't believe my luck!

That night I slept with all the Sherpas and Sherpanis attending to the Number Two Team, on a sleeping platform inside the largest of the two rock cabins. Strips of meat hung above the hearth at the opposite end of the room, drying in the smoke of a few smouldering embers. As Buddhists, Sherpas generally refrain from killing or hunting any living thing, but have nothing against eating meat provided someone else killed it. Sherpas wait at least a day before preparing the meat to let the soul of the animal seek reincarnation—perhaps in human form. I watched the slivers of yak meat slowly curl up at the ends and shrink, and listened to the hissing burners of the giggling Sherpanis, as they prepared tomorrow's mid-morning snack. I was a little apprehensive about returning to 'the hill', as Chomolungma was now affectionately known. In spite of everything Charlie had said, I knew tensions would be building up. High altitude made life uncomfortable and somehow encouraged personal irritations, no matter how small or petty, to grow and grow until they reached exploding point. Anything could spark the walking, talking time-bombs these climbers would become over the next few weeks. Perhaps the missing whisky case would set someone off … or perhaps my own incessant questions would flare a temper or two …

Notwithstanding my anxiety, it really felt great to arrive back at Base Camp the next day and see everyone again. For all my moaning, I really liked most of the guys a hell of a lot, and I had in fact missed them all terribly; even Min Moor and his lousy, vindictive jibes. I hadn't been gone more than a week, but in this environment where *everything* seemed to intensify, it felt like months.

After surprising Jill in the cookhouse, I went up onto the sundeck and surveyed the extent of the Tri-Nation camp below. The Japanese climbers had erected an archway out of spare ladders, and placed it on the track leading into the Base Camp area. A sign lettered across a side panel from one of their plastic packing boxes hung from the arch. On behalf of China, Japan and Nepal, it welcomed the Australian ambassador, Di Johnstone, to Base Camp. Among the neat rows of bright orange Dunlop-sponsored tents, the expedition's Japanese television crew were preparing their cameras in readiness for Di's propitious arrival. She, Peryman, Nick and the rest of the Number Two Supporters' Trek, were at least an hour away from Base, struggling slowly but surely up the mighty glacier.

Half unpacked boxes were strewn from one end of the Tri-Nation 'city' to the other. It would probably take weeks before they had their camp sorted out and running with typical Tokyo-like efficiency. The climbing teams were distinguishable by their colour-coded clothing. The Japanese were decked out in orange down suits, the Chinese in red and the Nepalese nationals in light green. Piles of brand new iridescent lime Koflach boots filled the corner of an open marquee-style tent. Several Japanese climbers were showing the novice Chinese contingent how to

Di Johnstone arrives at Base Camp with ABEE Chairman John Peryman (in red jacket).

strap crampons on the soles of their boots. I turned and said something to BJ about not being the only inexperienced moron on the mountain, but he was miles away, and didn't respond. I nudged him, but he just looked at me like he had seen the mystical light at the end of the tunnel.

'What's with BJ?' I asked Chris, who was brooding in another corner of the deck. 'I guess he's still a bit shell-shocked,' Chris offered. 'What from?' I asked with genuine concern. I always had the feeling that people suspected the motive behind *all* my questions was purely professional nosy journalism. Many of the guys were paranoid I would write their expedition book in a very scandalous, Joan Collins style. 'He fell down a crevasse on the twenty-eighth,' Chris said. I couldn't believe it! Here were all these experienced climbers throwing themselves down slots, like depressed lemmings over cliffs! What chance did I, a total klutz, stand up there? 'Don't look so shocked, Sorrel', Chris responded, 'He just fell down a slot near Camp Two. There's plenty of them up there you know.' No! I didn't know! 'And plenty of altitude floating around up there as well!' he added, rubbing salt into the wound. I had psyched myself up for the danger-fraught Icefall, but I had assumed the long walk through the Cwm wouldn't be as bad. This whole mountain was looming like a nightmare above me.

I tried to weasel the story out of BJ but he passed the buck onto Chris. 'You tell her mate, you pulled me out of it,' he directed at Curry. 'I may as well—there's nothing better to do. We aren't *allowed* to have lunch until the Ambassador gets here,' Chris said, revealing the reason for his long face and matching mood. At Base Camp there was only one thing worse than waiting for food, and that was not having any beer to go with it. This was definitely *not* the time to spill the beans about the missing whisky.

According to Chris, he and BJ were making their way through the Western Cwm together, towards a small snow-free patch of moraine they believed would be ideal for establishing Camp Two. The pair were roped together, and Chris was leading when he came to a slot only 15 centimetres wide. 'It was easy to see it

was overhung, so I jumped well clear of it and moved on,' Chris explained. 'Suddenly I was flat on the snow and BJ had disappeared. I was being pulled back across the snow towards the slot, but I managed to anchor myself with my ice-axe. BJ had collapsed the snow overhang, and fallen with it into the crevasse.' When Chris looked over the edge, BJ was about 6 metres down the hole, standing on a block of ice which had fortuitously lodged itself between the sides of the crevasse. It was very lucky for BJ they were roped together, and luckier still that Chris was in a position to hoist him out of the hole. 'BJ hadn't broken anything, but he was pretty scared. After about half an hour he reached the lip of the crevasse, but couldn't pull himself over it,' Chris continued, 'He was gripping out, scared and tiring really fast. I held his weight while he got his ice-axe out of his harness and anchored it over the edge. We both heaved, and he popped up and sort of wallowed over the edge.'

BJ, who'd been getting goose-bumps just listening to the story, said, 'I wasn't scared; I was *terrified,* mate; absolutely terrified.' It seemed a suitable time to ask the army major the terribly clichéd 'But why do you climb?' question. During most months of the year, BJ worked as an instructor in the Junior Staff Wing of the Land Warfare Centre, teaching all the captains in the Army about middle management. He had earlier gone to school at Barker College in Hornsby, NSW, with my childhood nextdoor neighbour and it was fascinating (and impossible!) to try and work out what made one become an architect, and the other a climber and an officer in the Australian Army.

I began by asking BJ what he thought of danger, and asked him if he didn't think climbing was just another, perhaps more socially acceptable, form of Russian roulette. 'I don't see that I'm here playing Russian roulette,' he replied. 'I'm staking my experience and judgement against the challenge. I've actually seen Russian roulette played for real in Rhodesia … 1979 … the guy's brains were blown out all over the bar.' I didn't think I needed to hear any more, but BJ went on. 'The good thing is, if you are going to die up here, at least it will be a sudden death, as opposed to a long, drawn out thing. The risk element (of mountaineering) has improved over the years, re frostbite care, etc. It's not like a 1920s expedition, when the train would pull into Delhi Station with half the returning team on board. There's this classic photo—the railway staff sweeping up all the bandages and toes off the platform; it's the most obscene thing I've ever seen.' BJ cut the gore for a while, and started rationalising his climbing philosophy with better chosen, if scholastically jargoned, words.

'I review danger objectively, and try to make a sensible assessment of it, based on circumstances here (at Everest) as they are, and the *total* implications of any assessment I have to make.' Sensing my confusion, BJ added, 'What I'm referring to is that I've got a family—a wife and an eight-month old baby girl—and I *definitely* want to return to Australia.'

I was pleased to learn he didn't have the do or die attitude some of the climbers were maintaining towards the mountain. 'We lost someone on my first big expedition to Ganesh IV,' BJ said. 'Avalanche … that's the objective danger. It's like traffic; you could get hit by a bus. I know it's not of the same order, but it's the same indicator of random selectivity.' While BJ believed there was always a risk involved in any sort of achievement, he recognised that the danger element in mountaineering served to heighten the achievement itself. But danger and the thrill of living close to death were not the reasons BJ gave when I asked him why he found the sport so satisfying. 'I need to contrast my everyday life,' he said, 'and then of course there's the friendships. On expeditions, you're with like-minds—people who share the same values. There's a good variety of people who are climbers; it gives you an opportunity to meet those people in an area of common interest. You can develop more meaningful relationships than, say, over a beer in a pub, because you share common dangers and experiences. I'll remember Chris Curry pulling me out of the slot forever, even though I would have done the same for him.'

It was early days yet, but BJ was obviously determined to put his survival ahead of his aspirations to reach the summit. In terms of the climb, he was more interested in being a team man; being part of a team that successfully put someone on top, rather than fulfilling a personal ambition to reach there himself. 'I'll carry oxygen for someone else if they've got a better chance,' he said, 'The team is all important—that's something the Army has brought out in me.' It was a pity this admirable attitude hadn't surfaced in too many of the other soldiers …

Just as we finished talking, Norm, who had been scanning the glacier for signs of the Number Two ABEE Supporters' Trek, gave a shout. 'They're on their way!' he called, 'Lady Di—yes, I can see Peryman and a bunch of yaks just coming into view.' Everyone collected on the sundeck to watch the 'official' arrival and Austin followed the Japanese film crew down to the archway to make the 'official' welcome.

By dinnertime, everyone had recovered from the long wait for lunch and the shock news concerning the whisky. There was nothing anyone could do about the latter anyway, and since the immediate need for alcohol had been met by Nick's and Di's gifts to the expedition, everyone seemed content.

Jill and Wanchu pulled out all stops for the meal, and somehow managed to turn a few meagre supplies into a veritable

Terry McCullagh, John Peryman and Austin Brookes drink a toast to Ambassador Di Johnstone.

feast: chicken in coconut milk, fried rice, yak curry, potatoes and of course, pudding. We had split into two groups to eat, but afterwards all the climbers and trekkers crammed into the mess tent, for the customary speeches, toasts and celebrations. Gota Isono, Mr Asawa, Narayan Shresta, Ang Norbu (the Tri-Nation Expedition sirdar) and two noted Nepalese climbers named Ang Rita and Ang Purba, all came up from 'the Jap camp' for the official welcome. Much to everyone's delight, they presented our team with two bottles of Suntory whisky. (My, news travels fast!)

Lady Di made an impassioned speech and Tony Delaney—our expedition doctor, who had arrived at Base Camp the day before Bruce, Peter and I left to climb Island Peak—couldn't resist getting his Bicentennial joke in. 'Di, we really shouldn't be calling this a Bison-tennial; they don't have bisons here in Nepal,' he mused, 'We should be calling this the Australian Yak-tennial Everest Expedition.' Groans were stifled, Di laughed and as usual, Jon Muir cracked up, no doubt for anticipation of the evening, rather than appreciation of Tony's pun. Jon was already high on the talk of booze; drunk on the mere sight of the bottles of whisky.

'The one good thing about high altitude, is you don't need very much grog to have a really good party!' Austin declared as he popped the first champagne cork. Everyone cheered. After three tiny sips each, there wasn't a sober head in the house! A furore of talk and laughter erupted from the crowded tent and flowed like lava out into the still, pitch night. An avalanche peeled off the West Shoulder of Chomolungma, but no one took much notice. The ambassador had come to tea; she'd brought champagne and boosted morale, and no one was particularly concerned about anything else—least of all the Mother Goddess. It was time to kick up the old heels and party. There was no need to even think, let alone talk, about the mountain. It would be there, in all its frightening glory, tomorrow. Cheers!

7

Restless White Sherpas

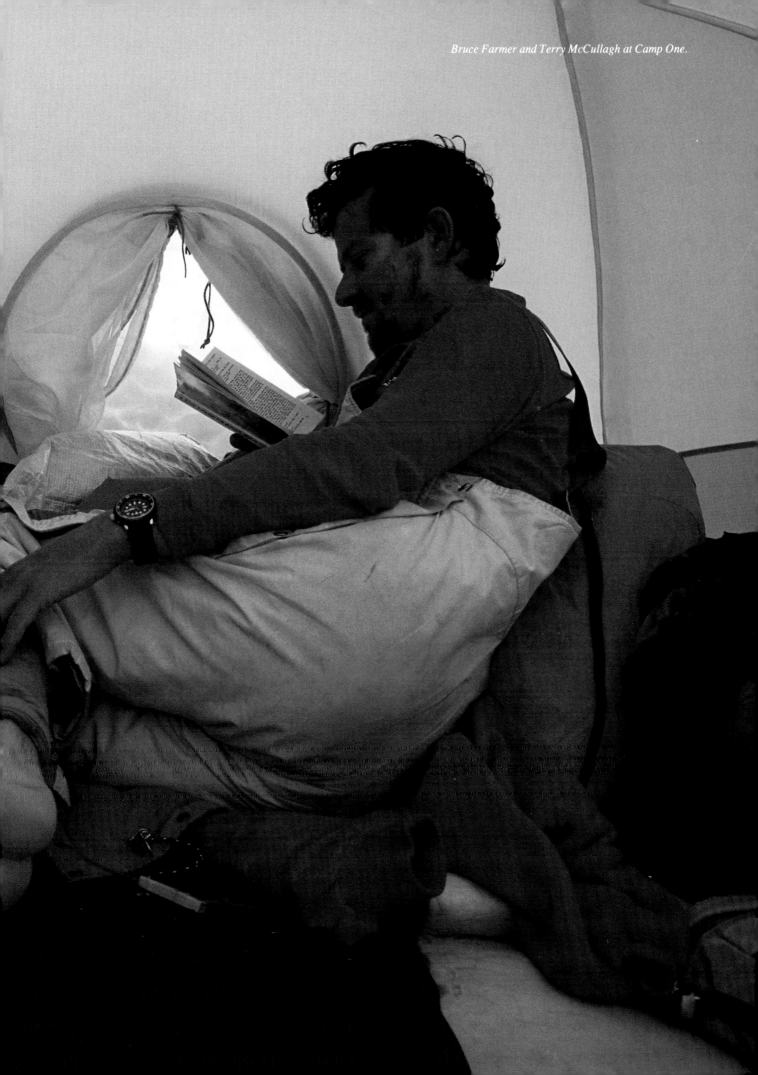

Bruce Farmer and Terry McCullagh at Camp One.

Chapter Seven

Restless White Sherpas

As he looks at the mountain the climber's heart swells with joy and pain. It is so beautiful and yet so inaccessible. Oh! to set foot on those virgin slopes—even though death waits poised above!

Edmund Hillary,
in *Himalaya*

Zac Zaharias at Base Camp.

Ambassadors do not drop in on expeditions every day. To the best of our knowledge, Di's visit amounted to something of a world first. An Indian ambassador visited an Indian expedition to Everest in 1965, but since he died during the visit his journey didn't count. There was no shortage of well-wishers and supporters trekking in and out of Base Camp, but Di's visit was special and significantly boosted team morale. We didn't have a live-eye satellite set up to beam reports of our progress back to Australia; if Australians were interested in what we were up to, they had to come to us.

It was a shame the media had expressed such little interest in receiving expedition updates to keep the public aware of our progress. The attention of the press would only be drawn if someone made it to the top or died in the attempt. Even the custodian of Australia's pioneering 'spirit of adventure'—*Australian Geographic* publisher, Dick Smith—couldn't care less about our team's endeavour. In his expert opinion, climbing Chomolungma was not an adventure; primarily because it had been climbed before. The fact that none of the ABEE members had ever *personally* reached the summit of the mountain, simply didn't bear mention. Dick's advisers maintained our expedition would set the sport of mountaineering back thirty years, and undermine the precedent Tim Macartney-Snape and Greg Mortimer had set with their lightweight-no-oxygen climb in 1984.

Our expedition was too big for the purists, and too small for the popular press. It was a real slap in the face to read a full-page feature article on the impending Tri-Nation Expedition published in the top-selling Sydney daily newspaper, just prior to our departure from Australia. The journalist had really done his homework—which was more than I can say for the handful of reporters who had turned up at our pre-expedition press conference. I'll never forget being asked, 'Is Mt Everest the highest mountain you ever want to climb?' Unbelievable, but true!

While we valued every little bit of moral support we could lay our hands on, nothing, absolutely nothing, could make up for our great lack of physical support. We had no Sherpas to find and consolidate our route up the mountain, or locate and stock safe campsites. Unlike the expeditioners of yesteryear, not to mention the Tri-Nation teams of today, the ABEE climbers could not just lounge around sipping coffee and nibbling biscuits while Sherpas ferried their burdens to and fro. The ABEE members had elected to be their own porters, and wore their 'white Sherpa' hats with pride. They were determined to 'take the hill' alone, and that meant an unprecedented amount of toil.

A typical day for a white Sherpa began at 5 a.m., with a quick breakfast of eggs à la Jill (anything from hard boiled to scrambled) and *chapatis,* coffee or tea. Whether people came to the mess tent fully dressed and prepared for the day's climb, or whether they ate breakfast before packing their rucksacks and strapping on their harnesses was a matter of personal choice. Either way, the teams were usually away by 6.00 a.m., carrying what constituted one of many 'payloads' up through the Icefall, and beyond to Camp One or Two.

A 'payload' comprised either stores and equipment to stock a camp, or ladder sections, ropes and snow-stakes to reinforce or repair a route. How far a white Sherpa travelled in a day, depended on the destination of his particular load.

Austin and Norm spent hours, days even, calculating what would be needed in the various camps. They had worked out an ever-changing schedule which ensured the route-finding and building tasks were shared between the four climbing teams, and similarly, tabulated an equal distribution of the camp-stocking loads. All up, a whopping 1355 kilograms of supplies, including forty-three high- and low-pressure oxygen cylinders, had to be lugged up onto the mountain.

From Base Camp to Camp One or Two the climbers could feasibly carry loads weighing 12–20 kilograms, but higher on the hill, carries between Camp Three and the 8000-metre South

102

Sherpas assisting the Tri-Nation Expedition and our own white Sherpas carrying loads through the Icefall. (Bruce Farmer)

ladder sections, 175 snow-stakes, 750 batteries for torches Walkmans and radios, 1000 Gaz gas cylinders and of course food to feed the masses while they were away from Base Camp. The food constituted close to half of the 1355 kilograms and was quite different from the type of supplies Jill had at her disposal in Base Camp. Although there were no potatoes, fresh vegies or eggs, there were plenty of crowd-pleasing high-calorie chocolate bars and sweets! Zac had really done an incredible job working out a variety of menus and estimating quantities into what he called 'four-man-day high-altitude ration packs'. Each pack, contained in a nylon drawstring bag Zac's wife Janet had sewn, held enough food to feed four men for one day. Alternatively of course, the pack would also satisfy two men for two days or one man for four days.

There were 264 four-kilogram ration packs in all and an additional twenty-four smaller 'summit packs', weighing 2 kilograms each. At least ninety of the former were held in reserve at Base Camp, but the rest were destined for the hill. Zac had worked out six different combination menus and named them after the famous mountaineers Shipton, Tilman, Tenzing, Hillary, Whillans and Bonatti. To avoid people favouring one menu and looting other packs for 'the pickings', Zac didn't label any of the food bags. There was no way of knowing if you were dining on a Tenzing or a Tilman, until you cracked open the pack.

All six menus had breakfast, lunch, dinner and snacks, but the variety in each was quite different. You could start the day with a cereal, such as Weetbix or muesli, with some sort of dried or reconstitutable fruit and healthfood bar to finish. Lunch would include dry crackers with tinned salmon, tuna, smoked oysters or mussels and cheese, Vegemite and peanut butter, washed down with a powdered fruit juice and followed by a chocolate bar or two. The last meal of the day was everyone's favourite: dehydes! Yes folks, pure, nothing fresh, nothing tasty, all preservatives and colouring added, individually packaged dehydrated dinners! Oh how deceiving such labels as 'Veal Italienne' and 'Roast Pork and Gravy' can be! Luckily Zac had had the foresight to

Col would amount to only 7 or 8 kilograms. In real terms, that meant most climbers would have to make two or three trips into the Icefall with ladders and ropes, three trips from Base Camp to Camp One, another five or six load carries right through from Base Camp to Camp Two and at least three trips up to Camp Three from the Western Cwm. If they still had any energy left, they would have to do at least one carry to the South Col, before returning for a final summit attempt. As an indicator of just how daunting a task that really was, Pat figured it would take one person a six-day round trip to get just one oxygen cylinder up to the South Col. Austin was beginning to wonder if his team had bitten off more than they could chew.

Apart from the oxygen, the loads included tents, sleeping mats and bags, 7000 metres of rope, 80 metres of aluminium

Jill's culinary creations gave the climbers food for thought; meal-times at Base Camp were followed by meetings, arguments and lengthy discussions.

include a variety of herbs and spices in each ration pack, and enough just-edible freeze-dried mixed vegies, peas and potato, to compensate for the tasteless (but admittedly practical) main courses. There were stacks of powdered soup and sauce mixes as well as sweet biscuits, pudding and/or rich fruit cake, and a tremendous variety of beverages: teas, herbal teas, fruit teas, coffees, fruit drinks and drinking chocolate as well.

Clearly the oxygen cylinders posed the greatest problems for Austin and his merry team of white Sherpas. Many argued they wanted to try and climb the mountain without supplementary air, claiming that the small amount of benefit it would give climbers outweighed the extra effort needed to get it up to the Col in the first place, not to mention the added burden of carrying it through to the summit. The cylinders, regulators and breathing apparatus had all been especially designed and provided for the expedition by the Sydney-based company Phillips Diving and CIG, and were without a doubt among the best and lightest systems ever to grace the slopes of the mighty Goddess. But even so, they still weighed 7.5 kilograms each.

Regulated to flow at a rate of 3–4 litres a minute, the high-pressure cylinders would last an optimum 10 hours each. Going

Camp One, above the Icefall.

on previous recorded times, it would take about 12 hours plus to summit and return to the South Col, which meant the climbers would each need two cylinders to top out and return. On Austin's calculations, 150 kilograms of equipment needed to be carried to the Col, and the minimum oxygen requirements (presuming not everyone would be fit enough to make a summit attempt) accounted for 110 kilograms of that total.

Ultimately, the decision to use oxygen during a summit bid would fall to an individual's discretion, but from Austin's point of view, he had to think of the team, and ensure enough cylinders were in place to keep both options open for *everyone* anticipating a summit attempt.

I remembered reading about the various hair-brained schemes that had been suggested to the 1953 British Expedition, regarding the oxygen issue. In those days full cylinders weighed 13 kilograms apiece, so they had even greater cause to ponder alternative ways of getting air to the Col. One suggestion which they had considered quite seriously was to take along a big mortar and fire the oxygen cylinders like bombs from the Western Cwm up to the South Col. God knows how they envisaged stopping them from shooting straight over the 8000-metre pass and flying off into Tibet! Another idea recommended that the expedition lay a pipeline all the way up the Lhotse Face and beyond, and pump

oxygen supplies through it from a depot in the Cwm. A series of 'taps' along the pipeline would allow climbers to swig air from the supply when necessary. Considering Hunt's team had, at one stage, contemplated attaching hydrogen balloons to themselves to sort of 'half float' up the great Mother Goddess, it was small wonder they reviewed these proposals so earnestly.

Hunt eventually conceded that the only way to get oxygen to the Col was by backpack; using of course, high-altitude porters' backs for the bulk of the work. They had a total of 45 eighteen-kilogram loads to carry to the 8000-metre mark—at least five times as much gear as our own expedition. But that was hardly a reason for our poor white Sherpas to celebrate. The magnitude of their undertaking was only just starting to sink in. It was one thing to sit in an air-conditioned boardroom in Sydney, deciding the team could 'take the hill' without the assistance of professional high-altitude porters, but quite another to struggle and toil, day after day, up and down, up and down through the notorious Icefall and the avalanche-prone Western Cwm, unaided. The climbers were becoming dissatisfied with the slow progress of the expedition and demoralised by the task they had set themselves.

After making his first carry all the way through to Camp Two on 2 April, Zac Zaharias recorded these feelings in his diary:

The trip to Camp One took me four to five hours. I arrived around 11.00 a.m. and was quite tired. I was carrying 12 kilograms plus personal gear and I certainly didn't feel strong … Camp Two looked so far away … It was so far that human figures were hardly distinguishable. I was totally devastated. It took me two hours to get to the turning corner. I was encouraged by the beauty of the Cwm and the fact that at last I could see the South-West Face of Everest, the Lhotse Face and the South Col. All these years of reading and planning, and at last, I was actually seeing the places of my dreams … I plodded on, stopping every thirty paces. At this rate I'd never get there … Slowly I inched my way to the camp. At about 4.30 p.m. I reached the foot of the last gully, which leads to the camp. Terry McCullagh and Bruce had just dumped their loads and were on their way back. They tried to convince me to leave the load there and return straight away. I was sounding exhausted, but convinced them that I wanted to continue; I was only ten minutes away. They waited for me while I plodded the last few metres to camp, dumped my load under some rocks and returned. It had taken me nearly five hours from Camp One. I was demoralised. I had another four carries like this to make. I had difficulty in breathing due to my laryngitis, and anyway, at this rate I would *never* climb the mountain. People were carrying from Base Camp to Camp Two and back in about eight to nine hours. How could I even have a chance? What was the point? I didn't want to be a yak for the others …

Zac wasn't the only one whose performance suffered through illness. Several guys were losing weight rapidly due to the altitude, and with deteriorating condition, they were more likely to catch whatever bug was floating around. Mick Pezet and Min

Moor had already dropped 10 kilograms each. Hardly a day went by without someone coming down with something. Phil Pitham was plagued by a terrible cough which got so bad that Doctor Tony sent him down to Thyangboche to recuperate. He returned a few days later, feeling '10 feet tall and bulletproof', but still wheezing. My tent was right next to Phil's, and at night you could hear his tortured, lung-racking attacks. It was scary stuff, believe me!

Phil's was the worst, but not the only, 'high-altitude hack'. Dinnertime in the mess tent looked and sounded more like pill-popping time in a hospital cancer ward. As if the nagging coughs weren't enough to handle, well over half the guys had had the dreaded diarrhoea—more than once. There was nothing worse than having a sudden attack on one's way through the Icefall. Invariably it was impossible to get one's harness, overalls, pants and longjohns off in time … which usually necessitated a rest day and a trip to the washing hole.

Diarrhoea attacks aside, the team frequently took advantage of sun-filled rest days, and bathed at the expedition's private 'beach'. If nothing else, it was an attempt to maintain some level of hygiene and ward off at least a few diseases and ailments. Between Base Camp and the foot of the Icefall, a horseshoe ring of tall ice-fins erupting from the glacier made the bathing area quite secluded. A windless sunny day, a bucket, a cup and a sledgehammer were all you needed for the perfect 'dip'. After breaking through the thick layer of ice covering a small stream running through the glacier, it was possible to scoop cupfuls of the melted ice into a bucket. It made a very cold shower! With the warmth of the direct sun and reflected heat bouncing off the white-finned amphitheatre, you could actually regain feeling in your skin after about half an hour. Heaven help anyone who crapped their pants on an overcast, blustery day!

Apart from washing bods and clothes, there was plenty to do on a rest day in the life of a white Sherpa. There were books to read, games to play, mountains to meditate upon, photojournalists and cooks to whinge to, Jon's tape collection to bop to, bare tent walls to stare at and much, much more. Pity there was no grass to sit and watch growing … Letter and diary writing filled in a few of the long, seemingly endless Base-Camp-bound hours, as did joke-telling sessions and eating competitions. Lambo usually won the latter, hands down.

To alleviate boredom for a few hours one day, James Strohfeldt initiated a session writing letters to 'sponsors we should have had'. Realising posters and women were two things they most needed in the mess tent, Mick Pezet suggested the team write to Kylie Minogue and ask her to send a picture for the bare canvas wall. Weeks went by before they received their prize *and* a hand-written note from the teenage superstar:

To all the expedition members,
Hi! How are you all? I hope you're coping with the cold. If it makes you feel any better, the weather here is disgusting! … and very cold as well. However, I do feel for you all and admire your efforts. Thanks for your letter and I hope that I can brighten up home base in some way.
Hang in There,
Best wishes, Kylie X

To alleviate boredom at Base Camp, James Strohfeldt studies
formulas and form.

Mail days were always eagerly anticipated, and either filled
people with joy (if they got letters) or massive doses of depression
(if they didn't). There was nothing worse than watching
disappointment sweep over people. Some of the letters got
passed around for general reading but others were taken to an
individual's tent and read in private, over and over again. Each
word meant so much in this cold, alien place on the other side of
the world.

Of the 'general' letters, my favourites were the ones Mick
received from his little sisters. They were always classic and
never failed to spark a smile on the faces of the saddest letter-less
climbers.

But letters, meditations, jokes and domestics aside, the greatest
amount of time at Base Camp was spent planning. Night after
night there were discussions and day after day still more
discussions. In spite of all this, people never stopped complaining
about the lack of communication around the place. The Inner
Sanctum was begrudged by the Chook Union and constantly
criticised for keeping their fray in the dark. The expedition had
only just established Camp Two, and the white Sherpas were
restless. They were getting toey and starting to, as BJ put it,
'jockey for positions'. Although Austin was adamant that
everyone would get a crack at the summit, the Chook Union was
rather suspicious. There were rumours circulating that a 'Summit
Team' had already been picked and those not 'in' with Austin
were destined to simply carry loads for the lead climbers. I could
scarcely believe some of the unfounded remarks I heard, and
passed most of them off as spiteful paranoia. Austin said
everyone would have a fair go, and as the leader of the expedition,
everyone should have believed and trusted him. Rumours at sea-
level were bad enough, but up here, they were down right
dangerous.

Fear of being denied a chance to stand on top of the world had
actually invaded some individuals' thoughts long before progress
had advanced the expedition to Camp Two. Several weeks

beforehand, after a particularly frustrating day, one climber
found cause to scrawl in his diary:

> I was absolutely ropable at lunch when I found out that there
> had been an Inner Sanctum meeting, which Peter Lambert—
> our illustrious leader of Lambert's Layabouts—hadn't
> attended. What's more, and not surprisingly, we had our role
> changed and got stuck with Zac's Yaks' task of improving the
> route in the danger zone … There was hardly justification to
> give us the dangerous job. Obviously being friendly with
> the leader helps. I've obviously ruined my chances by
> being a trouble maker. I'll not be surprised by anything that
> happens now.

Sadly, such fears failed to pass; on the contrary, they gathered
momentum. 'You ain't seen nothin' yet …' BJ assured me, after
one particularly volatile after-dinner meeting. 'This is just the tip
of the iceberg. It's the same every expedition—all the politicking
and concern. This is nothing.'

But I found BJ's 'nothing' totally unacceptable, in human
terms. The 'nothing' had been a full page of complaints,
suggestions and demands written and delivered to Austin by Jim
Truscott. He had a certain way with words, our Jim, and his list
included sensitive issues such as criticism of Austin's laid-back
style of leadership. It also drew attention to minor, even petty
points, like 'inadequate ventilation in the mess tent' and a
suggestion to hang a noticeboard somewhere where messages,
dates of mail runs and times of meals were detailed. Jim was used
to orders—receiving and giving them. He hated inefficiency,
and if dinner was only five minutes late, he didn't hesitate to hurl
abuse at Jill and her band of Nepalese helpers. He was disturbed
the leadership hierarchy had not made any arrangements re a
deputy overall leader, should something untoward happen to
Austin. The list went on and on, with many complaints being
fired like arrows towards the bane of his existence, Zac Zaharias.

The outcome of the volatile meeting saw Mike Rheinberger
elected as a deputy leader and placed in-charge on the mountain.
A non-smoking ban was placed on the mess tent and Norm was
instructed to make some sort of memo board. When the latter
appeared the following morning, the first notice to grace it read
something like this:

1. For public speaking lessons, see Jim Truscott.
2. For red cross parcels, see Jim Truscott.
3. Anyone wanting a little after hours R and R in the form of
   some malicious S and M should contact [yes, you guessed it]
   Jim Truscott.

The joke was taken in good humour, and with some tensions
resolved, life at Chomolungma settled.

Apart from a few highlights, like Jill's home-made Easter
buns on Good Friday, and chocolate eggs on Easter Sunday,
Base Camp was a pretty boring place over the following week.
The eggs had been hand-delivered by Di Stubbs, a friend of
Lambo's from England who trekked into our camp one day and
stayed for a while. She was happy to be at Base Camp and our
team were equally appreciative of her company. Any friends,

family or 'official' ABEE supporters and AAA trekkers were welcome, as it was always good to see some new faces and hear new jokes at Base Camp. Uninvited trekkers were not usually made to feel so at home, though. They were tolerated for fear of giving Australia a bad, unfriendly name. Basically the climbers only voiced their objections when individuals or small groups of them arrived with insufficient clothing, expecting to be fed, looked after and entertained.

The only place to go to escape trekkers and relieve the Base Camp blues, was up. Life on the hill itself was anything but boring. Routine, yes, but never dull. Most climbers, even though the load-carrying was back-breaking yakka, preferred to work than lounge around Base Camp. Chris was so agitated by the slow progress of the expedition he had started carrying other people's loads up the mountain. *Anything* was better than doing nothing—even doing too much.

The Tri-Nation Expedition had started climbing at last and finding one's way along the route through the Icefall was worse than contending with sale-crazed crowds of shoppers on George Street. As expected, there were a few teething problems associated with sharing our route. Every morning there were queues at each ladder, and with all the to-ing and fro-ing it's a wonder no one was accidentally bumped off a headwall or into a huge crevasse. The Tri-Nation porters and novice Chinese climbers didn't understand the 'one person at a time' principle on ladders and rope sections, so the Aussie climbers were constantly looking over their shoulders before scaling a wall or crossing a crevasse to make sure they didn't have company. The Icefall was dangerous enough without the added risk of having someone disturb your balance midway across a ladder, or having to detach yourself from the fixed rope to allow someone to pass.

In the relatively short time our team had been working on the mountain many seracs had toppled and new crevasses opened. According to the experts, there seemed to be less movement in the Icefall than in previous years. Ang Rita, who, like Sundare, had summited Chomolungma four times, believed our route was quite safe, largely due to the lack of snowfall during the preceding winter. On 6 April, the day after he passed that comment, the 'Bowl' (an area about the size of a football field two-thirds of the way through the Icefall) completely collapsed. The ice depression slumped a further 5 metres, twisting and destroying ladders and burying hundreds of metres of fixed rope. Surprisingly, many of the crevasses in the area closed, rather than opened, so when the climbers had resurrected the route, it was actually safer and easier than the original.

On 7 April, I made my own first journey right through the tortured, twisted ice-forest with Austin. The other guys were accustomed to the route and its conditions now, so much so that Chris, Paul, Jon and James were able to make their carries from Base Camp to Camp Two and return before afternoon tea time. Austin assumed it would take me *three days* to get to the 6400-metre camp, but I guessed he was being kind, and overestimating my abilities so as not to embarrass me in front of his men. Well … I had to take photographs, remember? I had to stop a lot to compose pictures and change film, and wait for seracs to come crashing down for action shots, and recover from slips, spills and avalanches, and …

What a place! Words would never do it justice. Photographs would hint at, but never capture its immensity and magic. The lower areas of the Icefall where Austin and I had often ventured on practice sessions—those bits on which I had used up all my adjectives and best descriptions—were hardly worth mentioning now, after my first glassy-eyed scan over the rest of the Icefall. I spent over eight hours in the icy labyrinth—loving every minute of it visually, and hating every second physically. My legs ached. My hands ached. My shoulders ached. Every single muscle in my body screamed in agony. I had no idea climbing was so damn hard. And I wasn't even carrying a load.

I collapsed at Camp One and slept like a log all night, but sleep did little to repair my physical state of exhaustion. Gradually I was beginning to respect my team mates and appreciate their past efforts, and those which still lay before them. After splitting open a ration pack and divvying up the breakfast spoils, Austin and I headed off from Camp One, and up into the Western Cwm.

The Cwm is a hauntingly beautiful place; an enormous long valley fortressed between the colossal walls of Chomolungma's West Shoulder and Nupste. From Camp One at the top of the Icefall the route hugs the West Shoulder and weaves through a maze of bottomless crevasses. It crosses the valley and heads towards Nupste, turns and centres itself for a head-on collision with the dwarfed Lhotse Face—a Himalayan princess, crowned by the South Col. The awesome black summit of Chomolungma, regally sitting on the right side of Lhotse, slowly comes into view as the 8-kilometre Cwm curves to meet it. Camp Two is nestled

Wanchu, our Nepalese cook, displays Jill's hot-cross buns on Good Friday.

at the end of the valley on a pile of grey boulders and glacial moraine, slave to the elements, cowering beneath the queen of all mountains.

It was a hell of a long way through the Valley of Silence (as the Cwm is known) particularly once you had the camp location and the summit in sight. The route just went on forever, and every step forward failed to draw you closer to your goal. If it wasn't for the mind-blowing beauty of the surrounding mountains, it would have been the most dispiriting, laborious walk of my life. I vowed I would never again criticise the climbers for their emotional outbursts or petty squabbles. I was ready to whinge and spit blood over anything, I felt so disheartened. Instead of ridiculing their anxiety, I promised to be compassionate towards it. Instead of condemning their egos, I would worship them; they would never get to the top of Chomolungma if they didn't believe they were bigger and better than the 'black bitch' herself. Success in climbing and mountaineering was proportionate to how immortal you believed you were. From discussions I had had with most of the team members, I knew only about half of them had what it would take to reach the top of this hill: an unshakable *knowledge* (not questionable belief) that the challenge was well within the realm of their capabilities, and a rock-solid commitment, a strong, binding conviction, to 'summit at all costs'. It was a frightening attitude, considering the number of people who have died attempting to conqueror Chomolungma. I hoped to God that such unequivocal assuredness would be tempered by sound mountaineering judgement and commonsense higher up. But for now, those climbers definitely had the edge on the others. Psychologically they had what it takes to get there, and all they needed was a little luck with the weather.

The Western Cwm, a beautiful valley fortressed between the colossal walls of Chomolungma's West Shoulder and Nuptse.

And speaking of weather, when we finally reached Camp Two the sky began clouding over for the first time in days. We shouldn't have been surprised by the sudden change; it was after all 8 April, and the monk from Pangboche who conducted our Icefall blessing the previous month, had forecast snow would fall on this day. By jingo, that holy man was better than Lennox Walker! I hoped his other prediction about the expedition's success would prove to be just as accurate.

Camp Two at this stage consisted of a couple of pitched tents and a few scattered piles of supplies. Debris from previous expeditions lay in the moraine rubble; anything of value had been scrounged by Jim, who had gone up to the camp alone, following his articulate outburst about expedition leadership et cetera. He was doing a great job organising loads as they arrived at the camp and had cleared enough sites for five dome-shaped tents, to be erected in due course. He was a funny bugger really, and seemed happier up there on his own than he ever had at Base Camp. He joked around with Terry, who had arrived with Zac and Van Gelder about an hour before Austin and I, and even managed a smile when I made Austin a hot lemon brew. Weeks later, I found out that Jim had been using the battered saucepan I'd used to mix the drink in for a night-time pee-bottle. I should have guessed something was up. Displays of genuine human warmth were unusual for Jim.

With the sky growing so ominously dark, Austin didn't want to hang around too long at Camp Two. We finished our brew and started back for Camp One. It was a bloody long way, but all downhill, and by Austin's expectations, it wouldn't take more than two and a half hours—if we flew. I was as exhausted as I had been on reaching Camp One the previous day, and only moved when Austin, Zac and Terry threatened to disembowel me with their ski poles.

Pat and Min Moor turned up at Camp Two just as we were

From Camp Two, climbers watch in awe as clouds fill the Western Cwm. (Chris Curry)

preparing to leave, so I got another five minutes grace sitting on my butt while Austin chatted to the two new arrivals. Min looked terrible; even worse than I did! His wife, Julia, had trekked into Base Camp with one of the AAA teams and Min had taken a few days off from climbing to accompany her back as far as Gorek Shep.

After Julia's parting, Min ran into Sundare, who was having a binge-break from the Indonesian Pumo Ri Expedition. Judging by the look on poor Min's haggard face, it was quite a heavy session which didn't end—even when Min tried to leave and stagger back to Base Camp. Sundare had spiked Min's water bottle with alcohol, so every time Min tried to rehydrate, he just became more inebriated. He passed out somewhere on the Khumbu Glacier and woke up after the sun had set, shivering and covered in his own frozen vomit. He managed to stumble back to Gorek Shep, where Sundare was still drinking rapaciously. Min fell asleep, and during the night Sundare finally comatosed himself by swilling the five bottles of beer Min had purchased to share with his team mates back at Base Camp.

Pat and Min decided to stay at Camp Two for the night, so we left them to set up another tent, and walked back to Camp One. Well, Austin walked, I crawled.

By morning, still more cloud filled the sky. It hadn't actually snowed yet, but it was just a matter of time before the monk's prophecy would be realised. One day out wasn't bad. Zac's Yaks got away to an early start, shifting their personal gear and two 4-kilogram food bags each up to Camp Two. They intended staying up there for four or five days in order to reconnoitre a route over the Bergshrund—a huge crevasse which ran the length of the Lhotse Face and separated the mountain from the Western Cwm—and begin fixing ropes up the Lhotse wall itself. Austin abseiled off down the big headwall and I (the chicken, remember?) took the ladder-route into the Icefall. My shins were killing me for some reason, and after a piddling half hour

climbing *downhill,* my legs were stuffed. Putting one foot in front of the other caused shooting pains to race from my toes to my shoulders.

My body was wimping out, and I found that really infuriating. I'd trained for this damn climb for at least five weeks! Bloody legs! I wanted a trade-in! As I fumed to myself about my total lack of agility and strength, I tried to heed Austin's plea of speed. He wanted to clear out of the Icefall as quickly as possible and get down to Base Camp before it started snowing. I trudged down an upright ladder mounted on the side of a massive headwall just before the Bowl, unclipped from its safety rope, reclipped into the next fixed rope section and turned to start plodding down a 0.5-metre-wide 'ramp', which led down the lower half of the wall. I tripped and fell straight over the edge of the ramp. The instinctive thing mountaineers usually do when they fall is anchor themselves with their ice-axe. I didn't, of course. I screamed and grabbed the rope I was clipped into with my teeth. I have no idea why that was my instant reaction, but so be it. The rope itself was anchored at both ends, so I didn't fall very far, but it was far enough to scare the life out of me.

To add insult to injury though, I couldn't get up the side of the wall and back onto the ramp. I was like a parachutist, caught on a powerline; just dangling stupidly in mid-air. I tried to kick my front crampon points into the headwall, but the surface was like powdery caster sugar and just collapsed beneath my feet. My ice-axe was just as useless. I was still gripping the rope with my teeth, convinced I would fall into a void if I let go, when Austin poked his head over the side of the ramp and called down to me. 'Moo! What the *hell* are you doing down there?' He was trying really hard not to laugh.

'I frigging fell here!' I cursed, still clenching my choppers.

'Git that out of there, Moo—I can't understand what you're saying with that bloody rope in your mouth,' Austin yelled. 'Don't you trust a 2000-pound karabiner?' So, I unlocked my jaw. Austin tried to soothe my fear by saying, 'That's better … now stop panicking … AND CLIMB OUT OF THERE BEFORE A BLOODY SERAC FALLS ON YOU AS WELL!'

'I can't!' I screeched back, blubbering something about my ice-axe and the consistency of the headwall's surface. Just at that moment, one of the Nepalese climbers swung off the ladder and grinned down at me. He got on one end of the rope I was fixed to and Austin got on the other. They hauled and pulled until finally my head popped into view, and then they lifted me up by the arms and yanked me over the ramp edge. I couldn't thank them enough. It took half an hour for Austin to coax me back into action but my legs didn't stop shaking until we were out of the Icefall altogether, and safely heading across the glacier to Base Camp.

We reached 'home' before the snow started falling. I was so relieved to be *alive,* I just stood on the sundeck hugging Jill and laughing my head off. I kept pinching myself to double check I wasn't dreaming. The nightmare was over now, I'd fulfilled my duty to the expedition and I was free to go home. Fair dinkum home, that is, not just back to my tent, but back to Australia! Prior to Austin's phone call on New Year's Eve, I had committed myself to three publicity tours across Australia, the US and the UK, and the first was scheduled to begin on 22 April. While the

An avalanche's bark proved worse than its bite at Base Camp. It was always a joy to return to the relatively safe confines of home after a day 'on the hill'.

ABEE struggled to attain the summit, I would be jetting around the world promoting the release of my first book. I'd probably be spending a lot more time above 8000 metres than they would!

Charlie Hart and Peter Allen were due to leave Base Camp a day ahead of me, so between the three of us, we were drumming up a lot of joy around Base Camp. It was impossible to contain our excitement, even though it filled some of the climbers with a deep sense of emptiness and longing. Everyone was beginning to miss their families and friends, particularly the guys with young children. Letters couldn't replace hugs, which was the one thing they all needed more than anything right now. The mountain was so impersonal, so unforgiving. As the expedition crept up the mountain, tensions would tighten and pressure-

cooker tempers would no doubt explode. Home would never feel so damn far away.

The communication issue had reared its ugly head again while Austin and I were away on the hill. People were already anxious about the final stages of the expedition and still speculating that the final assault climbers had already been chosen. Who's in the Summit Team? Who are their Sherpas? Why don't we know yet? Why isn't there any chocolate at Base Camp? (That question always snuck in, no matter what was being discussed.) When are *we* going home?

The snail's-pace progress of the expedition was frustrating everyone as well, and accounted for at least a third of the discontent expressed. According to Charlie's great computer-analysed 'master plan', the expedition was supposed to have already located Camp Three and fixed rope halfway up the Lhotse Face. As it stood, we had only half-stocked Camp Two and not even ventured beyond the Cwm side of the Bergshrund.

There was so much disillusionment floating around Base Camp you could almost cut it with a knife. Those who were not inclined to vocalise their worries and complaints, began airing their ill-feelings in diaries:

> In spite of Terry McCullagh's Chook Union, in spite of Jim Truscott getting outraged at the lack of communication and in spite of Austin Brookes saying he would discuss more matters with the team as a whole, silence reigns …

> Another area of mystery, is how we're going to carry to the Col …

> There's already been quite a lot of dissatisfaction with the leadership amongst some of the members of the Chook Union, but it's only recently I've added my voice. The major problem is failure to communicate … Austin argues that eighteen people is too many to make decisions. Maybe so (I disagree), but everyone should at least have the right to express their opinion, particularly now that we're facing the "going high stage" …

> The Army personnel, used to full briefings and lots of flow of information and a firm chain of command, find Austin Brookes hard to take. They give him a hard time—his leadership is very quiet, in some ways laissez-faire…

Austin held an impromptu meeting with the climbers who were hanging out at Base Camp and managed to restore some faith around the place. It would only be temporary, for as BJ had warned, this was only the tip of the iceberg. There were still weeks and weeks of work to complete before *anyone* would have a chance to go for the top, but the white Sherpas were restless and chafing at the bit.

8

Here's the Plan... and Here's the Plan Again

Confrontation in the Cwm as 'the plan' changes ... and changes again. (Rick Moor)

Chapter Eight

Here's the Plan... and Here's the Plan Again

Those who are hardest hit by change are those who imagine that it never happened before.

Elizabeth Janeway,
in *Man's World, Woman's Place*

Andrew Smith radios Base Camp for an update on 'the plan'.

The climbers eventually reset their sights on the lower half of the hill. There were routes to find, ropes to fix and loads to be carried. This mountain would not be climbed if people didn't put the summit at the back of their minds for a while, disregard their differences and just get on with the laborious task.

As Pat's, Mike's and Lambo's teams ferried loads up to Camp Two, Zac's Yaks worked relentlessly day after day on the Lhotse Face. They successfully fixed a route through the Bergshrund and on the lower half of the Face, but stopped just one and a half rope lengths (150 metres) short of the Camp Three site. They were relieved by Terry Tremble, Paul and Chris, who completed the task in a day by quickly locating the site for the third camp—a precarious perch littered with the remains of an American expedition tent, at 7300 metres. They fixed the rest of the rope and dumped the payloads they were carrying and returned to Camp Two well before sunset on 13 April.

On the following day, Pat returned to the high point with Paul and together they dug out three platforms on the steep face for the expedition's tents. They pitched one, and spent their first night at the new camp—albeit a little uncomfortably. They were not acclimatised to the higher altitude and suffered headaches and loss of appetite as a result.

On 15 April Terry McCullagh and Min Moor made a carry to Camp Three and returned. On the 16 April Lambo and BJ left Base Camp on a similar run and the next day Dad's Army went up the hill, intent on staying for a week. They planned to make two carries each from Camp Two to Camp Three, before returning to Base Camp for a rest.

With co-operation and concentration focused on the immediate situation, everything was going smoothly at last. Well ... almost.

There were still some fairly bitter outbursts at Base Camp, notably instigated by Terry McCullagh. He was becoming obsessed with his anti-Zac campaign, and seized every opportunity to criticise his team leader's efforts towards the expedition planning—particularly with regard to Base Camp food supplies and the unwritten policy on trekkers.

Terry was disturbed by the treatment the AAA trekking groups were receiving when they arrived at Base Camp, and launched a scathing attack on his adversary. Terry believed the Army trekkers should have been given an open invitation to stay at Base Camp as long as they wished and abused Zac for advocating otherwise. Chris was present at the session, and supported Zac, claiming that *any* trekkers were a pain, ate the expedition's food supplies, contributed diseases, such as coughs and colds, to climbers, and robbed people of their privacy.

Terry's outspokenness was starting to backfire—while some of the team members enjoyed his bullying, most were starting to realise his outrage was a little over the top, and potentially destructive for team morale.

After yet another aggressive attack on the 19 April, targeting Zac's bungling of the Base Camp food resources, Chris was so infuriated he wrote: 'Terry's mouth is now, without doubt, bigger than his brain.' Zac, who had put a hell of a lot of effort into the food portfolio, was the first to admit he had miscalculated the amount of time people would spend at Base Camp, and thus the amount of food they would require. He never let his real feelings show, but wrote of the outbursts:

What really pissed me off was the tone of the discussion. It was an emotional attack by Terry McCullagh and Min; there were obviously other issues under the surface. To the others, it was a storm in a teacup ... Terry had done little for this expedition and was its most vocal critic. He was complaining about a shortage of food, but part of the problem was due to this open-arm policy on trekkers! ... I didn't get to bed until 3.00 a.m. I find that I cannot handle criticism, particularly when it is emotive and vindictive. I take it to heart and have to chew it over. Terry may have slept well after getting it off his chest, but I didn't. Why do people have to be such bastards?

There was really no need for Terry to raise the food issue over and over again; the expedition had already sent Jill down to Namche to buy more supplies, and she was due to return to Base Camp any day.

So far, the ABEE had really paved the way for the Tri-Nation team. While his men laboured backwards and forwards with loads, Austin had a number of discussions with the other expedition's leaders. It was agreed their Sherpas, who were already responsible for maintaining the Icefall, would now pioneer the route from Camp Three through to the South Col. That meant the only tasks now resting on the shoulders of our own expedition were primarily load-carrying ones. As soon as the Tri-Nationers fixed the rope between Three and the Col, our boys could establish their higher camps and finally position themselves for a summit bid.

While Dad's Army were making their consecutive carries up the Lhotse Face, the Tri-Nation Sherpas were working on the last fixed section of the route, and anticipated it would be finished

The Lhotse Face. (Bruce Farmer)

around 26 April. Their expedition chiefs still had every intention of reaching the summit on 5 May, but realistically, our team could not hope to make so much as an attempt until the middle of the month.

On the morning of 21 April, Austin and Norm (who had taken to climbing like a duck to water) left Base Camp early for Camp Two. They were going to make a stock-take of all the resources now in place and amend their lists for the remaining carries to the Col.

Shortly after their departure, there was an emergency at the Tri-Nation Base Camp. No one could rouse the Japanese doctor. Tony, Carol and Jim Van Gelder rushed over to assist the fifty-five-year-old. A crowd of people gathered around the expedition's hospital tent as the three medics tried to revive the Japanese doctor, using oxygen and external cardiac massage. After half an hour attempting to resuscitate their patient, Tony, Carol and Jim desisted. The doctor was pronounced dead. The Tri-Nation climbers, in particular the Japanese contingent, were stunned, and spent the rest of the day in mourning.

Back at the Australian Base Camp, a lively discussion was

underway concerning the need for a Camp Five above the South Col. People were growing impatient for the summit again ...Many of those arguing against Austin's wishes for the extra camp (claiming they could make a summit bid from the Col), hadn't even carried to Camp Three yet! Still, they were anxious to resolve the issue by consensus, and agreed they should have a full-team meeting as soon as Austin and Dad's Army returned to Base Camp.

Mention of Dad's Army led to further debate. Some of the climbers felt that Mike's team was up on the mountain 'waiting indefinitely' for the Tri-Nation Sherpas to fix the rope through to the Col. They believed they were trying to 'position themselves' for the summit. They were stalling their load-carrying so they could move straight through with a load from Camp Two to the Col.

People were growing steadily more suspicious of each other, not to mention Austin's leadership. There was talk of Mike conspiring with Austin in order to get his team on top first, and the 'Summit Team has already been picked' theory was aired again.

The Camp Five issue was eventually resolved on 23 April. The 'against' case maintained that too much additional effort would be required to put the camp in place. It would be easier for climbers to make their summit bids straight through from the Col. Austin explained he wanted the expedition to have the extra camp for safety reasons. In this he was strongly supported by Mike Rheinberger. He wanted it positioned at around 8300 metres; 300 vertical metres above the Col. In spite of strong contention, only five people voted against his plan. It would take a lot of extra equipment, time and effort to establish the camp, and even though it would consist of only one tent, oxygen, a stove and emergency food supplies, it meant everyone would have to carry an extra 2 kilograms to the Col. The debate had been unusually civilised, and ended without rancour.

Ill-feelings were laid aside again on 25 April. It was Anzac Day, and Norm made sure everyone knew about it, including the Tri-Nation Expedition. He simulated a couple of dawn bomb blasts by setting two full Gaz cylinders alight, then delivered rum and coffee in bed to all those Aussies who hadn't yet stirred. Everyone assembled on the sundeck, where Min made an impassioned speech. 'A lot of us don't think of Anzac Day in the traditional spirit it was thought of. It's not a war-mongering occasion; it's not a time to glorify war or remember war. It's simply a time to remember those Australians who gave their lives in various causes, whether we support those causes or not.' He then reflected on his own more recent experiences, saying, 'In my own service I've had five soldiers who have been killed in the last few years; it's also a time to remember people like that. In our service, we have to often do things that are above and beyond the call of duty, so I just ask you to have a think about those in the past who, through no cause of their own, have died for their country'. His speech was followed by the obligatory one minute silence, then the expedition moved down into the mess tent. By this time they had been joined, briefly, by several

Climbers carrying loads on the Lhotse Face above Camp Three. (Chris Curry)

members of the Tri-Nation Expedition, including Major Taba, the LO from the Nepalese Army, and a Chinese soldier.

The guests stayed for breakfast and listened intently to a spiel from Zac, explaining the significance of Anzac Day. They excused themselves after an hour, leaving the Australians to continue their celebration alone. The chilling 'And the Band Played Waltzing Matilda' was wafting out from the ghetto-blaster, but its melancholic strains were barely audible above the rowdy din of the climbers, as they immersed themselves in yet another aspect of the Anzac Day tradition—alcohol.

There wasn't a lot to go around, and God knows where the rum and Scotch came from—the last time anyone had so much as sniffed the stuff was at the ceremony with Di Johnstone over three weeks ago. Pat called Mohan, the liaison officer, over and told him, 'I have one task for you on this expedition: you have to go down to the Tri-Nation team and ask them for two bottles of whisky.' Jim Truscott yelled, 'Kerosene will do!' which brought a roar of laughter from the rest of the team. Pat continued, 'If you don't come back in half an hour with the whisky ...'

'...shoot yourself,' Jim interjected.

Mike articulated the plea again, stressing the urgency of the request. 'Today is a very important day, Mohan. We need much grog,' he said with a serious tone. Mohan dutifully went to beg what he could from the expedition's neighbours, and returned with a bottle of beer and a bit of Sherpa *rakshi*.

Zac had brought his Australian Bush tapes over to the mess, and everyone took turns at slurring along with the many verses of 'The Man From Snowy River'. Everyone talked at once, laughing and stirring each other about any and everything. There were only three climbers absent from the party—Mick Pezet, Terry Tremble and Chris—who were all up on the hill working.

Above the chatter and raucous laughter, Pat's voice suddenly boomed, 'I wish to alert the leader of the ABEE that we have a crisis on our hands. It is only 9.30 a.m. and we've run out of alcohol.' It wasn't much of a crisis—they were all as drunk as lords anyway, and more alcohol would merely have produced more casualties. The soldiers were not holding their liquor as well as they were able to at sea-level!

Austin was thrilled to see his team enjoying themselves for a change. He was recording the occasion on the small tape recorder he used as a diary, and towards the end of the morning, he added a note of commentary over the crescendo of laughter. 'Anzac Day, 25 April ... celebrated in a style only Australians can manage' ... he began. 'There is really a genuine ethos that spans Australia. We share a heritage, which in older countries is often regional, rather than national.' He was moved by the demonstration of good feeling he was witnessing again amongst his men, and finished his 'diary' entry by confidently stating, 'If we can keep this unity going, we will take the hill.'

There was no time to waste the next day nursing hangovers. Austin and Norm made an early start on their planning. They were still trying to work out a realistic programme for load-carrying to the Col. Pat, Min and Zac's Yaks eventually got away from Base Camp and started their behind-schedule trip up to Camp Two. Together with Mick Pezet and Terry Tremble, Pat and Min planned to move up to Camp Three and then make the first carry to the Col, now that the Tri-Nation Sherpas had finished consolidating the route. Zac's Yaks were moving into position to make the second set of Col-carries.

Aside from Jim Van Gelder, who moved like a steam train regardless of the snow conditions and weight of his pack, everyone moved up the hill very slowly indeed. Min only got as far as the first Icefall ladder, and had to turn back. The others battled on, and finally made Camp Two late in the afternoon.

The weather had settled into a pattern, and now snowfalls were the order of the afternoon. If each fresh fall consolidated on the otherwise glassy iced Lhotse Face, it would make climbing to Camp Three a great deal easier. If it didn't, it would make the treacherous slope even more dangerous by increasing the risk of avalanche.

After having a cup of tea, Zac made radio contact with Base. He was more than a little surprised to learn Austin had been attempting to raise him since 3 p.m. to detail some significant changes in the overall plan. At a meeting the day before Anzac Day, Austin had decided Zac's team would carry 10.7-kilogram loads to the South Col then drop back to Camp Two to pick up a 7–9-kilogram load which they would carry through to the Col on their way to the summit. The new plan required they boost their initial loads to a daunting 12 kilograms. Austin had based his latest decision on the assumption that only twelve carries would be made to the Col, not the original sixteen, as it was now anticipated Mike's team would only make one carry to the Col, and push straight through with the supplies to establish Camp Five. They would make their first bid for the summit on the same trip.

A shock wave rocked Camp Two. It looked like all their worst fears had been realised. Dad's Army were going to get first crack at the summit. According to the new plan, Zac's team would make the second attempt, Lambo's team the third, and Pat's team would run up the rear.

Zac was quite happy with the second-pole position, but thought the 12-kilogram loads would be too heavy to carry high up the mountain. They were not Sherpas, and yet their payloads, when coupled with their own personal gear, would ultimately weigh 18–20 kilograms. It was too much for a climb to 8000 metres. His team members objected on the grounds that Mike's team were getting it easy, only having to make one carry up to the Col.

Pat, Mick, Paul and Terry Tremble were furious. They felt their team had been written off. It was assumed Min, Mick and possibly Pat wouldn't have the strength to make it much further than the Col, and a clause in the plan allowed for the 'leftovers' to join the other teams on their summit bids—a separate attempt of their own would be difficult to support, resource-wise.

The next day no one moved from Camp Two. Discussions raged all day, as people tried to come up with alternate plans based on the principle of equal opportunity. There was talk of people not going up to Camp Three, rather back to Base Camp— that is, going on strike. For some reason people had forgotten the objective of the expedition was to get *someone* on the summit in the Bicentennial year. The willingness to work as a team to achieve that had been overlooked in the rush to fulfil individual ambitions. Austin was desperately trying to give everyone a go, but at the same time remain realistic and true to the cause of the

expedition. He wasn't very good at communicating his ideas and opinions—especially over the radio. Bruce eventually came up with a plan which satisfied everyone at Camp Two: essentially it required climbers to make a successful carry to the South Col before they so much as qualified for a summit bid. He radioed Austin and detailed the idea. Austin listened, but wouldn't budge. There was no choice—accept his plan, or go home.

Several more climbers arrived up from Base Camp, destined to complete their carries up to Camp Three. Zac's Yaks were heading up to Three to stay. There was only one tent pitched on the site, and since Terry Tremble and Mick Pezet were already occupying it, their first task would be to dig more platforms out of the face and erect an additional two tents. Then they would make the first of their designated trips to the Col. Terry Tremble had already tried to carry just one cylinder of oxygen above Camp Three, but had given up a long way short of the Col. Mick hadn't been feeling well enough to move beyond the 7300-metre camp, so he was spending the day resting, and would hopefully join Terry Tremble on another attempt to reach to Col the following day.

There was a great deal of tension and disappointment in all camps over the next few days. No one was able to crack the Col, let alone the summit. Phil had fallen on his way up to Camp Three, badly bruising his shoulder. Apparently he thought he had clipped into the fixed line and lent backwards to rest for a moment. He slid over 150 metres down the face before managing to 'self-arrest' by falling into a small crevasse. He was bloody lucky; most falls on the Lhotse Face end fatally.

Terry and Paul, on behalf of Pat's Rats, had failed to reach the 8000-metre pass on what was their second attempt. Mick Pezet, who had teamed up with Zac's Yaks temporarily, had developed cold feet shortly after setting out on 30 April. Only twenty minutes later, Terry McCullagh started experiencing an alarming tingling sensation in his hands, feet and face; he joined Mick back at Camp Three, and on radioed advice from Doctors Tony and Chris, he descended on oxygen to Base Camp. The rest of the team, Zac, Bruce and Jim Van Gelder, managed to move 36 kilograms of the expedition's gear, including three high-pressure oxygen cylinders, higher up the mountain, but ultimately they, too, failed to reach their target. Bruce managed to get as far as the Geneva Spur, a buttress of rock just below the traverse to the South Col. Zac and Jim only made it through the 'yellow band'—a 150-metre thick band of yellow schistose limestone undulating across the Lhotse Face between 7550 and 7700 metres. They scaled the band via its narrowest but steepest point, exhausting themselves on the virtually vertical layers of rock protruding from the icy face of the mountain.

Their efforts did little to boost morale. The South Col was proving to be the most critical obstacle; if it could not be attained, there was no way onto the summit. The plan had to change. Again.

Austin went back to the drawing board. To add insult to injury, the Tri-Nation Expedition were celebrating as their

The view from Camp Three, perched on a narrow ledge on the Lhotse Face, made up for the discomforts of the camp site. (Bruce Farmer)

Summit Team left Base Camp to begin their straight-through assault on the hill. Their Sherpas had carried countless loads and established both Camp Four and Five, during our expedition's fruitless attempts to reach the Col. Perhaps the loads the white Sherpas were required to carry were just too heavy … they would either have to reduce them and make twice as many trips, or make their carries breathing supplementary oxygen. It was 30 April, and Austin realised he could no longer hold onto the ideal of allowing everyone a chance to make a summit bid. He reassessed the objectives of the expedition, and began structuring a plan which would force people to put their personal aspirations aside, and start working for the success of the expedition. After hours and hours of carefully analysing each climber's performance, he finally picked a Summit Team.

Austin alerted Camp Two that he would announce details of the new plan, nicknamed 'Plan 365', on the 7.30 p.m. radio schedule. By that time Zac's Yaks would have returned to Camp Three, and would be in a position to receive the broadcast. Everyone waited impatiently for the schedule. How would the plan have changed? Who would be favoured, and who would have their chances weakened?

Peter Lambert and BJ had joined the crew stationed at Camp Two, comprising Andrew, Pat, Min, Paul and Terry Tremble. Lambo and BJ were gearing up to attempt the next carry to the Col, and were not very impressed with some of the talk Austin's intention had sparked. Lambo wrote in his diary:

> Again the "conspiracy" theory has raised its ugly head. Paul (and Pat to a lesser extent) considered that Austin and Mike Rheinberger were plotting to place Mike's team in the position to go for the top. I was quite astounded. I could not believe that someone like Austin would volunteer to be leader, then systematically go about destroying the morale of his team. I argued heatedly with Paul about this … I was beginning to think I was politically naive; and I got the feeling Paul and co. thought so too. Nonetheless, I could honestly say I had never seen any evidence to suggest that Austin was doing anything other than working his guts out to make the expedition succeed. I related how I had seen Austin working by lamplight late every night to readjust and refine plans. Terry Tremble then started to complain that the plans were changing too often! Again I was astounded. How could he expect the plan to stay the same on such a big mountain, with so many variables! … I thought Terry's expectations of Austin's leadership and planning were unreasonable and immature.

As Austin well expected, his new plan stunned everyone. A pregnant silence followed his announcement. He wanted six climbers in position at Camp Two to carry loads from Camp Three to the Col using oxygen. He then wanted two summiteers, Jon Muir and Chris Curry, supported by James Strohfeldt and Andrew Smith, to carry to Camp Four, again on oxygen. James and Andrew would establish Camp Five, making it possible for Jon and Chris to make their summit bid. This first attempt would be followed by a second, involving Jim Truscott and Mike Rheinberger, supported to Camp Five by Bruce Farmer and Phil Pitham. If resources, weather and time permitted, a third attempt

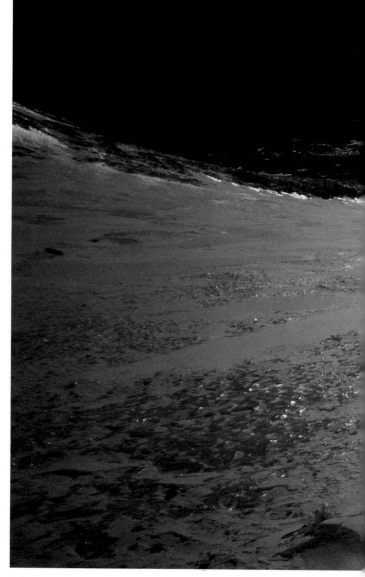

A lone climber makes another gruelling carry to Camp Three. (Chris Curry)

could be made, but at this stage, the participants would not be named.

Even Lambo, who had the utmost respect for his leader, had trouble digesting Austin's new plan.

> BJ and I and Pat's team were going to do oxygen-assisted carries to the Col in support of a Mike Rheinberger Summit Team. I am really perplexed—Is this it then? Is this to be the end of my chances? Austin was quite vague on the radio, so I put it to him bluntly: Would we have a chance, or were we out of it? Austin was non-committal. I was really concerned. I wanted Austin to tell me straight out; had he done so, I could accept it. But no, he said we would have a chance "just like everyone", after the first two attempts. Deep down I felt it couldn't be done—I didn't think we could support *and* also have a chance. I went silent on the radio; deep breathing and deep thought. What a personal dilemma! The worth of the team, versus the worth of all my efforts to this point! It was time for some rationalisation.

Discussions raged on long into the night. Pat's solution to the

debate came in the form of an immediate call for Sherpa assistance. A quick vote at Camp Two showed a 5 to 0 support for his idea, but a vote in Base Camp revealed a 0 to 9 defeat. If the expedition used Sherpas, they'd just be doing what everyone had done in the past; they wouldn't make history. BJ and Lambo then came up with a compromise: How about doing as Austin planned, to get some Aussies on top, *then* get Sherpas to help up the remainder of the summit hopefuls.

It was pretty useless trying to conduct the debate over the radio, so the next morning Austin and Norm trekked up to Camp Two to clarify 'Plan 365' and try and persuade people to work for the good of the team, and not themselves. Zac's team came down from Camp Three, so there was quite a crowd gathered in 'Parliament'. Camp Two had so earned its nickname because, as Chris Curry so eloquently put it, 'of the frequent question times, the heated debates, and the abuse that had come out of there recently'.

Those who could squeeze into the Camp Two kitchen tent did so, and the others gathered at the doorway. Lambo wrote:

The feelings were high—you could cut the air with a knife. Terry Tremble started out on an extremely rude and insulting tirade against Austin and his plans. Austin was becoming angry and upset to the point of tears. Pat joined in. I was disgusted by both Terry and Pat, so I jumped inside the tent to try and bring some sense to the discussions. Terry Tremble walked out and started heading back to Base Camp … The discussion cooled and eventually got fairly rational. It was all about the balance between team and personal goals—Pat continually harping that if we paid our $5000 dollars each, we should all get a go!

We eventually agreed to do the support climbing, and Austin agreed to see Kunga, the Tri-Nation's overall Nepalese leader, to arrange hiring Sherpas for the remainder of the climbers to have a go.

The crisis was over. The plan had been accepted by most, if grudgingly. Austin managed a smile, then set about working on yet more amendments to the load-carrying lists and calculations. BJ and Lambo helped Austin and Norm, as they were staying at Camp Two, and not high-tailing it with the others down to Base Camp for a rest. Min also stayed on at Camp Two, eager to team up with BJ and Lambo on their first oxygen-assisted support carry to the Col, scheduled to begin from Camp Three two or three days hence.

In spite of all the hours of planning and calculation, not to mention the emotional strain it weathered on everyone, the great, holy plan changed *again*.

The summit, as seen by climbers en route to the South Col. (Bruce Farmer)

When Austin and Norm made it back to Base Camp the next day, they were presented with suggestions for 'Plan 366'. There had been a long discussion at Base Camp in their absence, and Mike Rheinberger devised a plan which he felt would satisfy everybody; the individualists as well as their team-spirited leader. He knew his suggestions would not necessarily improve the chances of the expedition's success, but they would serve to rectify the current collapse of team morale. What they needed most right now was a little solidarity; not a half-hearted group of individuals running around with their noses out of joint. The Anzac Day unity, it seemed, had well and truly gone out the window.

In essence, Mike's plan meant his team, Jon, Jim Truscott, James Strohfeldt and himself, together with Chris Curry, would carry most of the stores needed to stock Camp Four, and one oxygen cylinder each to the Col. They would then return to Camp Two for a brief rest, then climb up again for the first summit attempt, carrying all their personal gear and just one high-pressure cylinder each. There would be no Camp Five. Their summit push would begin the hard way; from the Col itself. The second and subsequent teams would only have to carry their own *two* oxygen cylinders each to the Col, before returning for their own attempts on the summit, using all the gear Mike's team had put in place.

The two plans went to the polls. Mike's came out on top, 8 votes to 7. Unfortunately, Lambo, BJ and Min were up on the hill and out of radio reach. As it happened, they would have supported Austin's plans; but that news came far too late to turn the tables. Mike's plan was in. Interestingly, all of Dad's Army, including Mike, voted against Mike's plan, for while it put them in position for the first summit bid, the extra work it involved could prove to be a detriment to the overall team chance of attaining the summit. Chris interpreted the plan, writing:

It would give the whole expedition less chance of getting someone to the top, but would allow more people with less support to have a go and fail. It also allowed those who didn't want to use Sherpas to have a go first, and then the rest if they want to.

After the meeting, Austin returned to the office tent, and recorded his feelings onto his diary tape:

Theoretically, and I guess for all people practically, we are at an impossible stage. It seems in essence that both our plans would coincide—circumstances and logistics and everything else would force that. But there is still an essential difference in philosophy ie individual effort and opportunity versus the co-operative team approach. We had an open forum session because whatever plan we were going to choose the essential things were to have *unity*, to see that people understood the issues clearly, made up their own minds and got in behind one approach or the other. The point was to ease the divisions that had crept in. Why they crept in, of course, is another matter. In a way it is inevitable there would be differences at this stage of the expedition because people are tired and it's been a long haul.

Climbers are personally ambitious — they may well have understood that the team effort was important, but they obviously saw the greatest benefit for the team coming from individual success …

As fate would have it, Day One of the new plan was nothing short of disastrous. Andrew (who had volunteered to do a carry in support of Dad's Army) and Mike Rheinberger broke through the glacier on their way from Base Camp to the Icefall, and submerged chest deep in the icy waters beneath its surface. They had to return to Base Camp to dry (and thaw) out. Jim Truscott and Chris continued up to Camp Two, but Mike and Andrew's accident meant that Plan 366 was already a day off schedule. The other two members of Dad's Army, Jon and James, had decided not to use oxygen on their summit bid, so they were not required to make the first carry to the Col. They were free to wander down to Lobuje, or just hang out at Base Camp, and rest themselves for their attempt.

Higher on the hill, Min, BJ and Lambo were getting ready to try and 'crack the Col'. Bad weather prevented them from climbing onto the Lhotse Face, but they managed to dump half the oxygen supplies they would be carrying to the Camp Four site at the foot of the icy slope. They returned to Camp Two to wait for a better spell of weather.

Fortuitously, the next day was perfect. The three set out, but Min felt quite sick and turned back. BJ and Lambo reached Camp Three in the average time of six hours. When they arrived, the three tents were all but buried in spindrift and snow from the previous day's storm. Exhausted from the climb, they had to spend another hour digging out their tent.

On the whole of the Lhotse Face, which sloped at an average 40 degrees, there was no natural place to pitch a tent. Pat and Paul, and later Zac's team, had done their best to dig out and improve the site, but come what may, it was (and always would be) the lousiest camp on the hill. No one slept well there; it was just too cramped. Lambo described it:

Camp Three was easily the most loathsome camp on the hill. The narrow tunnel tents were the only thing we could fit on the face, and they were extremely uncomfortable. Since we were staying in the lower of the three tents, we also had the worst deal. Being the first tent people reached from Camp Two, there was a tendency for everybody to dump their loads there before heading back down. All the extra crap made the limited space even tighter.

It snowed again during the night, and the entrance to BJ and Lambo's tent was covered over. Lambo awoke with a severe headache and quickly realised he and BJ (who was feeling nauseous) were suffering from carbon dioxide poisoning. There was a lethal lack of oxygen in the tent, so Lambo frantically dug out the tent doorway. The list of dangers encountered in a high-altitude environment just never seemed to end. If it wasn't an avalanche, then it was the threat of cerebral oedema … if it wasn't a fall into a crevasse, it was hypothermia … if it wasn't frostbite, it was something else … on and on and on.

Just as the Japanese film and climbing crews had ordered, 5 May dawned clear. High up on the huge summit peak of Chomolungma, the Tri-Nation team were taking their last few steps towards victory—from both sides of the mountain. Lower down on the south side, Lambo was slowly pacing out a smaller, but equally significant success for the Australian Expedition.

The Tri-Nation Expedition, after successfully summiting on 5 May, bequeathed their Camp Four tents and left-over oxygen supplies to the Australian team. (Zac Zaharias)

BJ and Lambo had risen early, brewed and force-fed themselves with date biscuits. Loss of appetite was a common side-effect of high altitude, even for hollow-legged climbers like Lambo. The walls and roof of their tent were covered in hoar frost, and as the sun rose, it started dripping all over their sleeping bags and clothing. They spent a full hour getting dressed (and wet), then emerged from the tent to pack their loads.

Unfortunately BJ wasn't feeling well enough to make the first oxygen-assisted carry to the Col, so Lambo had to go it alone. It worried him a bit, since his only other experience of climbing to 8000 metres (on Broad Peak) very nearly cost him his life. On the push to attain that summit, Lambo carelessly allowed himself to dehydrate, his body temperature dropped and he became exhausted *and* frostbitten. If it weren't for BJ encouraging him

down from the summit, Lambo believed he would have killed himself during the descent.

Fearful of a repeat performance, he decided he had to concentrate on every move he made and every minute that passed. Every few steps, he would stop to think through what he called a 'body systems check', paying particular attention to drinking and eating enough high-energy snacks. Lambo recorded his journey to the Col in his diary:

I was carrying a tent and breathing from a low-pressure oxygen cylinder. At Zac's high point just above the yellow band, I had to pick up a high-pressure oxygen cylinder, a mat and some cooking sets. All in all it would be about 18–20 kilos to carry to the Col … I climbed across the snow slope to the yellow band. A short but steepish pitch at the start—a high rate of oxygen flow for that, then, once over the top, I moved up a short scrabbly bit of snow on rock. The rock under the snow made the short pitch extremely uncomfortable. I traversed

through the yellow band, then on a further rope length to Zac's Yaks cache … I was beginning to wonder whether the oxygen cylinder I was breathing from was worth carrying.

The snow on the next slope was about ankle deep, and I moved slowly across and up to the base of the Geneva Spur. I glanced up towards the summit of Lhotse every now and then, wondering how stable the slope was above me. Step slide, step slide, step slide—the movement of my feet and the Petzl jumar built up a rhythm. I counted my steps, aiming at taking forty steps before leaning over and resting on my ice-axe. At one of the anchors, I stopped for a while longer. The view down the Lhotse Face and right along the Western Cwm was spectacular. Above me the clouds were stringing out—blown off Everest and Lhotse by high winds. I had a drink; it didn't do me any good—I threw up on the spot …

It seemed to go on for ever; the top seemed a long way away for the whole climb. I started to worry about time now: would I get to the Col with enough time to descend safely to Camp Three? I decided, come what may, I would have to turn around at 3.30 p.m. I pulled myself up over the edge of the Geneva Spur. From there, I could see I would make it without any problems.

About a kilometre away, I could see the South Col. A couple of Sherpas were coming down the ropes and they said I had just one hour to go. It was an easy traverse around the spur and onto the Col. As I moved up, more and more of the Col came into view. It was a huge place, and as far as I could see, there were signs of past visits; tattered tents and oxygen cylinders everywhere …I picked up one of the cylinders and turned the top. Oxygen burst out of the nozzle. Great! I tried a few more, and found a second half full one. Perhaps we wouldn't have to carry up as many as we thought!

Just in sight of the Tri-Nation Camp Four, I dropped my load. It was great to be here; my second time to 8000 metres and I felt so much better this time around. I looked up the slopes towards the South Summit, trying to identify the route.

Hopefully I'd be back in a week or two to climb it. I met a couple of Japanese climbers and we took photos of each other. They couldn't speak English and I couldn't speak Japanese, so we grunted and smiled without learning anything from each other.

I started back down for Camp Three. It felt really good to have reached the Col with a load. I wonder what might have happened to team morale if I had turned back, or had an accident? I was beaming; just beaming all the way back to Camp Three.

When Base Camp received the news of Lambo's breakthrough, they were as jubilant as their victorious Tri-Nation neighbours. The Japanese had not only succeeded in their endeavour to put their expedition on the summit on 5 May, but had also managed to transmit the feat *live* around the world. The only downers in the whole day were the fact that no Japanese climbers from the south side managed to top out, and even though $A17 million worth of hard cash and technology had been invested in the project, the sponsoring television network in Japan only got to telecast five minutes of the event. Unfortunately the expedition's ultimate triumph coincided with the screening of a baseball match. The network didn't want to disappoint fans by interrupting the game with crummy satellite pictures *and* sound from the highest point on the globe!

Lambo's news that half full oxygen cylinders lay strewn across the Col pleased everyone. This was no time to be environmentally aware; the litter would be useful, and perhaps the Aussies could get away with carrying less of their own cylinders to Camp Four.

When Austin returned from extending his congratulations to the Tri-Nation leaders, he brought even gladder tidings. Kunga had suggested the Australian team may be able to take advantage of the Tri-Nation's Camp Four and Five facilities, once they were no longer needed by his expedition. That included the tents, whatever remained in the way of food and gas, and an estimated fifteen to twenty 800-litre cylinders of oxygen. Coupled with Lambo's discovery and triumph, it seemed a miraculous coup.

Over the next week additional carries were made by the team without any trouble at all. Lambo had not only overcome the physical obstacle, he had broken the psychological barrier it had imposed on the climbers. The day after his success, Jim Truscott and Chris reached the Col without oxygen and added two high-pressure cylinders, two regulators and masks and a dozen Gaz bottles to the cache.

On 7 May, Mike Rheinberger and Andrew also reached the Camp Four 'dump' without oxygen and took the high-pressure bottle total to five. Andrew decided to stay up with Mike's team to make another carry. A day later Pat and Norm used a low-pressure cylinder each to carry a sixth high-pressure bottle and what remained of Bruce's stash onto the Col. It was an amazing effort by Norm, the Base Camp manager who had never climbed before! He had done so much more than was expected of him, and even though he had no prospects at all of going to the summit, he willingly contributed to the load-carrying tasks of the team. His attempt to reach the Col had the blessing of all team members, and their praise on learning of his success was equally

genuine. Norm was one hell of a guy who deserved all the acclaim he received.

On 10 May, Terry Tremble carried a high-pressure cylinder to the Col, and Paul used oxygen to get another high-pressure and one low-pressure bottle up. Mike's team moved up to Camp Three, ready to make their second carry and summit bid. Everything was just dandy up there on the hill; everything but the weather.

Strong winds from Tibet continued to ravage the Col, so Mike kept his team stationed at Camp Three. The Tri-Nation team had made a second successful summit bid, but the two climbers responsible—Sundare and Karma, a Nepalese Army sergeant—had lost their snow goggles during the descent and were now severely snowblind and waiting up on the Col for assistance. Sundare had his fifth Chomolungma guernsey—at a price. If it had not been possible for a Sherpa to go to his aid, he and Karma could well have perished. They had spent five days on or above the Col waiting for and making their summit dash. The only people to have ever stayed longer in or above the 8000-metre camp never made it off the mountain. A team of four Indians in 1985 were held on the Col by storms for nine days. The last one died just ten minutes after the rescue party arrived. Six days was believed to be the maximum time anyone could spend at such an altitude and still have the strength to descend. Sundare and his partner were getting dangerously close to that cut-off point.

A point in Sundare's favour was that he was well acclimatised, having made a record-breaking ascent of Pumo Ri in eleven hours, prior to joining up with the Tri-Nation team. After a brief refuelling in Lobuje, he had climbed straight through to the Col, and probably would have motored on up to the summit, had it not been for the wind. Eventually Major Taba, who was keen to be responsible for getting the first-ever Nepalese Army representative to the top of the world, *ordered* Sundare and Karma to make their bid regardless of the conditions. They had obeyed.

The following day the wind continued to gust on the face, but by evening it was remarkably still. Sundare and Karma were helped down the mountain and Mike's team prepared to go up to the Col the next morning.

Jon and Chris had a particularly bad night in the cramped quarters of their tent, as Chris recorded:

I didn't sleep *at all*. The collapsing tent wall crowded close to my face. I couldn't breathe through my nose, so I got a terribly dry throat. For the first time in my life, I kept drinking during the night. Jon didn't sleep much either, and kept kicking his feet about next to my head. It was a very, very long night.

At 6.00 a.m. conditions were still good, and Mike's team got ready for their last trip up to the Col. However, by 7.00 a.m. there was a huge plume blowing off the summit, indicating very strong, high winds. Mike decided his team should descend, rather than risk having to spend time on the Col, waiting for a break in the weather. They had already spent a week at Camp Three and above, and most of the team felt too tired and drained to spend more than the minimum amount of time up higher. They

The South Col and wind-ravaged South Summit. (Zac Zaharias)

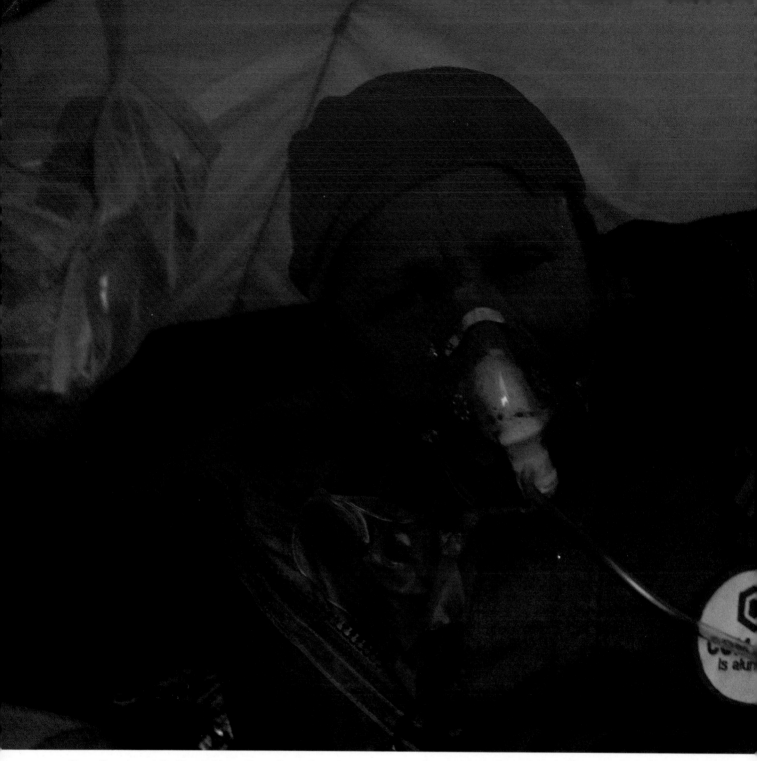

Bruce Farmer and Jim Van Gelder at Camp Four. (Peter Lambert)

would still have time for a second shot at the summit later in the month. Zac's Yaks, together with Lambo (whose team had disbanded since BJ had decided against going higher, and Andrew had hooked into Mike's team), were now at Camp Two ready to jump into position and make the expedition's first summit attempt. Now that the Tri-Nationers had formally handed over their Camp Four and Five to the Australian team, it was unnecessary for them to do a full double carry to the Col. Very few expedition members begrudged Zac and his team their position, although Mike's team, understandably, were a little depressed at the prospect of handing over the lead. Even Chris, who had not wanted to retreat, wrote:

We are now going to have teams moving through in rotation, so everyone at least gets a look in at 'going for it'. We were obliged to move up, and then down, because Zac's Yaks were hard on our heels. We couldn't have hung out at the Col for a couple of days; for lack of time, as well as condition. We are at the sharp end of the expedition now. It's going to be hell watching others have a go first. There's always going to be that feeling that if I'd only been a bit more forceful …

That night the forecast was for 60-knot winds at 9000 metres and temperatures (not including the wind-chill factor) of –30°C. But the next day, Friday the Thirteenth, things improved. When Zac, Lambo, Jim Van Gelder and Bruce reached Camp Three late in the afternoon, the temperature was a pleasant –10°C, and the

at all. Mick would be assisting Austin in carrying eight or nine oxygen cylinders up to Camp Two, and Phil had volunteered to maintain the route through the Icefall, now that the Tri-Nation Sherpas were leaving the mountain. His efforts did not go unnoticed, in fact Chris was moved to write:

> Phil is a hero. He takes on the most thankless tasks, and does them with passion and vehemence. Now he has taken on the preserving of our Icefall route from scavenging Sherpas (Sherpas make good retail out of used ladders, snow-stakes, rope, etc.) and maintaining it as well. A difficult task on your own.

Apart from summit-man-power, time was also starting to run out. All the expedition members were supposed to leave Base Camp on 27 May; just two weeks hence. Norm had already sorted out excess gear, and had arranged for yaks and porters to begin taking these loads down valley.

Prior to the Tri-Nation triumph, only one out of the last eighteen expeditions managed to reach the summit. We longed to add our names to the short-list of victors, but the chances of success were growing slimmer each day. The pressure was on.

On 14 May it was still snowing in Base Camp but Zac's Yaks were able to push on through the higher cloudy conditions to the Col. It was the first time Zac, Bruce and Jim Van Gelder had reached the 8000-metre pass. They had each used a low-pressure cylinder of oxygen this time, and found the going a hell of a lot easier for it. They dug out what remained of their group cache above the yellow band and added it to their loads. By the time they reached the Col, it was snowing lightly and visibility was poor.

They located the three bright orange Tri-Nation tents. They were thrilled to find them intact as it meant they wouldn't have to pitch their own smaller ones. They spent some time cleaning up the tents, then set about making themselves at home in them. This would be the expedition's first overnight stay on the Col, and thanks to the roomy Tri-Nation domes and availability of low-pressure oxygen for sleeping, Zac's Yaks would be a great deal more comfortable than they, and their predecessors, had been at Camp Three.

Sunday 15 May dawned clear and windless. Zac's Yaks spent the day scavenging cylinders of oxygen discarded all over the Col and sorted out what resources the Tri-Nation team had left. There was plenty of food, Epi-Gas and five half full and nine full oxygen bottles. In all, they now had nine Australian high-pressure cylinders, the Tri-Nation bottles, and six other smaller cylinders with about 2000 pounds per square inch (14 mega-pascals) in each.

However, when Zac's Yaks arrived at Camp Four on their summit attempt, they found only eight Australian high-pressure bottles. It became obvious that a member of the carrying parties had stashed a bottle. Such was the paranoia of some members of the team who felt they might miss out on a summit attempt.

Apart from the missing oxygen bottle, the main problem now at Camp Four was the missing Tri-Nation oxygen regulators. The Australian apparatus did not fit on the foreign cylinders,

wind above near the Col had eased quite noticeably. It was snowing in Base Camp, but Zac and his team were above the clouds. Sadly, Terry was not with them; he had turned around only half an hour out of Camp Two. He had been vomiting all night and felt too weak and nauseous to continue.

The climbers were dropping like flies. BJ was out, Phil Pitham had had so many accidents it was fairly obvious he did not want to risk a summit attempt, Andrew was weighing up his options but clearly leaning towards the 'giving up' elective, Mick and Min hoped to join the rest of Pat's team on their summit attempt but they had deteriorated so badly it was unlikely they'd make it beyond Camp Three, and now Terry seemed doomed to concede.

All of them were still keen to help the team effort in any way which left Zac's Yaks with little option but to use the Australian resources. Earlier discussions involving most of the expedition members had led to a general consensus that there should be an equal distribution of oxygen between the teams. Zac would not be popular if he failed to comply, no matter how sound his reasoning.

That evening, Zac moved out to a point above the Geneva Spur (in order to get clear reception) and radioed Austin. He announced his team would be setting out from the Col at midnight. Austin strongly advised Zac to consider only using four of the high-pressure cylinders on their summit bid, leaving the rest for a subsequent attempt. He suggested two of the climbers sacrifice their summit aspirations by 'plugging steps'— an exhausting and demoralising process—for the two strongest team members, in order to maximise the expedition's chances of success. Zac pointed out that there were still another eight high-pressure cylinders at Base Camp or Camp Two. Surely anyone wishing to make an attempt could carry up their own cylinder; after all, there was already sufficient food, sleeping bags, tentage and gas on the Col. Having alleviated the need for carrying these resources in their packs, there would be more than enough room for additional oxygen. Failing that, all they had to do was locate the Tri-Nation regulators and they would have another nine instantly useful bottles!

Austin had agreed that at this stage in the expedition Zac's Yaks had the best prospect of all to top out. They were in the right place at the right time. Zac clearly didn't want to jeopardise his team's chances by skimping on oxygen, nor risk making a mistake by picking the wrong summit pair. Austin stressed his suggestion again, but left the final resolution to Zac—adding that he would support Zac's decision, either way.

Zac went back to the tent and conferred with Lambo, Jim Van Gelder and Bruce. They agreed unanimously to use eight cylinders. No one wanted to accept Austin's judgement, nor forfeit their personal ambitions, as suggested. They were headstrong and 100 per cent certain they could make it; if they shared the step-plugging struggle, they would undoubtedly share the glory of success. Austin did not expect the team to reschedule their final intentions, so, confidence high, Zac and his Yaks melted snow, filled their water bottles, and rested up for their ultimate challenge.

There was no moon that evening, and at midnight, Zac's Yaks couldn't see a thing. They organised their gear, had one last drink and finally left the Col at 1.30 a.m. It was –30°C but, fortunately, very calm.

The cold continued to taunt the climbers until sunrise. As they approached the Japanese Camp Five site, the sky began to glow, but relief was short-lived, for the wind picked up quite suddenly. Lambo felt it biting through his multiple layers of Gore-Tex, down and Damart, and began worrying about the very real threat of frostbite.

From Camp Five, the snow deepened and became more unstable—powder snow on rock and ice-slabs. This wasn't going to be an easy day at all. They only pleasant thing about the early morning slog was the view—to the east lay Makalu and Kanchenjunga, to the West, Manaslu and the Annapurna Ranges. Jim Van Gelder had joked that he only wanted to climb

Zac's Yaks struggle through deep snow at 8400 metres. (Zac Zaharias)

Chomolungma to 'check out a new route on Kanchenjunga'. He had no idea the Mother Goddess would prove so demanding; he only managed a longing glance over to the smaller peak, then refocused his total concentration on the hill at hand.

It had taken them six hours to reach the Tri-Nation Camp Five; six hours to cover a vertical distance of just 350 metres. They suspected they would run out of time, but pushed on regardless. The snow went from knee to thigh deep. Bruce was out in front, blazing the trail up the 45–50-degree slope. He took three or four steps, then collapsed on the snow to recover. Thirty gasps later, he stood up and made another four steps, collapsed

again and recovered. After 100 metres, Zac relieved him, then in turn, Lambo and Jim plugged the way, at times actually having to dig steps with their ice axes. They had never done anything more exhausting in their lives.

Twelve and a half hours after leaving the Col, they reached the South Ridge, at 8580 metres. Chomolungma had beaten them. They would not have enough time to climb the final slopes leading to the South Summit, then traverse along the ridge to the top *and* return to the Col before nightfall. They were devastated. They had not overestimated their abilities; just grossly underestimated the severity of the conditions. They should have started out much earlier, or staggered their assault over two days, taking advantage of the Tri-Nation Camp Five.

It would be too big a risk to continue, and attempting to descend in the dark without oxygen was completely out of the question. They sat together for half an hour, each man silently swallowing his fate, then slowly began retracing their steps.

When the rest of the team learned that Zac's Yaks had not only failed to summit, but used the eight Australian oxygen cylinders as well, they were all furious. Austin's advice had been rejected in favour of what some perceived was selfishness. They called for a conference, to reassess the situation, and rethink the plan.

After the meeting, Chris wrote in his diary:

I was very forceful—fierce—in stating it was time people stopped wafting about in Fantasyland, and decided as an

expedition to back Austin Brookes. Every plan he's put up has been diluted or destroyed by self-interest. His plans have been designed to maximise our chances of getting someone on the summit, by having some climbers support the strongest. Conventional expedition tactics. But these jerks have got it into their heads that they can *all* climb Everest. It's amazing.

We resolved that we should go back to Austin's original plan of using a Camp Five, and of a big team carrying in support of two or three summiteers.

Pat's team missed the conference, as they had moved up to Camp Two in readiness for their own team summit attempt. Austin radioed them with details of the new plan, which, as one could well imagine, did not sit well with them at all. While Dad's Army (the original five minus Phil Pitham, plus Chris Curry) prepared to go up to the Col again, Pat, Paul and Terry Tremble decided to continue with their own summit plan.

Zac's team came down to Camp Two on 17 May, and Pat's team moved up to Camp Three the following day. On the way, Terry felt quite sick and returned to Base Camp. Pat and Paul were rock solid in their determination and continued on, finally reaching the Col late in the afternoon of 19 May—around the same time Mike's team (less Jim, who had had a last minute change of heart) settled into Camp Three. Terry McCullagh was climbing in support of Mike's team, and hoped to take a load through to the Col for them. There was the chance, of course, that he could join them on their summit bid, if he felt strong enough.

Dad's Army spent a reasonably comfortable night at Camp Three—everyone but Jon, that is. He spent the whole night vomiting up worms. Yes, *worms!* Fifteen- to twenty-centimetre-long roundworms. He was still having problems the next morning, and since he was unable to keep any fluid down, he had started to dehydrate. He had to go back to Base Camp. He had spent nine months on Chomolungma, trying to reach the summit. Nine whole bloody months! It didn't seem fair, but Jon accepted his fate with his usual good humour. There was always the possibility he could recover at Camp Two and rejoin his team mates on the Col—or go it alone if they were away before he returned.

The rest of Dad's Army made it up to the wind-ravaged South Col that afternoon, and prepared to wait, as Pat and Paul were doing, for a break in the weather. They waited ... and waited ... and waited. Hours became days. On the second day, Chris was already agitated and bored, writing of the experience:

Howling wind No movement. Lying about gets very tedious. There's a comic in our tent, but it's in Hindi. I look at the pictures over and over again. There's a woman who has incredible legs and wears a mini-skirt; real Hindi movie stuff. Even that gets boring ...

By 21 May, Terry McCullagh had become quite dehydrated and had to go down. Mike, Chris and James were having trouble communicating with Pat and Paul, even though their tents were only a couple of metres apart; the wind was so strong they could

At 8550 metres, Peter Lambert, Jim Van Gelder and Bruce Farmer abandon all hope of reaching the summit. (Zac Zaharias)

barely hear themselves, and no amount of shouting helped. It was too cold and windy to venture outside the tent for anything—calls of nature included.

With Terry on his way down, Mike Rheinberger and James Strohfeldt soberly considered the team's and their own chances of gaining the summit. Outside, the wind howled, temperatures hovered around −25 to −35°C and the weather forecasts were pessimistic. Mike was determined that he should not leave the mountain until he had given his best. James, too, wanted a go at the summit, but for him participation and doing his best for the team seemed to be sufficient. Mike was in a personal dilemma. He knew that in good health, Chris, Paul and even James had been faster through the camps than he. However, he had been a consistent performer, without sickness, and much faster than Pat. He believed the best chance of a team success would be gained by establishing Camp Five at around 8350–8400 metres, or by using the Japanese Camp Five, if its tent was serviceable. Clearly team success was more likely if two climbers were selected as the lead pair and the others moved in support, helping to break trail and carrying support oxygen.

In the solitude of their tent, Mike and James stewed over the situation until James won the upper hand and Mike agreed that they would support Chris and Paul in an initial summit bid the following day, provided the weather improved beyond the horrendous 50–60-knot winds which blasted the Col. Chris was called to the tent and concurred with the plan, although he indicated that he would stay for only one further day, being well aware of overall deterioration at that altitude.

Pat was called to the tent and the plan outlined. Pat was aghast and argued vehemently that the climbers' expedition contributions of $5000 should guarantee everyone a shot at the summit. There followed a bitter scene between him and Rheinberger who had been placed in control of all personnel on the Col. Invective flew on invective, fuelled by anger and frustration. Finally in disgust, Reinberger told Pat to exercise his own judgement and the meeting broke up in a bitter mood.

Outside, the wind howled and the evening radio schedule predicted continuing poor conditions. Later, Pat returned to Mike's tent, apologising for his outburst and promising to help in the carries. As it happened, the wind never abated and in the morning Chris and James decided to descend. Pat and Paul, who had already been on the Col for a day longer than the others, decided to stay, now joined by Mike. Pat had been keeping a record of everything he and Paul were drinking and eating in order to stay on top of the dehydration problem and felt confident they could hang on a few days longer.

Another day (23 May) went by. Personal differences temporarily buried, Pat, Paul and Mike prepared themselves to begin a summit push that evening, provided the weather relented. It didn't. When the next day dawned as gusty and violent as ever, Mike decided to descend.

Pat and Paul stayed. The winds had not eased since they arrived on the Col, but their faith in themselves remained as unshakeable as the mighty Mother Goddess herself. They would match the fury of the elements with their own dogged, powerful sense of determination. They would not be the first to break. It had to be the weather.

Paul catches Pat in action from the top of the world. (Paul Bayne)

9
Down Under on Top

Chapter Nine

Down Under on Top

In ordinary mountaineering terms, the risk isn't justifiable. I know that. But this is Everest, and on Everest you sometimes have to take the long odds, because the goal is worth it. Or so I try to tell myself…

Sir Edmund Hillary,
writing of the 1953 British Expedition

The elusive summit of Chomolungma.

Austin was breathless. His voice was agonisingly slow and raspy. He was tired and his lungs were aching from the powder snow he had inhaled while running from an avalanche the previous day. There had only been two potentially dangerous avalanches during the whole expedition, and both had targeted the tinny old leader. He slumped into the office tent, and switched on his tape recorder. He said nothing for a moment, just breathed heavily as if making a suggestive phone call. 'I guess the "Big E" has beaten me again,' he finally gasped between great gulps of air and sighs of depression. It was 10.00 a.m. on 24 May, and the expedition was drawing to an unsuccessful close. There wasn't an ounce of optimism left in his mind. It was over. The team had failed. After all the work—labouring backwards and forwards, up and down through the Icefall, the Cwm and the Lhotse Face—time had finally run out. Chomolungma had won again. The expedition had run out of energy, luck, and now time.

Pat and Paul were still up on the desolate South Col; still waiting for some magical force to abate the horrendous 60-knot winds. They would not move until the gods allowed them a chance to make just one summit bid. They had been there for five and a half days now, and Austin had every right to not only doubt the pair had enough strength left to make it to the summit, but also fear for their lives. No non-Sherpa had ever survived more than six days on or above the Col. Any attempt now would be touch and go. The line between life and death would be so fine, most mountaineers would not accept the risk, even if the weather and snow conditions were absolutely perfect for summiting. Most climbers would retreat while they still had the energy to move, unassisted. But Pat and Paul were not at all like most climbers.

The dogged pair were making very few radio schedules to Camp Two. It was not possible to make contact with Base Camp directly, so messages and reports had to be relayed down the mountain. To make matters worse, it was impossible to get a clear reception from Camp Four, so any contact at all necessitated

a 100-metre struggle through the howling wind to a point where the South Col met the Geneva Spur. The return trip to and from the lonely, claustrophobic tents on the Col took at least an hour to prepare for, and no less than half an hour to complete. Every step of the way was potentially disastrous—the climbers risked hypothermia, losing their balance and falling, or losing their fingers to frostbite.

Apart from these physical restraints, Pat and Paul were limiting their contact so as to avoid the inevitable: sooner or later Austin's pleas to abandon their vigil on the Col would turn to an order. There was a limit to the number of times they could argue for 'just one more day' and get away with it. That very morning Austin had tried to talk Pat and Paul into quitting while they still had enough strength in their bodies to descend unaided, but as usual, his request was met with the same unshakeable resolve that had brought the men to Chomolungma in the first place. They were there to conquer it, to 'take the hill', and damn it, they had no intention of coming down until they had at least given it their best shot. All they needed was a break in the weather. One lousy little break … And they promised Austin if it didn't come that night, they would indeed descend.

A number of climbers were packing up and preparing to leave Base Camp as well. The expedition's time was growing short. Some members had to return to Australia with prior commitments whilst others were required to get the expedition organisation in Kathmandu geared up for the return to Australia.

Van Gelder had to get his frostbitten toes down-valley and one climber had just had enough. It was just as well Chris Curry, although he resented the responsibility, was still strong enough to climb in the event of a rescue, and lucky Carol had stayed on to offer some professional medical support at Base Camp as the team doctor had left to organise an elephant safari.

Min Moor, Mick Pezet and BJ were the weakest of the climbers and all in desperate need of rest. All three had lost between 10 and 15 kilograms of weight, but they were adamant that they would stay on the mountain until the bitter end. Despite their condition, they were prepared to help in any way and firmly believed in the 'all hands on deck' principle. The Australian Army were lucky to have such men on side, and I take back every harsh word I've ever said about Min Moor. He was worth his weight (not that there was much left of it) in gold.

If, by some miracle, Pat and Paul made it to the top *and* managed to survive, they would be declared heroes. In the eyes of the media, and therefore the public, they alone would drink from the champions' cup. In the rush to raise the victors high on a pedestal, the efforts of people like Min, Mick and BJ would be completely overlooked. Our society never acknowledges the players, only the winners—we never hear about any individual Olympic competitors unless they bring home gold. So, it was unlikely anyone would hear about the gutsy gallants of our own sporting endeavour. All praise to them.

The tension cog at Camp Two and Base wound on another

The debilitating effect of altitude is obvious in these 'Mr Puniverse Contestants'; (left to right) Zac, Min, BJ, Mick, and Lambo. (Zac Zaharias)

notch. Pat's and Paul's determination had long passed its 'admirable' stage, and of the climbers left, most believed their obstinacy was irresponsible. Anxiety and fear turned to anger, as perseverance turned to perversity. Pat and Paul had put their own lives on the line, but in the event of a rescue, others would also be at risk. Chris Curry vented his growing hostility towards the maligned duo in his diary:

They're bloody-minded fools and want to be heroes. I don't believe that, even if they had perfect conditions, they'd have the strength to summit. Austin had warned them, "Remember, you're not Sherpas." They've obviously forgotten. So what's the point in getting an endurance record for living above 8000 metres? The Lhotse Face is getting icier and more difficult every day—descending maybe even more hazardous if they exhaust themselves with a vain summit attempt. Today Austin, via radio contact with Camp Two, was adamant Pat and Paul had just one more day (25 May) to have a shot at the top, and Paul said they'd have to go for it, whatever the conditions. But agreements have gone out the window. So has loyalty to leadership. Austin has been having to deal with spoiled and/or delinquent children who haven't been getting

their own way, for weeks. Pat and Paul's behaviour is incredibly irresponsible. How are we going to cope if they can't get down for some reason? If we had the means, Pat deserves a court martial. This "do or die" stuff is shit.

At 9.00 p.m. that night, Pat radioed Camp Two, where BJ, Terry McCullagh and Mike Rheinberger were keeping a lonely vigil to hold the communications open to Base Camp, to say that the wind had died down a little, and he and Paul were going to start ascending from the Col in half an hour. In spite of all the ill-feeling, everyone wished the emaciated pair the best of luck. Austin resorted to sleeping pills for some relief from worry, but before dozing off, he switched on this tape recorder, took a deep breath and recorded:

I guess the ultimate adventure is now for Pat and Paul. But everyone has obviously contributed to the possibility of the success of their attempt. All I want is that they get back in one piece. No mountain is ever worth disfigurement. Anyway, I hope that their strength, both in character and body, will allow them to succeed. It's obviously not as difficult as waiting; that *certainly* is not easy.

Up on the Col, Pat and Paul readied themselves for the climb. They had spent the whole day in separate tents preparing for their one and only assault on the summit, praying that the weather conditions would improve just enough to allow them that chance. They had boiled and brewed all day, forcing themselves to drink and eat in order to restore a little energy to their enervated bodies. Pat was so physically drained, just jiggling a tea bag up and down in his cup had become a major effort. Five and a half days on the South Col had really taken their toll. At 8000 metres above sea-level, the altitude had stripped what little fat Pat and Paul had on their torsos and was eating away at their muscle tissue. The sustained lack of oxygen had not only drained them of energy, but deprived them of sleep and now, one by one, their numbed brain cells were dying. It was a hell of a state to be in on the eve of a summit bid.

Pat made lists of what he was going to need and which pocket of his oversuit it could be found in. He double-checked he had everything, triple-checked, and just to be sure, checked again. Such meticulous preparations reduced the dangers and risks; if Pat was caught out higher up the mountain and forced to bivouac, he knew he would survive. Austin was sceptical, but Pat always carried a space blanket, spare food and a stove in case he was benighted, and had proved, while saving the life of the German climber on Broad Peak, that he could subsist above 8000 metres with nothing but these few meagre resources.

Pat had seven layers of clothing beneath his wind-proof suit. He was ready ahead of Paul, who took another hour and a half to ensure his socks and boots were completely dry and perfectly fitting. One could never be too cautious in attempting to prevent frostbite. When Paul had finished the task, he took out his small tape recorder and left one last message:

I don't know what to say. I think we can make it. I'm going to be pushing regardless of what it looks like up there; because

I've decided I'm going to climb the bugger. It's as simple as that. That's all there is to it … In weather like this, it's going to be pretty hard to get down again … I miss you guys … I better get moving … I'm just not interested in failing. I *am* going to get up this hill—*for sure*. See you guys soon. I sure as hell am looking forward to coming home!

At 10.15 p.m. Paul was finally ready to leave. He and Pat put their oxygen bottles in their backpacks, turned on their head torches, zipped up their tents, and turned to face the mountain of all mountains—Chomolungma, the Mother Goddess of the Universe.

Paul looked down at his pack. It took him a couple of minutes to build up enough mental energy to just lift the thing onto his back. He had been psyching himself up for this particular moment for a year and a half. Pat had been dreaming of it ever since he learnt to climb, and most of his professional and extra-curricular efforts over the past five years had been directly geared towards making that dream a reality. Apprehension and the taped music of Pink Floyd had clouded their minds for five and a half days, but now their focus was clear. This was it. It was now or never.

Pat and Paul moved 100 metres towards the daunting summit peak. They stopped and looked at each other. They were weak and debilitated and Pat was clearly shocked to see Paul moving so slowly. He was used to watching the agile heli-ski instructor rocket along at the pace one ordinarily associates with a speeded up film. One hundred metres of horizontal, not even vertical, movement, and they were down. Down, but not out. They realised they were in for one long, hard day on the hill, but silently agreed they owed it to themselves to keep going. They searched their inner selves, and found the emotional and psychological energy they needed to continue. Their hearts and minds were going to the top and, God willing, their bodies would just have to drag along behind.

They plodded on, taking two or three steps per minute, and eventually reached the abandoned Tri-Nation Expedition Camp Five, sited at 8350 metres, at 3.30 a.m. They rested until dawn and somehow found the resources to keep going.

From the South Col to the summit there was really only one spot where it was safe to trip up. A 0.5 by 1 metre platform at the bottom of the Hillary Step (an almost vertical 15-metre rock step) was the only place where the two climbers would not be in danger of tumbling all the way down into the Cwm if they slipped. They had to be mindful of each step. They had to control where each foot landed, making sure it didn't so much as brush against the other leg. If a crampon point caught on a gaiter, it could be fatal. Paul and Pat's legs were like jelly already, so their concentration was critical.

There was no thought of turning back, they barred the negative suggestion from even entering their heads. In the back of Paul's mind, beyond the pain and suffering of each laboured step, he knew that this climb was something he really wanted to do. His inner voice coaxed him along, screaming, 'FORCE YOURSELF TO DO IT! FORCE YOURSELF TO TAKE ANOTHER STEP.'

Gradually Paul moved ahead of Pat, and by the time he reached the snow face leading to the South Summit, he was one

The final summit ridge, from the South Summit. (Pat Cullinan)

and a half hours, roughly 150 metres, in front. He climbed on. The snow on the face was so soft it collapsed beneath Paul's feet. He made no progress and had to punch both arms into the snow to spread the weight of his body in order to stop himself from taking two steps backwards every time he made one. He couldn't zig-zag up the steep slope—he would have undercut it and wound up riding on an avalanche with a one-way ticket to the bottom of the hill. He tried taking huge steps and kicking his feet into the face. Gradually he ascended the 70-metre section. It wasn't far, but Paul experienced it as if it had amounted to half the height of the entire mountain. It was mind destroying, and reaching the South Summit offered little relief.

The view from the South Summit gave Paul quite a shock. Like every modern day mountaineer, he had claimed the Hillary route was no more than a long walk. It was not, to his understanding, a technically challenging climb. But looking up to the Hillary Step, and along the summit ridge, Paul changed his mind. This was *real* climbing. The Goddess had saved her best till last.

Five metres from the top, Paul still wasn't totally sure he could make it. There was no sudden burst of adrenalin. Every step, right to the very end, required his all, and when he got there, he just curled up in a ball to protect himself from the wind. The only thought he had was, 'Thank goodness that's over. I don't have to go up anymore.' He was too tired to do or feel anything.

After a few minutes, Paul started to feel better, and slowly lifted his head to have a look around. It was 12.40 p.m. on 25 May. He was the 204th person ever to reach the top of the world. He was there. On top, damn it! Euphoria replaced pain. 'This is it! This is where I wanna be! Oh *yeah!*' Paul told himself. He couldn't afford to get too excited. He had to stay in 'concentration mode' if he wanted to stay alive. Plenty of mountaineers had reached the summit of Chomolungma and died during their descent. He could not focus on his success—only his survival.

Paul stood up, took off his gloves and snapped a photograph of himself and one of the world below. A few minutes later, his fingers were numb. They felt like ice. Paul realised what he had done. He shook his head. 'Oh you silly, silly boy …' he thought to himself, 'frostbite.'

He fumbled into his gloves and plugged his fists into his armpits to try and warm his fingers. Luckily, it wasn't too late. After about five minutes, feeling returned to his fingertips— albeit searing pain. He sat for a minute screaming in agony (and relief) and decided not to take his down mitts off again; no matter what.

Paul was not sure how far Pat was from the summit, but decided to wait for him, so they may share their victory together. He curled himself into a ball again and rotated slowly, absorbing the breathtaking sea of snow-crested peaks stretching out below him; a 360-degree panorama encompassing hundreds of mountains from Tibet in the North to Sikkim in the east and Nepal in the south and west. The wind was frigid and after about twenty minutes Paul became so cold he feared his shivering would

The summit of Nupste seen from the summit of Chomolungma. (Pat Cullinan)

shake him off the mountain top and send him plummeting to his death. Pat would have to stand alone on the summit.

Pat was less than 100 metres from the top when Paul met him on the way down. It was very windy, and difficult for either climber to talk. They went up to each other and leant shoulder to shoulder. Both men were utterly spent. Pat lifted his oxygen mask from his face and said, 'Congratulations. Well done mate.' Paul was too tired to respond. The couple stood leaning on each other, half holding each other up, puffing and gasping for several minutes. Pat looked up at the high point above him. 'That top?' he asked, wasting no energy on grammar. Paul looked around, and needed a rest before he could answer.

'Next one!' he croaked.

'Oh hell!' Pat moaned, wasting no energy on multisyllabic damnations either. Paul blurted out a warning not to spend too much time enjoying the top, and cautioned Pat to stay in 'concentration mode' and take care on the way down. There was nothing more Paul could do for him. Like Paul, Pat would be alone up there; dependent on his own resources. There was nothing they could physically do for each other. They were not roped together or clipped into a fixed line. They were completely at the mercy of the Mother Goddess, the weather and their own minds. If any suddenly snapped, they were as good as dead.

Pat knew, when he passed Paul, that he was definitely going to make it. He refused to get excited and just plodded on towards his goal. He just wanted the nightmare to end. It took him four hours and fifteen minutes to traverse the full 600-metre distance from the South Summit to the top of Chomolungma, battling against exhaustion and 20–30-knot gusts of wind.

Pat reached the summit at 2.15 p.m. He was overcome by a feeling of relief—the uphill part was over and now, thank God, he could at last turn around. He looked down at Nupste. For most of the expedition, for months, he had looked *up* at the mighty neighbouring mountain. From Base Camp, Camp One and Camp Two, the 7879-metre peak dominated the landscape, and now he was looking *down* 1000 metres onto its summit. It was a sight he would never forget.

Pat took off his pack. He planned to leave his oxygen bottle on the summit, along with the three cylinders and already tattered prayer flags left by the Tri-Nation team. The bottom third of his pack was full of sponsors' flags and stickers—he had hoped to be on top with Paul, and fulfil our supporters' wildest dreams, by snapping shots of their logos on top of Chomolungma. Alone, it would be a very difficult task indeed.

Suddenly a terrible feeling swamped him—from the feet up. If he didn't get oxygen, he was going to die. Pat was really worried, and couldn't get his oxygen back into his pack fast enough. There was no question now of how to organise props for the photo session, there wouldn't be one. Survival came first. Just for the record, he took a few pictures from the summit, stuck a 'Have a Go Australia' sticker on one of the Tri-Nation oxygen bottles, a 'Comalco' sticker which Bruce had given him on another, and then began his epic descent back to the South Col. He didn't take in any more of the view. He had reached the highest point in the world, and that was quite a feeling in itself.

Everything was below him; the entire world was at his feet. And five minutes was all he could spare in appreciation, if he wanted to live to tell the tale.

By this time Paul was making steady progress towards Camp Four. The descent required just as much concentration as the climb up—there wasn't the same pressure physically, but mentally it was even more fatiguing. Paul had been going virtually non-stop for sixteen hours. His head was spinning. He ran out of oxygen about 300 vertical metres from the summit, somewhere on the South Ridge, and was having trouble stopping his thoughts from drifting. Every now and then he had to anchor himself in the snow and shake his head violently to correct the focus of his attentions. He would look out at the view for a minute and prepare himself for the next big mental effort of putting one foot in front of the other. About halfway down the summit peak, he started hallucinating.

A 15-metre long slug was inching its way up the Lhotse Face towards a large cave. Paul could see the slug's silvery trail, and watched it as it moved. The vision was totally realistic—he even considered exploring the cave after climbing onto the Col. His mind wandered onto daydreams that made very little sense, and every few minutes he would catch his concentration napping and scream to his mind, 'Hey! Get back here!' and keep going.

A little further down, he saw an aluminium man; an android, Star Wars-type of creature. He had his hands on his hips and was obviously waiting for Paul to descend a particularly steep pitch. In Paul's mind, there was nothing strange about seeing an android at all—there was snow here, a few rocks over there, clouds up above and an aluminium man below. No worries. His only thought was that it was a real pity he couldn't stop and talk to the man for too long, because he knew he had to keep going down. It was a shame really—Paul hadn't talked to too many aluminium men before, so it would have been an interesting experience. By the time he reached the point where the creature

Pat added 'Have a Go Australia' and Comalco stickers to discarded oxygen cylinders marking the actual summit. (Jon Muir)

had been standing, Paul's mind had muddled onto some other hallucination.

He eventually reached Camp Four at 6.00 p.m. Twenty hours had lapsed since Pat's parting radio communication, and Paul knew his team mates stationed at Camp Two and Base would be anxious for news of their ascent and, more importantly, confirmation of their safety. He dragged himself out of the tent with the radio. He looked up at the summit peak so he could accurately report Pat's position. He scanned his weary eyes up the various lower gullies. He searched the all too familiar rock bands. He shifted his gaze onto the upper reaches of the peak and followed his own descent route down. There was no sign of Pat. He hadn't been that far behind. Paul was frantic. He peered up higher still, towards the South Summit. Pat was just below it, descending the torturous snow slope. Oh-oh … trouble. There was only one and a half hours of light left, and Pat was at least five hours away. There was no way Paul was going to radio *that* piece of information to Base Camp. The last thing Austin had said to the summiteers was '*No bivvies,* Pat, and that's an order!' He would freak, knowing Pat was about to be benighted. It would be less of a worry for everyone if Paul just kept quiet.

Paul watched Pat for a while—he was moving so incredibly slowly. Paul was punch-drunk from exhaustion, but struggled into Pat's tent to melt some snow and fit a sleeping oxygen mask onto a fresh low-pressure cylinder, in readiness for his partner's return. He went back to his own tent and did the same for himself, then lay down in the doorway of his tent to continue watching Pat's descent.

It was 8 p.m. Pat was halfway down. Paul left his boots on in case Pat needed help, and threw a couple of sleeping bags over himself to keep warm. He peered into the dusky darkness, and glued his eyes to Pat's minute torchlight. He knew Pat only had to hiccup at the wrong time, or *think* about the hiccup, and he'd be gone. He was worried, really worried, and scared. He felt responsible for Pat in a way, because Pat had told Paul he wouldn't keep going if Paul chose to turn around. To a certain extent, Paul had encouraged Pat to go on, and now there was

nothing he could do to help him. He *knew* there was nothing he could do, particularly given his own deteriorated state, but that didn't stop him from feeling guilty. He had been guiding climbs for years so his 'feeling responsible' was an automatic response—even though Pat was not a novice, and had undertaken the challenge fully aware of the risk involved. Paul was so tense, he was sure he would stay awake until Pat reached the Col. He didn't. Just after Pat traversed through the rock bands below the Tri-Nation Camp Five site, Paul passed out.

Way down the hill at Base Camp, passing out was the last thing anyone was capable of doing. They were too depressed and fearful to sleep. Austin tried to rationalise why they hadn't heard from Pat and Paul, trying to avoid the worst possible scenario. Pat and Paul could well be dead, but he wasn't about to admit it; not even to himself. At around the same time Paul had reached the Col, Austin sought solace in the office tent and recorded his feelings onto his taped diary:

This is a worry. We've been in contact with Camp Two all day, and there is no news from Camp Four. It's twenty hours since they left the Col for the summit. Their oxygen would have run out by now. There's no message from Camp Four. I guess there are a lot of possibilities really: one is that they are at Camp Four and they're tired and resting; two, they started later and are still high up and on oxygen; three, I guess it's difficult not to face one of these possibilities …

His voice cheered up for a moment when he spoke next.

It certainly wasn't as windy today as it has been—from down here it didn't look that windy at all. I guess another possibility is the radio just doesn't bloody work.

Austin paused for a long time, then lapsed back into 'morbid mode', saying:

The people at Camp Two are worried. The people here are worried. We'll send a team of climbers to Camp Two tomorrow, and if Mike and Terry McCullagh are feeling good, they may start off towards the Col, and have a look around. I guess Pat's slow; he isn't in a triathalon. He had this incredible determination and courage which I guess has stood him in good stead in the past, but there are times when we have to desert mountains … GEEZ I WISH THIS RADIO WOULD GO!

Austin switched the tape off, before his imagination was carried away remembering the few times his climbing colleagues had died in action.

Pat did make it back to the Col, but not until 11.15 p.m. His epic summit journey had taken a gruelling twenty-five hours to complete. He, too, hallucinated: pink elephants, giraffes and chalets on the Col. At one point he thought the Col was Charlotte Pass in New South Wales, and planned to pop in on Tony Delaney, the resort's resident doctor, when he reached his hut. Pat's oxygen had run out on the Hillary Step, and it took him six hours to stagger his way down to the abandoned Camp Five site. He actually thought he had reached the Col, and on realising his

miscalculation, very nearly freaked out. He had taken six hours to *ascend* to the Tri-Nation High Camp … and since he seemed to be taking just as long to descend … he needed that sort of shock like a hole in the head. He picked up the oxygen cylinder he had dumped on the way up. It was a quarter full, so he fitted his regulator onto it, turned it on and started down towards the real South Col. It made a world of difference to his mental state, but it still took him forever and a day to arrive at the Col.

After overshooting the Camp Four site by 100 metres, Pat finally collapsed inside his tent at 11.15 p.m. His return journey to the summit had taken twenty-five hours. Paul woke sometime after midnight, and was relieved to hear Pat snoring. He stayed conscious long enough to reassure himself the sound was real, and not hallucinated, then rolled over and drifted back to sleep.

The sun struck Base Camp at 7.30 a.m. Jill looked at her clock: thirty-four and a half hours had passed since Pat and Paul's last radio contact. She was too depressed to get out of her sleeping bag, but so lonely in her gloomy thoughts she joined the others in the partly dismantled mess tent. But her team mates were all as depressed as she. Something must have gone badly wrong at the top.

Jon and Chris had left Base Camp at 7.15 a.m., and were speeding like bullets through the Icefall, anxious to climb as quickly as they could to rescue, if it wasn't already too late, the two silent climbers. Ironically, Jon was feeling stronger than he'd felt all expedition. He had rested for several days and taken enough prescribed drugs to kill even the most stubborn of his wriggling roundworms. Zac and James were half an hour behind Jon and Chris in support; their job was to take oxygen to Camp Two and relieve BJ, Terry and Mike, who by this time had spent eight, six and five days at the camp respectively.

At 8.30 a.m. Austin's radio crackled. Reception was bad, but unmistakably it was Paul's voice, relaying something to Camp Two. Everyone in the mess tent raced towards the radio. Austin listened, his pulse racing. He heard Camp Two ask, 'What time did you top out?' Christ! It was a double victory! Not only were the pair alive—they had summited as well! Austin's concern for Pat and Paul's safety was so consuming, he had completely forgotten about the ultimate success of his team. He was ecstatic. Jill was ecstatic. Base Camp broke into a frenzy of laughter, tears and joy. After ninety-seven days on the expedition; after what would have to be a record seventy-five days on the mountain itself, they'd made it! The Australian Bicentennial Expedition had bloody well taken the hill!

After Paul had delivered his news, he said he and Pat would pack up and leave the Col that afternoon. They both needed a good rest, but were capable of descending without help. Austin radioed Zac and James, who turned around and returned to Base Camp. Then he quickly prepared a message for the Australian Embassy and dispatched a mail runner to take it to Mountain Travel's office in Lukla.

Chris and Jon did not hear of Pat and Paul's success until they reached Camp One and radioed Base Camp. They were a bit confused as to why Zac and James had not appeared in the upper half of the Icefall, but all was quickly revealed. Chris and Jon were over the moon! Pat and Paul were safe, so they could turn their rescue bid into a summit assault! This possibility had been

The Nuptse/Lhotse wall from 8300 metres. (Zac Zaharias)

in their minds the whole time, and after much debate, it received Austin's blessing. Certain conditions accompanied the leader's consent, however. They could not, under any circumstances, repeat Pat and Paul's endurance performance; 'Kamikaze climbing' was o-u-t, *out!* They had to be back at Base Camp on 30 May. They could not rely on any support from the other climbers; Austin could not ask it of his men, particularly when most of them were so mentally and physically drained. Clearly, Chris and Jon didn't have much time to waste. They shot through to Camp Two as fast as they could.

But bad news awaited their arrival. There was every chance Paul would need help on the Col; Pat's condition had deteriorated dramatically. Actually, Pat hadn't taken any fluids or food; he hadn't spoken, urinated, or even rolled over since he had returned from the summit, and Paul, who initially assumed Pat would be OK was starting to worry. He tried to make light of it over the radio, just letting Austin know that Pat 'wasn't feeling the best', and off-handedly stating they had decided to stay another night on the Col before descending.

Another night? In total, that would mean *nine* days on or above 8000 metres. Austin's elation turned to fear. Nine days at that altitude was suicidal.

Chris and Jon left Camp Two at 4.00 a.m. the next morning; Friday, 27 May. If, by some miracle, Pat and Paul were able to come down alone (thus enabling Chris and Jon to resume their own push for the summit) Terry McCullagh vowed he would stay at Camp Two in support of his colleagues. He was a team man, through and through, and was furious when he learned so many climbers had deserted Base Camp. Chris had earlier asked for someone to relieve Terry, BJ and Mike, even if only until Pat and Paul were off the mountain, but for safety's sake, given the condition of the Icefall at this time, Austin elected to leave them where they were. Ever since the Tri-Nation Expedition left the hill, it had been impossible for the Australian team to effectively maintain the route through the Icefall. Day by day as ladders twisted, seracs toppled and snow softened to a slippery sludge, the icy labyrinth became more and more dangerous.

By mid-morning, Jon and Chris were at Camp Three. They hadn't heard anything from Camp Two or Base about Pat, so they had a quick brew and pressed on. To speed up their ascent, they turned on their oxygen cylinders. If it was a matter of life and death up there, every second was vital. Jon was petrified

about the possibility of finding Pat, and maybe Paul as well, dead. As he moved up towards the Col, his mind was clouded with memories of Craig Nottle and Fred From, the two Australians who had died on Jon's 1984 Chomolungma Expedition.

Down at Base Camp, Austin was beside himself. Paul had not radioed in to say what was happening. Minutes felt like hours, and hours passed like lifetimes. Jill and Carol offered all the emotional support they could, but Austin was slowly sinking to emotional depths far deeper than any he'd ever experienced before.

On the Col, Pat had made an amazing recovery, and at 10.00 a.m. he and Paul began their long climb down the hill. Oblivious to the fears and anxiety their lack of communication was causing, they left the radio in the tent for Jon and Chris. Even Paul's energy reserves were running low, so he avoided making an extra trip to the edge of the Col to radio Base. He figured he and Pat would be in Camp Two's line of sight before long anyway.

At 10.00 a.m., the same time the summiteers left the Col, Austin entered his office tent and turned his tape recorder on. He couldn't hide his emotions. He didn't know where to start, or exactly what to say. He was so deeply depressed, his thoughts were scattered and his words chilled with gloom. His breathing was still laboured from the inhaled avalanche powder.

A beautiful day; absolutely still … a perfect summit day, I guess—not a cloud on the horizon; just a fluffy white one over Lobuje Peak, but that's all …

Austin was having trouble broaching the point. He paused for quite a while.

Our problem of course is news from Camp Four … Chris and Jon are now at Camp Three, and from Three to Four they'll be on oxygen, so they should make good time. Terry and the guys at Two are waiting it out … However it seems unwise to commit what resources we have at Base Camp until we have more news. So … it's a waiting game … mucking about, tidying up Base Camp, packing gear, getting ready to burn off what rubbish we have. Everyone is edgy. James is sitting nearly crying on the altar mound, playing doleful tunes on his mouth organ … Jim Truscott is in the tent. Mohan and Sonam are busy as usual: Mohan is washing his clothes … all in all it's a very difficult time.

Jon and Chris were the first to know that Pat and Paul were alive and capable of returning to Base Camp unassisted. They saw the weary but jubilant heroes emerge at the top of the Geneva Spur, and met them as they descended beyond it. Neither couple could have been happier. The tables, *all* the tables, had turned in their favour. Again, the rescue was off and the summit bid was on.

The four were as high as kites as they greeted each other. 'How do you feel, Paul?' Jon asked. With a grin stretching from ear to ear and a bit beyond, Paul answered, 'I'm just feeling on top of the world!' He was really chuffed. So was Pat. 'Go for it

Looking towards Makalu from 8300 metres. (Zac Zaharias)

145

Chris Curry at 8300 metres, during his ascent. (Jon Muir)

mate;' Pat said to Jon, 'If I can do it, I've got no doubt that you can!' Jon was optimistic, but he knew the Himalayan mountains and weather patterns well enough not to make too many assumptions. This was, after all, his third expedition to the great Mother Goddess. 'I believe it, but I've heard it all before!' he laughed.

Pat and Paul continued down, wishing Chris and Jon good luck. Hell, they were going to need it! To keep their promise to Austin, they would have to reach to Col in good time that day, start for the summit that night, get from the Col to Camp Two on 29 May and race down the Cwm and through the Icefall on morning of the 30 May. From Base Camp to Base Camp, Pat and Paul's summit push would go down in history as being, undeniably, the slowest. If they made it off the mountain on 28 May (allowing for an overnight stop at Camp Two) their 'dash for the summit' would have taken them an epic fourteen days to

complete. Chris and Jon had a maximum of five days to top out and turn around.

Meanwhile, at Camp Two … Terry had his binoculars fixed on the upper reaches of the mountain. He had seen Jon and Chris disappear near the Geneva Spur, and shortly after caught sight of two figures descending from the same location. He couldn't see the figures clearly enough to ascertain whether it was Pat and Paul coming down, or Chris and Jon returning. He radioed Base Camp, and kept watching. Time ground to a standstill at Base Camp.

An hour ticked by before Terry could positively identify the climbers. At last, everyone could relax. The worrying and waiting game was over. It must have been very very marginal up there, but Pat and Paul were past the worst of it and making slow but steady progress towards Camp Three.

The triumphant duo plodded into Camp Two at 7.00 p.m. Never in their lives had they pushed themselves so hard. Never in their lives had they reaped such a huge reward. They blurted

out their summit stories to the wide-eyed, head-shaking trio at Camp Two. Somehow relating the experience made it more real for the two summiteers. They'd done it!

Chris radioed in from the Col to say he and Jon would leave for the summit at midnight. The weather report indicated winds of only 20 knots. If all went well, they would put the icing on the cake! What an amazing finish the expedition was having! Since 24 May, people had been drawn through the whole emotional spectrum. It was a real shame so many of the team members were not there now to savour Pat and Paul's success and shout support for Chris and Jon's forthcoming attempt.

That night Austin tuned into Radio Nepal, just in case the news of his expedition's success had reached Kathmandu. The only report that mentioned Chomolungma was one which detailed the particulars of a ceremony held at the palace to commemorate the Tri-Nation success. The king had awarded orders to nineteen Nepalese, six Chinese and eleven Japanese team members, and the long report named each recipient. When Major Taba, the

Nepalese Army officer who filled the role of liaison officer, was mentioned, everyone in the mess tent laughed. Min Moor wailed, 'All he did was sit around, play cards and drink piss!'

On a later broadcast, the Australian success was announced. Unbeknown to the expedition members, the news had not only reached Kathmandu, but Australia as well. Di Johnstone had already received telegrams from the Australian Prime Minister, Bob Hawke, and Major General Gration. Good news *always* travels fast—even on foot!

Chris and Jon spent several hours preparing themselves for the last leg of their virtual non-stop ascent. It was the third time Chris had been on the Col in as many weeks. Thanks to the roundworms, it was Jon's first time above Camp Three. Since he intended to make his summit bid without oxygen, Jon had not been required to make the initial 'compulsory carry' of high-pressure cylinders to Camp Four. While Chris was slightly wilted from his constant to-ing and fro-ing, Jon was fresher than the proverbial daisy.

Given the season's abysmal conditions, and Austin's imposed time constraints, there was now no question of who would, and who wouldn't use oxygen. The issue tonight was simply, who would get to use the last set of Australian high-pressure cylinders and who would have to make do with the scavenged Tri-Nation system. Since Chris had carried two Aussie bottles to the Col, he was clearly entitled to the familiar, lighter set. But when Jon tried on the awkward, foreign breathing apparatus, it interfered with his use of the movie camera. Chris (the softie), offered to swap systems. 'And that's when karma left me. Or ran out, or whatever it does ...' he wrote later, in his diary.

At midnight Jon and Chris were ready to leave. Cloud, which had earlier threatened to prohibit their attempt, was lifting off the Col, revealing a bright, near-full moon ... and very thick, black storm clouds in the south-west. 'Well, whatcha reckon?' Jon asked, looking over to the intimidating, swirling tempest. It was their only day. If the weather directly above them turned bad, they'd just have to retreat. They had nothing to lose. They buckled up their packs, fitted their oxygen masks, and started on up the hill.

After climbing for three hours, Chris's first oxygen cylinder ran out. He was horrified. The Australian bottles were lasting a minimum of ten hours at a 3 litres per minute flow rate. Three Tri-Nation cylinders were supposed to be equivalent to two Australian ones, so Chris's reaction was not surprising. He wasn't going to have enough oxygen to make it. His only option was to turn down his regulator to 2 litres per minute, and hopefully make the summit before his remaining supplies were depleted. But it was Catch 22; less oxygen meant a slower ascent. Inevitably, he started losing ground to Jon.

Just on light, he caught up to his partner at the Tri-Nation camp site. Jon had melted some snow and prepared a brew, and was comfortably lounging back enjoying a cigarette. Chris was cold, tired, and anxious about his equipment. He couldn't believe how strong Jon looked; nor how anyone could even *think* about smoking at that altitude. He shook his head and silently collapsed down next to Jon.

Jon was keen to keep moving, and in his haste to join him, Chris spilt quite a bit of the melted snow. Anywhere else in the world it wouldn't matter, but up there it was simply *not* the thing to do. Keeping hydrated was the key to survival, but melting enough snow to do that was a painfully slow process. Every drop of water was as precious as life itself.

From Camp Five, Chris and Jon moved up onto a steepening snow slope. Chris struggled behind Jon, losing ground as it became increasingly harder for him to climb. He wrote in his diary later:

> The snow was loose and unconsolidated and was actually more difficult for me, the second climber, than Jon, the first. It fell away underfoot, and a lot of steps made no ground at all; or even landed me lower than where I'd started. I lost more ground to Jon. He topped the ridge and waited a while, and took some film of me ascending the face … It was a real struggle for me to keep going to the ridge. Jon had moved off. I expected a straightforward ridge line to the South Summit: a little relief. But as I came over the ridge, I saw we had to go up another snow slope that looked *huge*. Dismayed, I slumped on the ridge.

Jon was literally speeding on towards the summit ridge. Chris heard him stop and change to his second oxygen cylinder. He was nearly there, and only halfway through his supply!

Chris pulled himself together again and kept going, but rather than following Jon's line of ascent along the wind-slabbed, firmer snow, he tried to take a more direct line up the snow slope and wasted time and energy, as Paul had done several days before, struggling in the deep soft snow of the 70-metre face. He gave up, and rejoined Jon's route. Then his second oxygen cylinder ran out.

Chris stabilised himself on the slope and changed his regulator and breathing apparatus over onto his third and final cylinder. It leaked. He tried to adjust it. It still leaked. It just wasn't fair … He buried his head in the snow and groaned. He had lost. At 8700 metres—just 174 vertical metres from the summit—he sat for a minute or two contemplating his fate, then began his descent in silence. Later, he wrote:

> I could weep. But I haven't—yet. This is the third time I've been knocked off the top rung by bitter twists of fate. First with the Rhodes scholarship, then with the Australian rowing team, and now with climbing. Each fall has set me off on another ladder. So I wonder what will become of this one? Where to, cruel Fate? Someone once said, "Good things come from the sides of mountains, not from the tops." *He* must have failed too …

Ironically, Jon had so much oxygen left when he reached the South Summit, he turned up the flow-rate to 8 litres per minute. He danced all the way to the top. Pat had struggled from the South Summit to the top of Chomolungma in four and a quarter hours. Jon knocked it off in forty-five minutes. The conditions on the summit ridge were perfect for cramponing, and Jon was loving every minute of it. He felt fantastic! Never better!

When he got to the top of the Hillary step, he was undoubtedly the happiest man in the world. He knew he'd make it; *nobody*

The view from the summit (when Jon was there). (Jon Muir)

turns back from that position! A lot of climbers over the years have turned back from the South Summit, but not from the top of the step. After three expeditions; after a grand total of nine months on the loftiest mountain of them all, Jon knew he had it 'in the bag'.

About 10 metres from the top, Jon looked at his watch. It was 11.14 a.m. on 28 May. Exactly one day short of Hillary's thirty-fifth 'Summit Anniversary'. Oh God, what a feeling! Those last steps … All Jon's Christmases had come at once!

He stood on top, thinking 'Na, na, na na, na—I'm the king of the castle!' He was delirious with joy. He got out the radio, and

tried to contact those lower down the mountain. 'Jon to Base or Camp Two; Jon to Base or Camp Two, over.' All he could hear was the crackle of static and a faint voice, struggling to be heard.

It was Terry down at Camp Two. 'This is Camp Two, Camp Two. I've got you loud and clear—over.' Terry yelled. Mike Rheinberger raced over to join him, saying, 'He's on the summit, is he? He must be!' Jon confirmed his position, screaming, 'I'M ON THE SUMMIT!'

'WHAT?' came the incredulous reply.

'I'M ON THE SUMMIT!' Jon yelled again.

'YOU'RE ON THE SUMMIT???' Terry asked.

'YEAH—I'M ON THE TOP!'

Reception was bad, but as Jon repeated his success over and over again, the realisation of it all gradually sunk in. Tears started welling in his eyes. The third time *had* worked the charm!

Terry was equally emotional. It was goosebump material just talking to someone standing on the summit! It was the next best thing to being there! He was cheering and whistling and congratulating Jon. He said, 'Oh well done, you bloody … Oh! well done, mate, well done! Where's Chris?—over.' Jon wasn't sure. Terry passed the radio to Mike, who congratulated his old climbing buddy, saying, 'Well done, Jono. How do you feel? Listen can you copy me? Get Chris to get a photograph of you holding the radio. Somehow get a photo of a Philips radio up there would you?—over.' Our sponsors would have been thrilled with Mike's sense of responsibility. But it was one thing for Jon

Pat Cullinan holding the flag of 1 Commando Regiment at Camp Four, with Chomolungma in the background. (Paul Bayne)

to promise he would try, and quite another to actually fulfil the deal. He had a hell of a lot on his mind up there, including the memory of Craig's and Fred's deaths. Jon could feel their presence, up there on top of the world. He could feel they were with him, and knew they had been, in spirit, all the way up the massive summit peak.

Down at Base Camp, Austin had heard most of the radio conversation and passed his best wishes on to Jon, via Camp Two. He couldn't contain his excitement. He was thrilled; *another* Aussie on top, and another one, presumably on the way!

Pat and Paul were safely off the mountain and about to celebrate their own triumphant return to Base Camp. Pat was especially jubilant, for his success heralded the end of his climbing career. He had pulled off a spectacular hat-trick; he'd made the first ascent of Tseringma Peak on Gauri Shankar, summited Broad Peak and now crowned his achievements by conquering 'the Big One'.

Norm had welcomed Pat and Paul home by firing off two Gaz cylinders in a mock two-gun salute, and champagne corks were about to pop in the mess tent. Before Austin started the proceedings, he switched on his tape recorder to record his feelings:

What a great feeling! It's been a great team effort, and I guess this is the culmination. Without them [Pat, Paul, Jon and Chris] obviously there wouldn't have been a success. But equally, without the *team* they wouldn't have been in a position to give us that success. It *has* been a team effort; we've had our ups and downs and disagreements, but in the end everything has come together. I haven't had a team that deserves success more than this …

As Jon enjoyed the silence of the mountain-top, the sweeping views and realisation of his dream, Base Camp went wild, and revelled in the team's success. Everyone gave little speeches as they toasted the two summiteers present, and the two on the hill. No one knew about Chris's problem with the foreign oxygen system, and all assumed he would soon join Jon on the summit.

But Jon remained there alone. He looked over into Tibet, and down the route Tim Macartney-Snape and Greg Mortimer had used in 1984, when they became the first Australians to ever climb Chomolungma. He thought about his own previous expeditions and the efforts of all his team mates on this one. He was particularly grateful to Mike and Terry for staying at Camp Two, and to everyone who had stuck it out at Base Camp as well. He thought about Pat and Paul's ascent; it was hard to imagine, since his own journey from Base Camp to the top had taken a record-breaking fifty-two hours.

At thirty-seven, Pat was the oldest Australian to climb the Mother Goddess. Jon, at twenty-seven, was the youngest. He looked at his watch and realised he had spent fifty-five minutes on the summit, absorbed in the view and consumed by thoughts and memories. Time flies when you're having fun. He didn't want to leave; he felt so good up there. He couldn't wait to stand on that summit again, without oxygen. He thought to himself, 'I've spent longer than any other Australian up here—and I'll be back!' Success had sated Pat's thirst for climbing, but Jon … well Jon was just like most mountaineers, really—he was still obsessed.

Appendix One
How the Australian Bicentennial Everest Expedition Began

The history of our expedition began in 1980. Tim Hughes, a young Melbourne-based mountaineer, was in Nepal working with Sir Edmund Hillary and Australian cinecameraman, Mike Dillon, on a film about Sherpa festivals, when he conceived the idea. He felt the Bicentennial year would be an appropriate time for an Australian expedition to Chomolungma, and 'booked' the South Col route for the projected attempt. Popularity of expeditions to the 8874-metre peak had steadily increased since the advent of lightweight 'alpine-style' ascents, so it was important to secure a permit for the preferred season and route from His Majesty's Government of Nepal well in advance.

Shortly after lodging the initial application, Tim took time off from filming to join friends and fellow members of the Southern Australian (Melbourne) Section of the New Zealand Alpine Club (NZAC) and attempted to climb Changabang, a 6864-metre peak in the Garwhal Himal region of India. Tragically, Tim was killed at the end of the successful expedition when he slipped and fell from the track during the walk-out.

His companions were devastated by the accident, but vowed to make Tim's 'Chomolungma '88' idea a reality. Peter Allen, one of the Changabang climbers, returned to Nepal in 1981 and confirmed Tim's 'booking' with a $1000 down-payment on the then $A2000 permit fee. At that time, Peter had only been on a few expeditions and felt it was pretty audacious to be contemplating the highest of the high Himalayan 'hills'. But seven years lay between 'now' and 'then', so he and his climbing colleagues were confident they would have plenty of time and opportunity to gain further experience and practice before facing their greatest challenge.

Around about the same time, members of the Australian Army's Alpine Association (AAA) were putting together a ten-year plan of activities, which naturally encompassed the Bicentennial year. Major General Gration, then the Assistant Chief of Defence Force Staff, had long supported the Army's involvement in mountaineering as a peace-time pursuit, and as the patron of the AAA, he suggested Chomolungma as the Association's goal for 1988.

Prior to his appointment as patron of the AAA, Gration was actually its president, and had been since he revitalised the disbanded club in 1975. Gration had first set his sights on the highest mountain in the world in January of that same year, when as a colonel, he led a group of soldiers to Everest Base Camp, under the Army's new Adventure Training Programme. It was the first time such an activity had been undertaken by the Army, and proved a resounding success. Gration was inspired by his first glimpse of Chomolungma, and saw it not only as an awesome mountain, but a distant objective for the armed forces. Perhaps one day soldiers would conquer the mighty peak. Perhaps in 1988. Not only would it coincide with the nation's Bicentennial celebrations, it would also give the Army plenty of time to gain the expertise and experience necessary to tackle such an ambitious project.

The major general's dream slowly gathered momentum as the AAA increased its membership and expedition activity. Gration lent constant, invaluable support to his men as they took up more challenging climbs and bigger mountains, strategically preparing themselves for his ultimate plan. First mention of the possibility of organising an Army expedition to climb the great Mother Goddess occurred with the news that Tim Hughes had already 'booked' the favoured South Col route, for a party of Australian civilians. Not disheartened, Gration and the AAA committee (with the lanky ex-SAS troop commander, Major Pat Cullinan, presiding) decided to apply for a permit to climb the great mountain via an alternate route. In 1983 they successfully secured permission to ascend Chomolungma using the West Ridge approach, during the same pre-monsoon season as Peter Allen and company.

Peter's original plan involved a close-knit group of eight (which included climbers Mike Rheinberger and Andrew Rothfield) ascending via the 'normal' Hillary, or South Col route, without the aid of supplementary oxygen or Sherpa support teams. The AAA's intention was for twelve servicemen and a corresponding number of high-altitude porters to climb using oxygen as desired or required. The Army tended to have a traditional, Hunt-style approach to climbing, summed up by their desire to 'conquer Everest', rather than to climb her. Philosophically, as well as logistically, the two teams couldn't have been further apart. But just before the AAA received confirmation of their application to climb the West Ridge route, Pat Cullinan (as the AAA president and newly appointed chairman to the Army's Everest Committee of Management) visited Peter to discuss the possibility of the two teams joining forces.

The lightweight Melbourne contingent—all members of the Southern Australian Section of the NZAC—were just not interested in being part of a full-scale, military 'assault'. Talks were amicable, but fruitless.

Since it was obvious that the paths of the two teams would cross many times before and during the set pre-monsoon expedition season, it was important for both parties to maintain good relations, regardless of their differing plans. Zac Zaharias, who was also involved in the Army planning, invited Peter Allen to join him and other potential 'Everest team hopefuls' on an Army expedition to Nilgiri North, a 7061-metre peak in Nepal's Annapurna region. The expedition was a great success and Peter had the opportunity to get to know Zac, his partner Peter Lambert, and several other Army climbers.

By late November 1983, shortly after the Nilgiri Expedition, it was clear the two groups would need to combine in order to attain support from the Bicentennial Authority and to avoid battling each other for other financial and equipment sponsorships. The Southern Australian Section of the NZAC and the AAA had independently applied to the Authority for official sanctioning of their expeditions as Bicentennial events. The Authority thought an expedition to the world's highest peak was worthy of a financial grant as well as Bicentennial endorsement, but would only support one such endeavour, not two.

A meeting was held at Bonegilla, near Albury, and although both teams would maintain their original objectives, they would unite under a common banner in order to receive the endorsement. They formed the Australian Bicentennial Everest Expedition (ABEE), and nominated a committee of six; three members were nominees of the AAA—Pat Cullinan, Peter Lambert and Zac Zaharias—and the others (Peter Allen, Andrew Rothfield and Michael Rheinberger) represented the Southern Australian Section of the NZAC. It was agreed the ABEE would climb the mountain in two separate but simultaneous attempts, and, conditions permitting, they would also try to traverse the peak from either one or both directions, that is, some climbers would ascend via the West Ridge route and descend from the summit on Hillary's South Col route, and/or vice versa. Peter Lambert and Peter Allen agreed to prepare and lodge a new, joint submission to the Australian Bicentennial Authority.

Expeditions are incredibly expensive undertakings and with limited resources for sponsorship available in Australia, both parties agreed to enlist the help of a professional consultant to assist them in their fund-raising activities. They estimated they needed a minimum of $350 000, and tentatively selected John Peryman, managing director of a Sydney-based firm called Copeland Consultants, to orchestrate and manage the daunting marketing task. The sententious consultant used to be a major in the Army Reserve, and was recommended to the expedition by Major General Sharpe, Commander of the 2nd Division. His position as financial consultant to the ABEE was confirmed at the inaugural meeting of ABEE Ltd on 14 May 1984.

By this time, the Australian Bicentennial Authority had given the thumbs up to the joint expedition, although official endorsement would not occur until October 1985. Both Major General Gration and the prime minister of Australia, Bob Hawke, had agreed to be its patrons. As president of the AAA, Pat Cullinan prepared a lengthy submission (essentially focusing on the AAA's West Ridge side of the ABEE) in order to get the sponsorship ball rolling. It detailed everything from projected budgets to logistics, and was presented on 12 October 1984 to the Army's chief of operations, Major General Smethurst, at a planning conference, organised to ascertain the extent of military support available to the expedition. The outcome of the conference was crucial, as it would profoundly affect so many areas of expedition expenditure.

Support was provided in principle, and the expedition received permission to proceed as an authorised Army activity. This established the framework for provision of funds and more detailed support as the planning of the expedition progressed. Smethurst authorised use of the military system, that is, communications, ground transport, etc., to assist in the expedition planning, and supported the request that all participating military and Army Reserve personnel be classed 'on duty' for the duration of the expedition. This meant pay and rations would be available, as per standard military exercises.

On the military side of affairs, involvement by any individual was subject to their immediate boss' discretion; but clearly Major General Gration's patronage would be advantageous in influencing the final decisions of those in command. The military committee members decided not to select their final twelve until after the planned AAA 'warm up' expedition to Broad Peak in Pakistan, scheduled for June–September 1986.

To strengthen the bond and gradually whittle down the barriers between the civilian and military contingents, members of the Southern Australian Section of the NZAC were invited to join the Broad Peak and subsequent Army climbs. Aside from this, the civvies were involved in their own 'practice expeditions', with Mike Rheinberger and Peter Allen joining the NZAC's own Chomolungma extravaganza in 1985. The fourteen-man team was led by Austin Brookes, and climbed from the Tibetan side of the mountain via the North Face. Although unsuccessful, Peter and Mike gained a very valuable hands-on insight into the unique environment and conditions of Chomolungma, which contributed greatly to the development of the ABEE plan.

Board meetings were held every three months, with monthly executive meetings; all of these meetings and the planning being done in addition to the participants' normal jobs. As the weeks, months and, indeed, years rolled on, the ABEE modified its climbing plan, equipment lists, strategies and stores requirements. About the only thing that didn't change was the principal objective of the expedition: to get an Australian, or Australians, onto the summit of Chomolungma in the Bicentennial year. Ideas and plans detailing exactly how that would be achieved were the topic of numerous board meetings. It was quite clear that some of the Army participants were experts in the 'broad-brush' style of approach, but the civvies (with their substantial mountaineering experience) had a more realistic idea of what, in detail, was needed. Both groups had to compromise their basic philosophies and plans, and after months and months of 'in-house' conflict, an amicable 'master plan' was finally drawn up. The two teams would drop their two-route, two-philosophy strategy, and concentrate their efforts onto one route: the South Col. The decision *not* to use Sherpas in the ascent and the total team count of twelve to sixteen climbers was a difficult one for some of the AAA members to swallow, as it meant fewer of their candidates would be selected.

Sponsorships were sought and gained during this period, and one major sponsor, Proplan (a Brisbane company specialising in critical path planning and programming), offered the expedition its management services. Charlie Hart, the company's managing director, compiled computer diagrams of the ABEE's new climbing plan and developed a programme to catalogue all the expedition's stores and equipment.

When the time came to select team members, close to 100 applications were received and processed. From the outset, it was agreed that every expedition member, civilians and servicemen alike, had to make a financial commitment of $5000 to the expedition, and wherever possible, contribute man-hours to the preparation and paperwork, estimation and accumulation of equipment needs, and securing of additional monetary and resource sponsorships.

One person throwing heart and soul into the cause on behalf of the AAA was Jim Truscott, then a training and operations officer in the Headquarters Field Force Command. Well supported by the colonel of operations, Andy Mattay, he lobbied Major General Smethurst, and successfully secured the use of the RAAF's C-130 Hercules Aircraft to fly the expedition's equipment and stores to Kathmandu. That alone saved at least $15 000 in freight costs, but Jim went on to bid for and attain $32 000 for travel, $25 000 for freight and cartage, $10 000 from the Central Army Amenities Fund, $16 000 to buy general stores and $5000 from the Peter Stuckey Mitchell Adventure Training Award. John Peryman also obtained $20 000 from the RSL's Armed Forces Overseas Fund (AFOF). To say the Army were playing a significant role in bringing the expedition to fruition was not an overstatement. Their input, thanks largely to people like Jim and Major General Gration, was far above and beyond the wildest expectations of everyone in the ABEE.

Other monies came from various Australian companies and corporations, and equipment and clothing were either donated outright, or made available at cost, by many major Australian and overseas manufacturers and distributors. Tee-shirts and postcards were designed and sold by the climbers, and numerous raffles organised to further boost the ABEE's coffers.

From June 1987, the expedition moved into top gear. The next few months proved to be the busiest and most hectic with equipment specifications being finalised, orders being placed and items delivered. The expedition was now being controlled by the Executive with Austin Brookes at the helm and with Peter Allen and Zac Zaharias doing the bulk of the co-ordination and organisation. Zac put Charlie Hart's computer services to the test—it was no small feat for an expedition to keep track of everything, especially when the stores included some 1000 varieties and weighed a total of 6 tonnes. But Zac had the lot under control and could locate any item, from a pot scrubber to a high altitude tent, in a matter of minutes. Peter and Zac put in hundreds of hours of work including numerous meetings and telephone calls in their own time, quite a mean feat when considering that Peter lived in Melbourne and Zac in Brisbane. Although less involved, Austin was beginning to get a feel for the organisation as the newly appointed leader and was impressed with the apparent smoothness of the project.

By November, all the bulk stores assembled at Malabar Rifle Range in Sydney had to be weighed, checked, tested and packed before being ferried out to Richmond Air Force Base for loading onto the C–130. Zac, Norm and Lambo controlled the delicate operation which took a full week, as equipment had to be individually itemised and then carefully distributed amongst loads to minimise any losses, ensuring each load weighed no more than 30 kg to facilitate cartage by porters or yaks. In early December, the stores—which included 51 oxygen cylinders, 264 four man day ration packs, 40 specially designed aluminium ladder sections, ropes, tents and other climbing hardware—were flown to Kathmandu. The last major obstacle was to get the six tonnes of equipment through the notorious Nepalese customs. Stories abounded of expeditions not getting off the ground due to the inability of the equipment to be cleared from customs. Lambo's careful planning paid off as the equipment was cleared within four hours of arrival, a record, and cause for much celebration as the hard part was over.

It was now imperative to finalise team selection and attend to all the last minute details of the expedition. Mike Groom, one of the civilian members of the ABEE, had to pull out because of frostbite sustained on an expedition to Kanchenjunga in 1987.

Peter Allen, who had spent more time than most (as ABEE secretary) planning and preparing for the expedition, decided to assume the role of assistant Base Camp manager and not to attempt to climb. He had recently 'acquired' a complete family— a wife and two sons—and with the birth of another Allen (a girl named Sophie), Peter's sense of responsibility outweighed his desire to climb Chomolungma.

Andrew Rothfield, who had acted as ABEE treasurer since the company's inception, found his medical studies and young family of greater importance, and decided not to leave Australia at all. That, needless to say, left a few openings on the team for last minute recruits. The total climbing contingent swelled to eighteen, not including the expedition leader, Austin Brookes, the Base Camp manager, Norm Crookston, the cook, Jill Trenam, and Charlie Hart, who was joining the expedition to help out at Base Camp for a little over two months.

Last to join the party were Jon Muir, an experienced climber and deft cinecameraman, and me, the photojournalist. Jon was sponsored by the Australian Broadcasting Corporation (ABC), who, in return for forking out Jon's $A5000 member's fee, would receive exclusive footage for a planned series of television news bulletins. Jon was introduced to the ABEE committee by Mike Rheinberger, who had somehow found the time to accompany Jon on another attempt to climb Chomolungma during the 1987 post-monsoon season.

Many of the climbers and support party met for the first time at a function held in Sydney, just two days prior to the team's departure for Kathmandu. Peter Allen and Norm Crookston were the only two unable to attend as they were already in Nepal, on their way to the mountain in order to establish the expedition's Base Camp.

Speeches and cocktails flowed through the evening; lots of backslapping and handshaking and thankyou calls to sponsors. Our major proponents met the climbers and the climbers met each other. Everyone involved in the organisation—everyone responsible for the expedition becoming a viable (logistically and financially) event—received certificates and accolades, and the expedition was bestowed with various sponsors' flags to fly from Base Camp, and if possible, the summit. The Australian Bicentennial Authority, who had granted the ABEE a whopping $50 000, presented Austin with an enormous green and gold flag bearing the official Bicentennial logo. There were more speeches, more cocktails and more handshaking, then eventually the evening drew to a close. Most of the climbers went home to pack, and spend what little time remained until 'take off' with their families and close friends. Chomolungma was a cold, barren, lonely sort of destination, and farewells were not made any easier by the very real possibility that one may not return.

After eight years in the pipeline, the members of the Australian Bicentennial Everest Expedition were poised to embark on their challenging adventure. The climbers had raised all the experience, the expertise, the support and the sponsorship they needed. Clearly, the hardest part of the expedition was over. All they had to do now, was get to Nepal, climb Chomolungma, and plant the Australian Flag on the roof of the world.

Appendix Two
The Team—Personal Profiles

Name: **Brian Agnew**
Date of birth: 13 December 1954
Occupation: Major, Instructor at Junior Staff Wing, Land Warfare Centre

BJ was the leader of the Ganesh IV Expedition in 1981, a member of the British Army Expedition to Peak 29 (Nepal) in 1982, and deputy leader of the expedition to Broad Peak (Pakistan) in 1986, during which he achieved a successful summit ascent. His other interests include water polo, bird watching and travel.

Photograph by Peter Lambert.

Name: **Austin Brookes**
Date of birth: 9 November 1937
Occupation: Teacher

Austin has spent 34 years climbing the mountains of the world. He was the leader of the 1959 Sarek Expedition, the 1976 Cerro Stokes and Aconcagua expeditions, the 1981 Molamenqing Expedition and the 1985 Chomolungma Expedition. Among his other interests are skiing, kayaking, scuba diving, sailing, education and reading.

Name: **Chris Curry**
Date of birth: 25 April 1953
Occupation: Doctor, Emergency Medicine

Chris has climbed Pumori (Nepal), Kedarnath (India), Kommunizma and Kodjenevskaya (USSR), Aconcagua (Argentina), and McKinley in Alaska. He has also had alpine climbing experience in Scotland, Europe, the Andes and New Zealand. Skiing and photography are two of his other interests.

Name: **Paul Bayne**
Date of birth: 9 August 1956
Occupation: Mountain and heliskiing guide

Paul gained most of his climbing experience at Mt Cook in New Zealand, where he has been a climbing guide since 1979. He also made the first solo ascent of the Balfour face of Mt Tasman. As one of the three members of the Everest Expedition who reached the summit, he describes the moment:

'Reaching the summit was unforgettable—a feeling of incredible privilege, and the relief that everybody's effort was not in vain.'

Photograph by Zac Zaharias.

Name: **Pat Cullinan**
Date of birth: 6 October 1950
Occupation: Army Major, Second in command of Special Air Service (SAS) Regiment

The highlights of Pat's climbing experience (Tseringma Peak in 1980, Broad Peak in 1986 and Everest in 1988) are for the most part in the Himalayas, although he has also climbed in Africa (Victoria Emanuel Peak in 1982). His other interests include parachuting, running, backgammon and 'taking it easy'. He describes the ABEE as:

'A once in a lifetime challenge.'

Name: **Anthony Delaney**
Date of birth: 16 June 1947
Occupation: Doctor, ski guide; Major, Commando Regiment (Army Reserve)

Tony's previous climbing experience includes reaching the summit of Mt McKinley in 1982, and an expedition to Broad Peak in 1986. His other interests are sports medicine, skiing, surfing, scuba diving, sailing, martial arts and languages.

Name: **Bruce Douglas Farmer**
Date of birth: 25 January 1947
Occupation: General Manager
Comalco Aluminium
(Bell Bay) Ltd

Bruce has spent 24 years climbing, mainly in New Zealand. His expedition experience includes being deputy leader for the 1977 Southlan Patagonian Expedition; the first ascents of Cerro Stokes, Cerro Pyramide, Cerro Mitre; and the third ascent of the east face of Aconcagua. In 1981 he was deputy leader of the New Zealand Himalayan Expedition and in 1985 of the New Zealand Everest Expedition. Bruce's other pastimes include scuba diving, bush walking and sailing.

Name: **Terry McCullagh**
Date of birth: 2 July 1958
Occupation: Army Major, 1st Field
Regiment

Terry's climbing experience includes five seasons of alpine climbing in New Zealand and reaching the summit on both the 1983 Nilgiri North Expedition (Nepal) and the 1986 Broad Peak Expedition (Pakistan). His other interests are free-fall parachuting, rock-climbing and running. Of the Everest Expedition he comments:

'I would describe the South Col as the most depressing place on earth—extreme cold, hurricane force winds, no oxygen and no McDonalds.'

Name: **Jon Muir**
Date of birth: 7 March 1961
Occupation: Professional mountaineer,
guide, instructor, lecturer
and film-maker

Jon's climbing experience is extensive. Some of his most important climbs include a 1982 ascent of Changabang, a solo ascent of Matterhorn in 1983 and the discovery of new routes on a 1986 ascent of Shivling and a 1987 ascent of Kedarnarth (India). Before the Bicentennial Everest Expedition he had already reached the west ridge of Mt Everest on a previous expedition.

Name: **Peter Lambert**
Date of birth: 2 December 1957
Occupation: Major, Royal Australian
Signals Corps

Peter reached the summit of Mt McKinley (Alaska) in 1982, Mt Nilgiri North (Nepal) in 1983, Tent Peak (Nepal) in 1984, and Broad Peak (Pakistan) in 1986. He has also spent a number of seasons climbing in New Zealand. Some of his interests are cycling, swimming, bushwalking and cross-country skiing.

Name: **Richard Moor**
Date of birth: 30 May 1955
Occupation: Army Major

Richard has had a variety of climbing experiences, from a Cook's tour of the Mexican volcanoes, to several trekking peaks in western Nepal. He was also a member of the AAA expeditions to Broad Peak (Pakistan) and Mt McKinley (Alaska). Richard's other interests include rock climbing.

Name: **Michael Pezet**
Date of birth: 20 April 1960
Occupation: Car radiator
repairman; Corporal,
1/19 Bushman's Rifles
(Army Reserve)

Michael has spent a couple of seasons climbing in New Zealand. He has reached the summit of Chulu West and Pisang Peak in Nepal and the summit of Mt McKinley (Alaska). He also took part in the Broad Peak Expedition (Pakistan). His interests include bushwalking, canoeing, swimming and dancing.

Name: **Phil Pitham**
Date of birth: 5 July 1958
Occupation: National Purchasing Manager.

Phil spent ten years climbing in New Zealand and in 1981 he was a member of the Ganesh IV Expedition. He reached the summit of Mt McKinley (Alaska) in 1982 and was also successful in reaching the summit of Mt Nilgiri North (Nepal) the following year. In 1984 he was a member of the Devachen Expedition in India and also joined the Papsura Expedition in 1985. His other interests are bushwalking and cycling.

Name: **Andrew Smith**
Date of birth: 12 February 1964
Occupation: Navy Lieutenant HMAS Watson

Andrew has had varied climbing experience. He has spent several seasons in New Zealand and was a member of the Army Alpine Association Expedition in 1984 to Tent Peak in Nepal, and in 1985 he climbed Pisang Peak, Nepal. He also led the expedition to Mt McKinley (Alaska) in 1987. Andrew's other interests include art, antiques, music and cross-country skiing.

Name: **Terry Tremble**
Date of birth: 20 December 1958
Occupation: Teacher

Terry's previous climbing experience includes three seasons in New Zealand, two seasons in Europe (where the highpoints were successful ascents of the north face of the Eiger and the north face of the Grandes Jorasses), and in the Himalayas alpine-style attempts on Jannu and Kanchenjunga.
Photograph by Zac Zaharias.

Name: **Michael Rheinberger**
Date of birth: 6 October 1940
Occupation: Professional electrical engineer; Major (Army Reserve)

Michael's climbing has taken him all over the world. He has scaled White Sail and Changabang in India; joined expeditions to Kwangala, Kangguru and Everest in Nepal; and climbed Broad Peak in Pakistan. He also enjoys rogaining (a form of orienteering), nordic skiing, classical music and chess.

Name: **James Strohfeldt**
Date of birth: 9 March 1959
Occupation: Orthopaedic sports physician

James has climbed in New Zealand, the USA including Alaska, and the Himalayas. His other interests include skiing, triathlons, mathematics, philosophy and Zen Buddhism.

Name: **Jim Truscott**
Date of birth: 26 May 1956
Occupation: Army Major

Jim's mountaineering experience includes five seasons in New Zealand and expeditions to Ganesh IV (Nepal) in 1981 and Broad Peak, Pakistan in 1986. He has also had extensive experience in rock climbing. His other interests include cross-country ski racing.

Name: **James Van Gelder**
Date of birth: 2 February 1961
Occupation: Doctor

Before ABEE, James' most important climbs were successful attempts on the summits of Mt McKinley in Alaska and Broad Peak in Pakistan. He has also made two unsuccessful attempts on Kanchenjunga.

Name: **Zac Zaharias**
Date of birth: 21 July 1956
Occupation: Major, Officer commanding Advanced Students Squadron, Australian Defence Forces Academy

Between 1976 and 1983 Zac climbed in the Southern Alps of New Zealand. He was the deputy leader of the Army Alpine Association and a member of the Ganesh IV Expedition (India) in 1981. As the leader of the 1982 AAA Mt McKinley Expedition (Alaska) he successfully reached the summit. He also reached the summit when he was the leader of the 1983 AAA Nilgiri North Expedition (Nepal), which included the first ascent of the south-east face. In 1985 he was a member of the Australian Kulu Expedition to India and climbed White Sail. Zac reached the summit during the 1986 AAA Broad Peak Expedition, which was the first Australian ascent of the mountain.

ABEE auxiliary team

Jill Trenam
Expedition Cook

Norm Crookston
Base Camp Manager

Peter Allen
Assistant Base Camp Manager

Carol Brand-Maher
Medical Research team

Ali Shah
Medical Research team

Charlie Hart
Assistant Base Camp Manager

Sorrel Wilby
Photojournalist

John Peryman
Chairman ABEE

Photographs of Jill Trenam and Norm Crookston by Zac Zaharias. Photograph of Sorrel Wilby by Austin Brookes.

Nepalese Base Camp Staff

Sonam Girme
Sirdar

Gowchan
Base Camp staff

Wanchu and Little Pasang
Cook & Head Cook-boy

Mohan Ali Singh and Mahander
Liason Officers

Sponsors

The expedition was very generously supported by a range of companies and organisations who provided us with substantial material and financial assistance. Our sponsors were:

Adidas	sportswear, bags and shoes
Armed Forces Overseas Fund (the RSL)	cash
Ansett Airlines	air travel in Australia and cash
Armed Forces Food Science Establishment	food research, high altitude rations
Arnotts Biscuits	biscuits
Australian Bicentennial Authority	cash
Australian Broadcasting Commission	cash and film
Australian Defence Forces	equipment, food, office supplies and facilities, accommodation, moral support, Telecom card, cash, air travel, medical supplies
Ausventure	trek organisation
BBC Hardware	aluminium ladders, tools and cash
Bellview Hosiery	socks
Boots	cash and pharmaceuticals
Boral Kinnears	fixed rope
Cadbury-Schweppes	confectionery
CIG Medishield	oxygen equipment and cash
Comalco	aluminium and cash
Cottees	de-caffeinated coffee
Damart Thermolactyl	clothing
Decor	kitchenware, plastic ware
Hanimex	cameras, film and cassette players
Jarrah Foods Pty Ltd	coffee
J & H	clothing
John West Foods	tinned food
Koflach Sports	climbing boots
Macpac Wilderness Equipment	tents, packs and clothing
MONT Equipment	sleeping bags
National Australia Bank	financial services, financial
Nordic Way	ski and climbing equipment
OPSM	eyewear, telescopes
Philips Diving Services	radios and accessories and oxygen equipment
Prestige Cookware	cookware
Proplan	project planning and computer services
Sentinel Insurance	insurance
Soccomin Fine Foods	food
Thai International Airways	air travel to and from Kathmandu, return cargo to Australia
Union Carbide	batteries
Wild Country	climbing and camping equipment
Wild Sports	climbing ropes and climbing equipment

For the transport of our personnel and equipment to Nepal we are particularly grateful to those who assisted us at Thai Airways and the RAAF. We would also like to record our gratitude to Sergeant Michael Herrick, who designed and built the best Icefall ladders ever made.

It would be impossible to adequately thank Diane Johnstone, Brian Pullen and the staff at the Australian Embassy in Kathmandu. Their help and hospitality did much to encourage the team and their efficient assistance meant a trouble free entry and departure for the members and their equipment.

Support Treks
by Peter Allen

As part of our objective of making the Bicentennial Expedition as accessible as possible to interested Australians and as a fund raising exercise ABEE offered two trekking opportunities in association with the expedition. These were a 19 day trek to Base Camp to visit the expedition and a 24 day trek to Base Camp which also included an excursion with expedition members to attempt nearby Island Peak (6100 metres).

These two treks were very successful, although the Island Peak climbers regrettably missed the summit due to poor weather. Diane Johnstone, our Ambassador to Nepal, and John Peryman, our intrepid Chairman, adventurously accompanied the Base Camp trek.

The expedition was very grateful to the support trekkers both for their financial contribution to the expedition but particularly for their encouragement and good company during their stay at Base Camp.

The Base Camp Trekkers	The Island Park Trekkers
Trevor Adams	Mark Carson
Colin Avery	Rosemary Farmer
Nick Deacock (leader)	Rodger Henning-Smith
George Goring	Robert Kinnane
Diane Johnstone	Laura Lombard
Sandi Johnstone	Desmond McCarthy
Greg Luz	Steve McDowell (leader)
John Peryman	Barry McGlashen
Sue Ross	David McInnes
Graeme Whitford	David Morgan-Brooker
Diedre Wilson	Mark Norden
	Robert Parker
	John Ross Reid
	Kieran Sell
	Andrew Webb
	Winston Sellars-Jones

Index

Numbers in *italics* denote illustrations